'In this brilliant provocation, François Debrix courageously calls us to shift our analyses from the body to body parts, and from terror to horror. Debrix tracks the horror of contemporary global politics in a number of settings, but also uses horror to put forth a most radical, and necessary, critical intervention against regimes of terror and security.'

Brent J. Steele, University of Utah, USA

'Human bodies litter the earth. Some obscured, some forgotten, some celebrated, some torn apart: these bodies have a physical, literal presence, a record of humanity written in flesh and bone. In *Global Powers of Horror*, François Debrix finally gives them the attention they deserve, tracing their political import and influence. The particularities of bodies, from the horrors of severed heads to the limits of embodied life, underpin our most resilient ideas about government, sovereignty, control, and discipline. Debrix's focus on this corporeal reality literalizes biopolitics and the topographies and theologies of life and death. It proves an essential guide to understanding the violence inherent to contemporary international politics.'

Kennan Ferguson, University of Wisconsin-Milwaukee, USA

GLOBAL POWERS OF HORROR

Global Powers of Horror examines contemporary regimes of horror, horror's intricacies, and their deployment on and through human bodies and body parts. To track horror's work, what horror decomposes and, perhaps, recomposes, Debrix goes beyond the idea of the integrality and integrity of the human body and focuses on parts, pieces, or fragments of bodies and lives. Looking at horror's production of bodily fragments, both against and beyond humanity, the book is also about horror's own attempt to re-form or recreate matter, from the perspective of post-human, non-human, and inhuman fragmentation.

Through several contemporary instances of the dismantling of human bodies and pulverization of body parts, this book makes several interrelated theoretical contributions. It works with contemporary post-(geo)political figures of horror—faces of concentration-camp dwellers, body parts of victims of terror attacks, the outcomes of suicide bombings, graphic reports of beheadings, recompositions of melted and mingled remnants of non-human and human matter after 9/11—to challenge regimes of terror and security that seek to forcefully and ideologically reaffirm a biopolitics and thanatopolitics of human life in order to anchor today's often devastating deployments of the metaphysics of substance.

Critically enabling one to see how security and terror form a (geo)political continuum of violent mobilization, utilization, and often destruction of human and non-human bodies and lives, this book will be of interest to graduates and scholars of biopolitics, international relations, and security studies.

François Debrix is a Professor in the Department of Political Science and the Director of the ASPECT Program at Virginia Tech, USA.

Interventions

Edited by Jenny Edkins, Aberystwyth University and
Nick Vaughan-Williams, University of Warwick

The Series provides a forum for innovative and interdisciplinary work that engages with alternative critical, post-structural, feminist, postcolonial, psychoanalytic and cultural approaches to international relations and global politics. In our first 5 years we have published 60 volumes.

We aim to advance understanding of the key areas in which scholars working within broad critical post-structural traditions have chosen to make their interventions, and to present innovative analyses of important topics. Titles in the series engage with critical thinkers in philosophy, sociology, politics and other disciplines and provide situated historical, empirical and textual studies in international politics.

We are very happy to discuss your ideas at any stage of the project: just contact us for advice or proposal guidelines. Proposals should be submitted directly to the Series Editors:

- *Jenny Edkins (jennyedkins@hotmail.com) and*
- *Nick Vaughan-Williams (N.Vaughan-Williams@Warwick.ac.uk).*

For a full list of available titles please visit www.routledge.com/series/INT
The most recent titles in this series are:

Security without Weapons
Rethinking violence, nonviolent actions, and civilian protection
M. S. Wallace

Disorienting Democracy
Politics of emancipation
Clare Woodford

Democracy Promotion as Foreign Policy
Temporal othering in international relations
Cathy Elliott

Asylum Seekers, Sovereignty, and the Senses of the International
A politico-corporeal struggle
Eeva Puumala

Global Powers of Horror
Security, politics, and the body in pieces
François Debrix

GLOBAL POWERS OF HORROR

Security, politics, and the body in pieces

François Debrix

Routledge
Taylor & Francis Group

LONDON AND NEW YORK

First published 2017
by Routledge
2 Park Square, Milton Park, Abingdon, Oxon OX14 4RN

and by Routledge
711 Third Avenue, New York, NY 10017

Routledge is an imprint of the Taylor & Francis Group, an informa business

British Library Cataloguing in Publication Data
A catalogue record for this book is available from the British Library

Library of Congress Cataloging in Publication Data
Names: Debrix, François, author.
Title: Global powers of horror: security, politics, and the body in
pieces/François Debrix.
Description: Abingdon, Oxon; New York, NY: Routledge is an imprint
of the Taylor & Francis Group, an Informa Business, [2017] |
Series: Interventions | Includes bibliographical references and index.
Identifiers: LCCN 2016037873 | ISBN 9780415741415 (hbk) |
ISBN 9780415741422 (pbk.) | ISBN 9781315725383 (ebk)
Subjects: LCSH: Biopolitics. | Human body–Political aspects. |
Political violence.
Classification: LCC JA80.D44 2017 | DDC 320.01–dc23
LC record available at https://lccn.loc.gov/2016037873

ISBN: 978-0-415-74141-5 (hbk)
ISBN: 978-0-415-74142-2 (pbk)
ISBN: 978-1-315-72538-3 (ebk)

Typeset in Bembo
by Sunrise Setting Ltd, Brixham, UK

CONTENTS

ACKNOWLEDGMENTS

This book started to take shape as I moved from Miami (FIU) to Blacksburg (Virginia Tech), back in 2011. Many of my colleagues at Virginia Tech have been strong supporters of this project, and I greatly benefitted from my conversations with them. I also had the chance to present a couple of this book's chapters to them, often in the context of the ASPECT Working Papers series. First and foremost, I owe a debt of gratitude to my wife and beloved colleague, Clair Apodaca, and I thank her as always for her love and support. At Virginia Tech, I would like to thank Danna Agmon, Paul Avey, Gabriel Blouin Genest, Brian Britt, Mauro Caraccioli, Priya Dixit, Rohan Kalyan, Chad Lavin, Tim Luke, Michael Moehler, Wayne Moore, Madhavi Murty, Scott Nelson, Trish Nickel, Luke Plotica, Besnik Pula, Andy Scerri, Tamara Sutphin, Janell Watson, Edward Weisband, and Laura Zanotti. Their comments and suggestions, and their fostering of a theoretically rich and analytically critical intellectual environment at Virginia Tech, and within ASPECT in particular, are constant sources of encouragement. Doctoral students and scholars in the ASPECT program at Virginia Tech (a program I have been honored to direct since 2011) have been wonderfully clever, smart, inquisitive, and thought-provoking. Over the years, they have made ASPECT into a top-notch theory PhD program, and, through their engagement with my work and with theory more generally, they have pushed me to be clearer but also more daring about my thinking and my writing. This book owes a lot to their passion and intellectual honesty. In particular, I would like to thank the terrific discussions, during and outside graduate seminars, on matters of biopolitics, thanatopolitics, the body, terror/terrorism, horror, ideology, critical geopolitics, critical international relations theory, security politics, postcoloniality, postmodernity, visual media and culture, and theory in general that I have had with Judson Abraham, Caroline Alphin, Ryan Artrip, Seth Bartee, Amiel Bernal, Katie Cross, Rikky Curtis, Claudio D'Amato, Komal Dhillon, Taulby Edmondson, Sascha Engel,

Tim Filbert, Johannes Grow, Darren Jackson, Eli Jamison, Holly Jordan, Jordan Hill, Mario Khreiche, Jordan Laney, Jenn Lawrence, Christian Matheis, Kent Morris, Mohammed Pervaiz, Francine Rossone de Paula, Mary Ryan, Jamie Sanchez, Melissa Schwartz, Aaron Stoller, Alex Stubberfield, Tyler Suggs, Anthony Szczurek, Josette Torres, Shelby Ward, and Mike Zarella. Likewise, many friends and colleagues across the profession have been enormously generous with their time. They have offered comments on chapters or sub-sections of chapters at conferences, while serving as discussants on panels, as a result of invited lectures, or through many informal conversations. For this project, I have gathered important feedback through various discussions and conversations with Jack Amoureux, Kellan Anfinson, Alex Barder, Tom Beaumont, Jane Bennett, Peter Burgess, Elisabeth Chaves, Mat Coleman, William Connolly, Joel Crombez, Miguel de Larrinaga, Jenny Edkins, Clara Eroukhmanoff, Kennan Ferguson, Simon Glezos, Harry Gould, David Grondin, Jairus Grove, Renee Heberle, Nick Kiersey, Mark Lacy, Daniel Levine, Mike Lipscomb, Georg Löfflmann, Ben Meiches, Himadeep Muppidi, Dan Öberg, Sam Opondo, Mat Paterson, Mark Rigstad, Andrew Ross, Sayres Rudy, Mark Salter, Nisha Shah, Sarah Sharma, Mike Shapiro, Joel Shelton, William Sokoloff, Ty Solomon, Vicki Squire, Brent Steele, Simon Stow, Alex Struwe, Nick Vaughan-Williams, Antonio Vasquez-Arroyo, Inna Viriasova, Cindy Weber, Jason Weidner, Geoffrey Whitehall, Yoshiko Yamada, and Andreja Zevnik. I am very grateful to the Department of Politics and International Studies at the University of Warwick, the School of Political Studies at the University of Ottawa, and the Institut für Politikwissenschaft at TU Darmstadt for their generous invitations to present early versions of some of this book's chapters. Finally, I am thankful to Jenny Edkins and Nick Vaughan-Williams, the Interventions series editors, and Lydia de Cruz and Nicola Parkin, the editors at Routledge, for their patience and their continued support over the years.

An earlier version of Chapter 1 appeared in the journal *Environment and Planning D: Society and Space*, Vol. 33, No. 3 (2015). A shorter and early version of Chapter 2 appeared in *International Political Sociology*, Vol. 9, No. 2 (2015). And a few substantially modified sections of Chapter 3 appeared in Priya Dixit and Jacob L. Stump (eds), *Critical Methods in Terrorism Studies* (New York: Routledge, 2015). My thanks go to the editors of these publications for allowing me to share my work with their readers.

This book is dedicated to my grandkids Elizabeth, Ethan, and Jeremy, who, as they know well, "have a lot of French in them."

INTRODUCTION

Global powers of horror

Sights of horror

In August 2012, in one of the most sordid episodes of violence perpetrated by drug cartels and related paramilitary groups in Mexico, a carful of decomposed body parts was found on a roadside in the state of San Luis Potosi.[1] In their unending wars against Mexican governmental forces and against each other, *narcos* have multiplied scenes of horror throughout the Mexican and sometimes the US south-west landscape, littering it not just with dead bodies (killed for treason, for supposed collaboration with the government or a rival group, for lack of cooperation, for defection from the group, or to send a message of terror to local populations) but also with gruesomely maimed and sometimes unrecognizable body parts. Documenting *narcos* terror, journalist Ed Vulliamy recounts how a Mexican federal police raid on a compound in 2009 stumbled upon a strange cistern with a putrid smell. As Vulliamy and a police captain "look[ed] inside one of the blue plastic barrels ... [they found] the gum of a lower jaw, with teeth still attached, that somehow escaped [the acid] dissolution" to which the bodies had been subjected.[2] And "at the bottom of one of the steel tanks, there [was] raw flesh and jellylike human tissue."[3] This presence and proliferation of what often looks like randomly scattered or released human flesh, tissues, and fluids reveals a mobilization of violence that not only makes use of the "simple biological fact of life," life as a mere natural condition of living/being, as Giorgio Agamben puts it,[4] but rather abuses it and renders even bare life superfluous. To quote Vulliamy, whose book *Amexica: War along the Borderline* (2010) investigates this grotesque carnage of the flesh in Mexico and nearby areas, what the *narcos* seem to be involved in is a violence on body parts that is "recreational" or, perhaps, takes place "for its own sake."[5] This violence "for its own sake" targets bodies, often dismantles them, and publicly displays limbs, organs, and chunks of skin and flesh. It does so not just to kill but, it seems, to disseminate human matter beyond any form of recognition or identification (at least, beyond the recognition of any whole or integral body). This "recreational" *narcos* violence leaves behind it fragments of human life in an attempt, perhaps, to signify that putting to death, even if done in an extremely violent manner, is not sufficient. Rather, pulverizing human bodies and lives seem to be the desirable effects of violence and destruction that render human matter irrelevant and indistinguishable from any other type of matter.

Reducing human bodies and lives to fragments, making use (and abuse) of these fragments, and, at times, learning to deal and, perhaps, live with bodily fragments are particularly common features of the violence perpetrated against humans and humanity in the long aftermath of the war on terror. The mere evocation of terror/terrorism today conveys images of destroyed human lives but also, and perhaps more poignantly, of hurt, maimed, and often broken and disjointed bodies. Responses to terror/terrorism, in the West and beyond, often in the name of security, are no different, particularly when the main form of reaction to terror is to send soldiers (human bodies, often) and to deploy military techniques and technologies (as alleged extensions of soldiers' bodies) to the war on terror's hot zones in order to defeat and, typically, to eliminate proponents of terror, terrorist sympathizers, or groups of individuals suspected of helping to propagate anti-American, anti-Western, anti-liberal, or anti-human(ist) ideologies. In fact, if we are to subscribe to Zoë Wool's arguments about life in the long post-war-on-terror era, fragmented life, fragmented bodies, and a fragmented humanity have become normal, almost expected, and possibly ordinary realities.[6]

Anchoring her thought to a richly detailed ethnography of the daily lives at the Walter Reed Army Medical Center of American veterans wounded in the Iraq and Afghanistan wars, Wool refers to this fragmented normality as the new "extra/ordinary."[7] In this new "extra/ordinary," fragmented bodies all too often become the taken-for-granted limit conditions for everyday life to take place, both in the West and in the non-West (although I am not suggesting here that spaces of fragmented life/being are equivalent or even comparable in the so-called West and non-West). In this new extra/ordinary of "afterwar life" (Wool's term), what Wool calls "configurations of the flesh" may end up feeling "comfortably whole" to some.[8] And yet "there is always something extra, and even as life stabilizes [for some, but not all, wounded bodies], it stabilizes in an extra/ordinary register."[9] Fragmented lives and bodies, if/when they seem to survive or, better yet, when they carry on living, must nonetheless learn to deal/live with the "uncertainty of bodily forms."[10]

Today, this "new knowledge of the world in fragments"[11] is often expressed and felt at the level of the body or, indeed, as and through body parts (injured, repaired, missing, reconstructed, dismantled, imagined, replicated, blown apart, etc.). Fragmented bodies and disseminated body parts, at home and abroad, seem to populate (geo)political realities and imaginaries. Although this seems particularly common today—on either side of the border—or when troops come back from "our" wars on terror, this is really not a new state of affairs. Elizabeth Grosz has remarked (far more optimistically than Wool might have) that human bodies have always been open to "fragmentations, fracturings, dislocations that orient bodies and body parts toward other bodies and body parts."[12] Moreover, the fascination with body parts, from both living humans and dead bodies, is an old one. For example, a desire to connect a human past to a human present for the sake of a human future has compelled generations of biologists, archeologists, anthropologists, and forensic experts (to only name a few scientific professions with a stake in the matter) to look for remnants of bodies and body parts—bones, often—in order to create "human remains collections" (many of which would later become, particularly in the nineteenth century, justifications for the creation of modern natural history or science museums in the West).[13] To dig up, to collect, and to "classify human bones"[14] has typically been seen as a noble and valuable scientific endeavor in the name of a better understanding of the human condition. More recently, in a slightly different register, documenting atrocities, war crimes, or crimes against humanity has led human-rights scholars to focus on body parts too and on what those parts may reveal about bodies that once were integral, whole, and alive (and about the conditions that led to these bodies' destruction).[15] Thus, beyond the fact of life or death, violently targeted body parts and fragmented human lives and bodies have long been the object of various modes of curiosity, attraction, and collection.

Even before the war on terror was initiated and named, some photo-journalists had taken it upon themselves to travel to war zones to take snapshots of disseminated body parts, perhaps with a view to trying to "repair and stabilize life and bodies and to regularize them in their appearance in contact with the world."[16] For example, renowned Magnum Agency photographer Gilles Peress spent time in the 1990s in both Bosnia-Herzegovina and Rwanda to document traces of genocides through a wide array of photos.[17] Close shots of hacked limb bones poking out of torn clothes in Rwanda or meticulous pictures of rows of muddy skulls dug out of mass graves in Bosnia (some of Peress's most gruesome yet famous images) focused on specific parts—or bits of crushed bones—in a way that could contribute to what I once called a "visual taxonomy of death."[18] In hindsight, I might have been better off referring to Peress's forensic photographic work as a visual taxonomy of fragmented bodies and disseminated body parts since his objective seemed to be not so much to document death but rather, beyond death, to "read bodily remains" (as Bella Brodzki puts it[19]) in the hope of trying to reconstruct integral human bodies or full lives from pieces and fragments that often no longer looked human.

Biopolitics, thanatopolitics, horror

A leftover brew of decomposed human flesh in Mexico. Extra/ordinary fragmented lives coping with a new uncertainty about (their) bodily shapes and forms in the United States. Bits and pieces of bone remnants, some with shreds of cloth on them and others found in muddy graves, that may or may not be human in Rwanda and Bosnia. What are we to make of such an insistence—at once narrative, visual, ordinary, exceptional, and geopolitical—on the human, human life, and the human body *beyond* any clear presence of human integrity, identity, or unity? Might we turn to theories of and about biopolitics to tell us how, in excess of a "politically qualified life" (*bios*), what has been called a "mere," "bare," or "natural/biological life" (*zoē*)[20] has been used and abused for the sake of power or to impose certain political configurations? As is now well known, particularly among critical (geo)political, security, or violence scholars, to make sense of issues of extreme violence at the level of individual and collective bodies theorists of the political have been tempted to look towards biopower and biopolitics, whether they have chosen to describe their critical efforts in these exact terms or not. By turning to biopower/biopolitics, they have recognized that, from classical territorial conquests by way of warfare to perhaps more contemporary wars of attrition, or from the concentration camps to policies of control/management of displaced populations, the biopolitical capture of lives and bodies has involved the destruction of those very lives/bodies. They have remembered that Michel Foucault famously argued that biopolitics emerged when the power of the sovereign shifted from a "right to take life" to a capacity to "let live."[21] Still, they have also been fond of noting that, as Agamben and Achille Mbembe have clarified, while Foucault's claim that biopower is concerned with the maintenance of human life and bodies is crucial, the capacity to "make live and let die" is never completely separate from the "old" modality of sovereign power and force premised upon a right to put to death. They have quoted Mbembe who tells them that biopolitics is also about "the subjugation of life to the power of death."[22] And they may have followed this assertion with another frequently cited statement from Agamben, who stresses that "if there is a line in every modern state marking the point at which the decision on life becomes a decision on death, and biopolitics can turn into thanatopolitics, the line no longer appears today as a stable border dividing two clearly distinct zones."[23] Thus, many critical theorists (and I count myself among them) may have come to understand that when biopolitics—the concern with the management and possibly the enhancement of human life/living at the heart of political operations and sovereign decisions—becomes the main motivation of political power, what Mbembe has called "the creation of death worlds" turns into a dominant modality of violence in both modern and late-modern (geo)politics.[24]

Agamben and Mbembe, among frequently cited theorists of the biopolitical condition, may have been able to help us understand how we may go from biopolitics to thanatopolitics (or necropolitics) or from the management and enhancement of human bodies and lives to the often planned eradication of humanity or, at least, of some parts of it.[25] For some populations' lives to be maintained or expanded, other populations (and individual bodies) must be sacrificed and their lives must be rendered pointless or obsolete. By now, thanks to some of the theorists mentioned above and many others, the passage from biopolitics to thanatopolitics can be theorized, mapped, described, and criticized as well. What is perhaps less well documented or conceptualized, however, including by scholars/ thinkers of the biopolitical/necropolitical condition, is the passage from biopolitics-as-thanatopolitics—or from "the creation of death worlds" in order to continue to make some lives live—to the dismantling of bodies and lives and to the production, display, and dissemination of body parts and human fragments. Put differently, how do we transition from a modality of the political that seeks to preserve life or that puts to death in order to maintain or establish power over some populations (even if by means of extreme violence) to another modality of destruction for which the fact of being alive or dead, or of being recognizable as a human body or not, is irrelevant or of no obvious political utility? How are we to make sense, if making sense is still possible, of the seeming shift from a violence that still cares about humanity or, at least, about human bodily integrity to a violence that thrives in fragmentation, proliferation, and the pulverization of human shapes or forms (and sometimes, as Wool may have it, still expects ordinary life to be lived as such)?

In a previous study, to which this volume is indebted (and that, in a way, serves as a launch pad for many of the arguments deployed here), my colleague Alexander Barder and I tried to offer some preliminary possibilities for tracking this expansion of extreme violence beyond biopolitics and beyond thanatopolitics.[26] We did so by employing the notion of horror and, in particular, by relying on philosopher Adriana Cavarero's opposition between terror and horror.[27] To briefly recall Cavarero's argument, whereas terror forces human bodies to run away in the face of violence and destruction, horror freezes.[28] To be terrorized is a visceral fear that pushes human bodies to turn away from the terrifying sight and to flee so they may survive (or attempt to, anyway). The preservation of life—trying not to die—is key to terror and squarely situates terror within a biopolitical framework whereby living, being, or surviving are crucial. By contrast, horror is beyond human survival.[29] The sight of horror brings paralysis to the human body. In so doing, horror takes over human life, not just by killing bodies but by dismantling them.[30] Horror does not merely replace biopower with necropower or biopolitics with thanatopolitics. Rather, horror directly assaults human life, including the capacity to die a human death. Put differently, horror does not concern itself with the question of whether the human body is alive or dead. Beyond life or death, the sight of horror leaves the human "undone," as the human body "loses its individuality."[31] As Cavarero summarizes, "extreme violence, directed at nullifying human beings even more than at killing them, must rely on horror rather than terror."[32]

Relying on Cavarero's thought regarding horror, Barder and I started to argue in *Beyond Biopolitics* that terror and horror have different ontological purposes. Terror seeks to scare off or force away, often by killing and, sometimes, by killing gruesomely. By contrast, horror does not care whether humans are scared or not (or whether they are scared in order to survive or are scared to death). For terror to fulfill its objectives, it is imperative that humans—or, at least, some of them—remain alive, that their bodies retain a capacity to move or be active, or that their lives continue to be lived even if in fear. As I show in the present study, it is also imperative for security and security politics (the so-called normal or expected responses to terror) that terror remain in a biopolitical or thanatopolitical register—that is to say, that terror continue to put certain human bodies to death while preserving others. Security politics and its mobilization of lives and bodies require terror's capacity to take lives away, to make death worlds. By contrast, horror's ontological purpose is negative or, better yet, it is de-ontological. As Barder and I put it, horror has the ontological unity of human life by way of the human body as its main target.[33] It wishes to do away with human ontology, perhaps with the metaphysics of human substance (more on this "metaphysics of substance" below). Thus, as Cavarero claimed, horror goes after the human by seeking to "undo its figural unity."[34] Where and when the human is recognized through the figure of the one, whole, complete, or integral body, in life as well as in death, horror's extreme violence pulverizes the human's shapes or forms. It breaks down the human body into parts, bits, pieces, shreds of flesh, tissue, pulp, and fluids, and it renders human matter indistinct from non-human materiality (whether organic or inorganic). Thus, through the body, horror appears to target unity, individuality, integrity, and identity. It attacks the image/form/idea of the one and the same, of the human and its alleged singularity. Assumed to be the sovereign figure/form of ontological unity, the human body/ human life is what horror sets its sights on, even if and when the human body has already been deprived of life (as we will see in several of the following chapters, horror's annihilation is often well in excess of the kind of violence that would simply ensure that bodies are killed). Finally, unlike terror, what horror often leaves behind, in the wake of its dismantling work, is a sort of world without humans, or a world in which to be human no longer holds any special privilege, as philosopher Eugene Thacker suggests.[35]

This volume is, once again, about horror. It goes deeper into some contemporary regimes of horror, into horror's intricacies, and into their deployment on and through human bodies and body parts. To track horror's work, what horror decomposes and, perhaps, recomposes, it goes beyond the idea of the integrality and integrity of the human body and focuses on parts, pieces, or fragments of bodies and lives. It is about horror's production of bodily fragments, both against and beyond humanity. At times, as suggested above, it is also about horror's own attempt at re-forming or recreating matter—a new type of matter, perhaps—from the perspective of post-human, non-human, and inhuman fragmentation. As the unending war on terror extends and expands, temporally and spatially, it multiplies opportunities for instances of extreme violence and destruction of human bodies and body parts, often in a kind of extra/ordinary way that is both exceptional and mundane, uncommon and yet so familiar.

Theorizing (with) horror

By tracking down horror and its violent intricacies through several contemporary instances of the dismantling of human bodies and pulverization of body parts, this volume makes several interrelated theoretical contributions. One such theoretical contribution has already been mentioned in the previous discussion. Theorizing horror and its undoing, proliferation, and recombination of bodies and body parts confronts us with the limits of the political, including the limits of (geo)political configurations that champion biopolitics-as-thanatopolitics but also of those that seek to antagonize the passage from biopower to necropower. Horror has no care or concern for the body undone, for lives destroyed, or for a lost humanity. On the contrary, horror relies on and thrives in these conditions. Horror operates beyond human limits, beyond human life. This means that, with horror, there is no hope for a reconstitution of humanity, for a rediscovery of traces of the human, for a revamped political (human) community, or even for a newly found capacity for human life/living through concepts such as precariousness, grievability, over-living, or *surviv-ance*, for example (as has been suggested by some critical theorists over the last decade).[36] In fact, theorizing horror means that one may become suspicious of recent theories of the political that have sought to reclaim human life—and, through human life, politics, too—by affirming that, even when life and the body have been blown to pieces, there can still be some hope for another life, for a "stub-born life," perhaps,[37] or for a "more-to" life.[38] There is, perhaps, among these theo-ries and theorists, a desperate expectation that, even in horror, something about the human will live on. Horror reveals such an ultimate political project (to reclaim life and humanity when all seems lost) to be particularly pointless or to be yet another one of those "cruel optimisms."[39] This does not mean, however, that horror is beyond life or, at least, beyond matter. Rather, horror is beyond life (including any sort of more-to life or over-living) and beyond matter to the extent that these are construed as essentially human, as being about the essence of humanity.[40]

Moreover, if horror is beyond biopolitics and beyond thanatopolitics, it is also beyond (geo)politics. Whereas terror and security's responses to terror are very much part of the contemporary (geo)political assemblage, no (geo)politics can attach itself to horror. Horror's violence is in excess of (geo)political rationaliza-tions. It may well be that one of horror's objectives is to dismantle (geo)politics and (geo)political formations, including those that, either on the side of terror or on the side of security, rely on the deployment of biopolitics-as-thanatopolitics. Horror renders (geo)politics powerless. For what kind of politics or political claims (territorial, biopolitical, necropolitical, etc.) could exist or persist beyond the human/humanity? Or, as Thacker prefers to phrase it, "if life is not exclusive to the human ... then the question becomes: can there be a politics of life in terms of the non-human or the unhuman?"[41] Perhaps horror's main target is precisely a certain (geo)politics of force, violence, and terror that, often deployed in the name of life and humanity, seeks to use and abuse bodies, whether these bodies are human or non-human.

Horror thus partakes of the crisis of the human/humanity. To theorize and track down horror, as this volume does, is also to think about the post-human and, per-haps, about the non-human. Consequently, this study may seem to align itself with some recent post-human theorizations that have diagnosed the limits of the human, or some non-human (often technological, objects-based) extensions or enhance-ments of humanity, or the capacity for matter other than human to, indeed, matter, act, or be dynamic and vibrant.[42] Detailing horror's violence and reflecting upon it (two main tasks performed by this study) appear to fulfill two key related mis-sions of post-humanist scholarship: to contribute to a "philosophical critique of anthropocentrism"[43] and to oppose humanism's "dualist conception of a rational, self-governing [human] subject whose [human] nature is transparent to itself"[44] and, furthermore, is "unmarked by its interactions with the object-world."[45] However, the theoretical reflections offered in the present study break ranks with much post-humanist or vibrant/new materialist scholarship because, far too often, in this genre of writing/thinking about the more-than-human (or about what may lie beyond the human), an agent-centric perspective remains, whether the agent is a human subject or actant or something else altogether. Too often, post-humanism is obsessed with questions about the promotion/preservation of life, a life that is claimed no longer to be of, for, about, or by humans but that nonetheless maintains a strangely human-centric form, appearance, or composition.[46]

By contrast, horror's violence onto the human, including its possible recombination with non-human matter, does not seek to account for a vibrant materiality of things or of matter in general (although it may abuse or take advantage of such vibrant matter). Rather, horror problematizes the human-body-versus-inorganic-matter duality in a way that does not leave space to reinsert metaphysical concepts about a lost humanity or about a recombined humanism into the realm of matter/life (something that, in my reading of post-humanism, too many theorists contributing to this scholarship end up doing). Put differently, post-humanists/new materialists/vibrant materialists often fail to rid themselves of the metaphysics of human substance—that is to say, of the belief that there must still be an essentially human or, if not human, at least human-like unity, entity, and, perhaps, agency as the guarantee for the whole world to be and/or make sense.[47] To borrow Thacker's language, the "negative ontology" that comes with horror may not always sit well with presently fashionable post-humanistic critical perspectives on the more-than-human.[48] By removing the weight of humanity/the human from the world, horror seeks to put an end to the metaphysics of substance. Horror opens up the "problem of thinking the world-without-us,"[49] whether the "us" is a human body or any new human extension or substitute principle.

Contrary to many post-humanist approaches, this study of horror and its violence stays with the human body. But it tackles the human body through its always already plural, disseminated, dismantled, pulverized, and possibly unidentifiable dimensions. In this way, in its tracing and tracking of horror's work, it is not the human/non-human bifurcation of bodies that this volume concentrates on. Rather, it is humanity itself, the fact of the human, and, indeed, as intimated above, the metaphysics of substance that are questioned by horror and, by extension, by the present study. It is the human as "the place of ceaseless divisions"[50] that this book, through its examination of horror, places center-stage. Thus, horror can also help us to rethink the question of the human/humanism in new ways. What if what is left of the human in and after horror or, more crucially, perhaps, what is left of life is what results from the incongruity of the extra/ordinary encounters between the human and the non-human in the aftermath of (geo)politics?

As already intimated, this study does not just track down or decipher horror and its violence for the sake of advancing a new concept of the human or even of the non-human. This book is, once again, very much about humanity and human bodies but in a critical and radical way. It uses the destructive force of horror for radically critical purposes. Thus, it has recourse to and works with horror, with contemporary post-(geo)political figures of horror—faces of concentration-camp dwellers, body parts of victims of terror attacks, the outcome of suicide bombings, graphic reports of beheadings, recompositions of melted and mingled remnants of non-human and human matter after 9/11—to challenge regimes of terror and security (and their insistent geopolitical claims) that seek to forcefully and ideologically reaffirm a biopolitics and thanatopolitics of human life in order to anchor today's often devastating deployments of the metaphysics of substance. Horror, once again, may enable us to reveal the so-called opposition between security and terror as a sham, as a false dualism that hides the (geo)political complicity between security and terror (and, just as scandalously, between security proponents and terror sympathizers). As I show in several of the following chapters, the point of view of horror critically enables one to see how security and terror form a (geo)political continuum of violent mobilization, utilization, and often destruction of human and non-human bodies and lives. The play between terror and security, their antagonism as much as their embrace (to start with, the fact that both need each other's actual or potential presence in order to remain operational and effective), is what enables biopolitics (the promotion of human life) and thanatopolitics (the violent production of human deaths) to appear as limit conditions for contemporary (geo)politics. Yet, by stepping out of biopolitics and thanatopolitics, horror can reveal how (geo)political strategies and tactics of security regimes are just as nefarious to life and bodies as terror/terrorism and vice versa. From the negative ontological perspective of horror, neither terror nor security has a prerogative over the use and abuse of bodies and life, in all their possible forms. In fact, often, security and terror, individually or in tandem, can provide an ideal platform for horror's own post-human violence.

Tracking horror

As I have tried to argue above, to track horror is also to become aware of its radical potentials and powers. This does not mean that this book is sympathetic to horror or its enormous work of devastation of human bodies and body parts. But it also does not condemn horror since to do so would be to express a political or ethical point of view—often, from the perspective of some sort of human-conscious or human-caring moral imperative—that becomes pointless once horror has started to undertake its pulverizing work. As the following chapters detail, horror is an ultimate challenge. Its critical force is unmatched. Thus, while horror demolishes and does not allow for a reconstruction or even a redemption of the human, it also can be revelatory.[51] The revelatory powers of horror are what this volume hopes to bring to the fore too, even if there is nothing salutary (for humanity, at least) about this sort of revelation. And, once again, what horror may reveal comes with horror's often unspeakable violence (and yet, as I also intimated above, the seeds of horror's violence may have been planted by human and political forces, like security and terror, and not by horror itself).

The first two chapters in this volume facilitate a theoretical as well as an empirical transition from biopolitical/thanatopolitical concerns with human life to the dismantling of bodies and body parts. Chapter 1 takes us back to biopolitical and thanatopolitical arguments about the capture of life in the camps. It offers two critical approaches to dealing with the kind of human life that finds itself relegated to the camps (concentration camps, refugee camps, and so on), or what I refer to as "camp life." To apprehend camp life, a shift in biopolitical theories from topographical understandings of camp territoriality to topological appreciations for the way the space of the camp is always in excess of its spatial demarcations is necessary. I suggest that Agamben and Judith Butler can offer us two perspectives on the topology of camp life that enable us to understand how the passage from life to death and from death back to life (or over-living) in the camp effectively and affectively operates. Topologies of camp life can also illuminate a salutary biopolitical potential that may be able to resist the harsh thanatopolitical topography of the camp, where human lives disappear and bodies are abused. Differently but also complementarily, Agamben and Butler claim that emergent topologies of camp life can serve as guarantees that the materiality of the camps, lives and deaths in the camps, and all sorts of operations of power onto bodies in the camps will not be lost, ignored, or forgotten. At the same time, I question Agamben's and Butler's respective topological reflections on camp life, and, in particular, I start to challenge their continued reliance on biopower. I end Chapter 1 by asking whether an insistent emphasis on the biopolitics of the camp/camp life (even if it is topological rather than topographically informed) can do justice to configurations of force, violence, and devastation in and beyond the camp that do not have the life or death of humans (nor their possible more-to life or survivability) as their main target.

On the face of it, Chapter 2 seems to be concerned with traditional (geo)political or international relations issues. This chapter revisits the relationship between sovereignty and security, or, to be more accurate, the relationship between the need to protect and preserve the life/integrity of the sovereign and the work of security politics. But it does so in a way that brings to the forefront of the analysis the problem of time (rather than the issue of space/territoriality that is more commonly tied to sovereignty and security preoccupations in international relations) and the question of the finitude of the life of the sovereign. I turn to theology in Chapter 2 to reconsider the close kinship between sovereignty and the politics of security and to highlight the role that questions of life versus death, sovereign violence, and the problem of time/temporality play in biopolitical and thanatopolitical regimes of security. In particular, I introduce the notions of *katechon* and *eschaton*. The function of the *katechon* in regimes of sovereign survivability is to restrain or fend off the attack of time against the sovereign, an attack that the sovereign and security politics often depict as the work of the *eschaton*. The *eschaton* is a figure or force that seeks to end time or that refuses to abide by the belief in infinite time that sovereignty/the sovereign body depends on. What I term katechontic sovereignty in this chapter is a complicity between sovereignty and security that mobilizes power, force, violence, and terror (in the name of the safety/life of the sovereign) in order to restrain or fend off the *eschaton* of finite time, or, to put it a bit differently, to cast away the uncertain, contingent, and non-eternal possibilities for human as well as sovereign life (since human life is often said to depend upon the survival of the sovereign) that eschatological time represents. By offering this theoretical revisiting of the relationship between sovereignty and security, this chapter reveals the fragility of sovereign constructs, their reliance upon katechontic violence and upon the terror of security politics, and the close kinship (as discussed above) between terror and security. It further demonstrates that the greatest challenge to the sovereign is not terror, since terror (that the sovereign and its security agents nonetheless falsely attribute to the *eschaton*) is always part and parcel of katechontic sovereignty, of security politics, and of the life/body of the sovereign. Rather, the greatest anxiety for sovereignty, security, and terror is horror, a horror "embodied" in the *eschaton* of time. Indeed, the *eschaton*'s horror opens up the political—or what is left of it—to the prospect of a radically different temporality, one according to which the life/body of the sovereign (and of the humans allegedly promoted and protected by the sovereign) is always potentially subject to finitude, to an absence of survivability or of a more-to life, and to an annihilating violence beyond sovereign and human redemption. Read in the context of horror, the figure of the *eschaton* transfers the terrorizing force and destruction of the sovereign and its security politics to the possibility of a violently horrific undoing of the permanence/eternity of human life, a horrific undoing that takes advantage of the sovereign body's ontological vulnerabilities, insecurities, and fears of fragmentation.

The next two chapters (Chapter 3 and Chapter 4) bring us in contact with contemporary instances of horror and with their fragmenting and pulverizing work at the level of bodies and body parts. They showcase horror "in action," even though they continue to explore the complicities between biopolitics and thanatopolitics, the devastating intimacies between security and terror, and the vulnerabilities of the human/humanity, particularly when the human/humanity has surrendered to dominant (geo)political configurations of security, terror, and violence. These chapters also show us that horror is not always what we expect it to be (for example, an added degree of inhumanity in and about terror) or where we expect it to reside (in the non-West, among "barbarian" or inhuman others, for instance). Finally, Chapters 3 and 4 foster a critical theorization of horror initiated in this Introduction and in the first two chapters of the book by insisting on horror's radically critical potentials and, above all, on its post-human or non-human assaults on the metaphysics of substance. What Chapters 3 and 4 showcase is not so much the advent of a new or differently critical theoretical framework of horror, but rather how horror operates as a chasm of and for theory, particularly of and for the theories that we commonly have turned to in order to think the (geo)politics of security and terror.

Chapter 3 starts with the scene of the 2013 Boston Marathon bombing and the figure of "Fallen Man," an individual who is seen on video as falling to his knees, whose body surrenders and lets go as a result of the blast at the finish of the marathon but who resiliently manages to stand up, walk again, and make it across the finish line. Fallen Man, I argue, becomes an iconic image in the post-war-on-terror

US/Western (geo)political landscape/mediascape. Fallen Man and other US/Western falling bodies (often, victims of terror) return to contemporary representations and rationalizations of security and terror to show humanity's power of survivability, its resilience and endurance in the face of terror/terrorism. But the icon of Fallen Man does not return by itself. It returns to contemporary (geo)political realities and imaginaries with a new visual emphasis on body parts (knees, limbs, heads, burnt flesh, loose skin, wounded organs, shattered bones, etc.) that, in the moment of the terror attack, are often unable to sustain the integrity/unity of the human body and human lives, give in to terror, and betray the entire/whole body. Thus, the iconography of terror that unfolds behind the image/symbolism of Fallen Man is a very precarious, insecure, and fragmented one. It is an image of human perseverance, resilience, or over-living that relies on a proliferation of dismantled bodies and disseminated body parts, as many narratives about the Boston Marathon bombing attack and its aftermath of (human) recovery have insisted on. Thus, with the figure of Fallen Man, it is in fact the horror of disseminated body parts that sets in and starts to take over official discourses and public/media representations and rationalizations about the ongoing (geo)political encounter between security politics and terror/terrorism in the ever present global war on terror. This horror of disseminated body parts, I go on to argue in Chapter 3, has a lot more in common with instances of suicide bombing and with the horror of recombined bodies and matter that immediately follow a suicide bombing attack, as theorists like Talal Asad or Cavarero have argued. I conclude this chapter by stating that, in cases of suicide-bombing attacks (most of which are still thought to take place "over there," in the non-West) but also in the presence of the so-called resilient image of Fallen Man as the new icon of security/terror in the West, a visual "repertory of horror" (as Cavarero puts it[52]) takes over regimes of representation and (geo)political rationalizations about terror and security. This visual repertory of horror directs our attention not so much towards the sign/symbol of a resilient and once again standing Fallen Man, but rather towards the sight of scattered, mingled, unrecognizable, and sometimes recombined body parts that, at the most, only have a few traces of the human in them.

Chapter 4 pursues this line of investigation about the leftovers of the human and human parts in the wake of horror's violence by switching the focus from terrorist attacks or the aftermath of suicide bombings to beheadings and severed heads. In mostly Western discourses and representations of the contemporary (geo)politics of security and terror, severed heads have made a comeback of sorts, particularly now that IS/ISIS/ISIL (the Islamic State) has been identified by security specialists, politicians, and media pundits as the new face of a terror that, often, is conveniently referred to as a matter of horror. Beheadings by "Islamic extremists," particularly in lands controlled by IS, often become an opportunity for Western scholars, pundits, journalists, and politicians to decry "their" monstrous inhumanity, an inhumanity that is contrasted to "our" Western humanity/humanism. Purposefully ignoring the fact that the West has its own (long, and at times revered) history of cutting off human heads and putting them on display, the more recent episodes of beheading in the context of the unending war on terror are qualified as an attack on the human or as an offense to the respect, dignity, and integrity of the human person and body. In a revamped orientalist discourse, the West, rightly or not, has identified Islamic head-cutters as the new "masters of horror," who can never be reconciled with Western/humanity's ideas and ideals. I wonder, in this chapter, if the severed head has not become our contemporary icon of horror, one that perhaps mirrors Fallen Man as the icon of terror (as detailed in Chapter 3). I interrogate the meaning-making powers of Western narratives and representations about severed heads, asking whether the obvious insistence on beheadings/severed heads in so many Western discourses of (geo)politics, security, and terror today is also not a way to try to tame or capture horror, to make it one's own. If the dismantling of the human and human body parts, starting with the head, perhaps, could become visible, representable, and possibly intelligible (even if we still abhor it), could there be some hope for the human/humanity after all, for the human body's recomposition and its survivability? More crucially, perhaps, could this provide "us" (alleged non-"barbarians") in the West with a new justification to go ahead and chop heads off and to pulverize bodies to the point of unrecognition too, as, for example, "we" appear eager to do by way of military drone attacks onto non-Western bodies/lives? Thus, this chapter ends with a critical reflection, enabled by horror, about who or what can claim a prerogative over regimes of preservation but also destruction of human heads today. What a fascination with severed heads and beheadings in the West, in our discourses on terror and horror, is meant to prevent is horror itself, and more crucially, perhaps, the questions that inevitably arise once horror enters the picture (for the questions that horror asks are also key to horror's incomprehensible powers). What cannot be asked, behind our discourses and representations about Islamic radicals cutting Westerners' heads off, but what horror nonetheless brings with it, is the question of whether the principle of differentiation between "us," defenders of humanity, and "them," anti-human monsters, can safely be maintained. What would it mean, I ask in the conclusion to Chapter 4, to think the unthinkable (to think with horror, that is), to entertain the possibility that "our" defense of the human is as much about the pulverization of the human and the dismantling of human parts as "their" so-called horrific assault on humanity?

By way of closing this study, I provide an Epilogue that takes horror back to the early days of the war on terror, to what supposedly initiated this war/(geo)political confrontation: the 9/11 attacks in New York City. I take horror back to 9/11 through this event's recent reconstruction in the National September 11 Memorial Museum at the World Trade Center in Lower Manhattan. In this revisiting of the 9/11 Memorial Museum, I pay attention to the way remnants of matter (organic and inorganic, human and non-human) are on display and appear to anchor the museum's narrative and mission. Unfinished, fragmented, and decomposed bodies and lives take pride of place at the museum. More importantly, perhaps, a blurring of human lives and objects is constantly at work. Fusion and confusion are key operating modalities of organization and meaning throughout the space of the museum. Human matter and what Jane Bennett calls the "thing-power" of non-human matter have come together,[53] often serving as substitutes for one another. The 9/11

Memorial Museum, strangely perhaps, becomes an evocation and, at times, a celebration of horror, particularly of a horror that is unleashed by way of an undecidability of matter or by a putting in common of bits and pieces that are neither human nor non-human. Thus, in a way, the museum seems to be able to metaphorize horror: a horror that dismantles, fuses and confuses, and possibly recomposes matter away from any sense of privilege that would need to be granted to human lives and bodies. Here, it seems, we are well beyond the metaphysics of human substance. It has been shattered. But there may nonetheless be ways to celebrate or, at least, to deal with what has been left over after the metaphysics of substance has been removed. At the 9/11 Memorial Museum, I wonder if we are not in the presence of another radically critical possibility provided by horror: the vision of the fused, confused, and undecidable human and non-human matter as that newly composed materiality that may give rise to some sort of liveliness (if not life) in which neither the human subject and its remains nor the non-human object and its remnants are to be found. While this may not amount to any sort of credible hope for a rediscovered humanity or for a survivability of human life, this kind of recombined/recomposed materiality may be all that horror can offer us (whatever this "us" may mean in the wake of horror).

Notes

1 Olga Rodriguez, "Mexico Violence: Eight Decomposed Bodies Found inside Car in North," *Huffington Post*, August 10, 2013, available at: www.thonline.com/news/national_world/article_63c73e1f-94be-5963-96f4-38b217bfff52.html.
2 Ed Vulliamy, *Amexica: War along the Borderline* (New York: Picador, 2011), p. 49.
3 Ibid., p. 49.
4 Giorgio Agamben, *Homo Sacer: Sovereign Power and Bare Life* (Stanford: Stanford University Press, 1998), pp. 2–3.
5 Ed Vulliamy, "The Terror," *Vanity Fair*, October 21, 2010, available at www.vanityfair.com/news/2010/10/drug-wars-in-mexico-201010.
6 Zoë Wool, *After War: The Weight of Life at Walter Reed* (Durham, NC: Duke University Press, 2015).
7 Ibid., pp. 8–9.
8 Ibid., p. 193.
9 Ibid., p. 193.
10 Ibid., p. 188.
11 As Wool puts it. Ibid., p. 191.
12 Elizabeth Grosz, *Volatile Bodies: Toward a Corporeal Feminism* (Bloomington: Indiana University Press, 1994), p. 13.
13 On this topic, see Samuel J. Redman, *Bone Rooms: From Scientific Racism to Human Prehistory in Museums* (Cambridge, MA: Harvard University Press, 2016).
14 Ibid., p. 19.
15 On this issue, see, for example, Adam Rosenblatt, *Digging for the Disappeared: Forensic Science after Atrocity* (Stanford: Stanford University Press, 2015).
16 As Wool puts it. Wool, *After War*, p. 189.
17 See Gilles Peress, *The Silence* (New York: Scalo, 1995) and Gilles Peress and Eric Stover, *The Graves: Srebrenica and Vukovar* (New York: Scalo, 1998). On the impact of Peress's photo-journalistic work on representations of international politics and foreign policy, see Liam Kennedy, *Afterimages: Photography and US Foreign Policy* (Chicago: University of Chicago Press, 2016), pp. 119–26.

18 François Debrix, "Post-Mortem Photography: Gilles Peress and the Taxonomy of Death," *Postmodern Culture*, Vol. 9, No. 2 (1999), available at https://muse.jhu.edu/article/27700.

19 Bella Brodzki, *Can These Bones Live? Translation, Survival, and Cultural Memory* (Stanford: Stanford University Press, 2007), p. 5. Differentially, Danchev calls Peress's approach a matter of "tracing the bones." See Alex Danchev, *On Art and War and Terror* (Edinburgh: Edinburgh University Press, 2011), p. 41.

20 Agamben, *Homo Sacer*, pp. 8–10.

21 Michel Foucault, *"Society Must Be Defended": Lectures at the Collège de France, 1975–1976* (New York: Picador, 2003), p. 241.

22 Achille Mbembe, "Necropolitics," *Public Culture*, Vol. 15, No. 1 (2003), p. 39.

23 Agamben, *Homo Sacer*, p. 122.

24 Mbembe, "Necropolitics," p. 40.

25 Michael Dillon and Julian Reid, *The Liberal Way of War: Killing to Make Life Live* (London: Routledge, 2009).

26 François Debrix and Alexander D. Barder, *Beyond Biopolitics: Theory, Violence, and Horror in World Politics* (London: Routledge, 2012).

27 Adriana Cavarero, *Horrorism: Naming Contemporary Violence* (New York: Columbia University Press, 2009).

28 Ibid., p. 8.

29 Ibid., p. 9.

30 Debrix and Barder, *Beyond Biopolitics*, p. 22.

31 Cavarero, *Horrorism*, p. 9.

32 Ibid., p. 9.

33 Debrix and Barder, *Beyond Biopolitics*, p. 20.

34 Cavarero, *Horrorism*, p. 9.

35 Eugene Thacker, *In the Dust of this Planet: Horror of Philosophy, Vol. 1* (Winchester: Zero Books, 2011), p. 9.

36 See, for example, Judith Butler, *Precarious Life: The Powers of Mourning and Violence* (London: Verso, 2004); Bonnie Honig, *Emergency Politics: Paradox, Law, Democracy* (Princeton: Princeton University Press, 2009); Didier Fassin, "Ethics of Survival: A Democratic Approach to the Politics of Life," *Humanity*, Vol. 1, No. 1 (2010), pp. 81–95; and Elizabeth Povinelli, *Economies of Abandonment: Social Belonging and Endurance in Late Liberalism* (Durham, NC: Duke University Press, 2011).

37 Judith Butler, *Frames of War: When Is Life Grievable?* (London: Verso, 2009), p. 62.

38 Fassin, "Ethics of Survival," p. 83; or Honig, *Emergency Politics*, p. 10.

39 Lauren Berlant, *Cruel Optimism* (Durham, NC; Duke University Press, 2011).

40 Although he does not invoke the figure of horror, critical anthropologist Eduardo Kohn offers a related sentiment when he calls for an anthropology that would "look beyond the human," one that would be satisfied that it "is not as if all life will end" even if the human/humanity is to be brushed aside. Eduardo Kohn, *How Forests Think: Toward an Anthropology beyond the Human* (Berkeley: University of California Press, 2013), pp. 221 and 227.

41 Eugene Thacker, *After Life* (Chicago: University of Chicago Press, 2010), p. 5.

42 See, for example, N. Katherine Hayles, *How We Became Posthuman: Virtual Bodies in Cybernetics, Literature, and Informatics* (Chicago: University of Chicago Press, 1999); Donna Haraway, *When Species Meet* (Minneapolis: University of Minnesota Press, 2007); Cary Wolfe, *What Is Posthumanism?* (Minneapolis: University of Minnesota Press, 2009); Jane Bennett, *Vibrant Matter: A Political Ecology of Things* (Durham, NC: Duke University Press, 2010); Diana Coole and Samantha Frost (eds), *New Materialisms: Ontology, Agency, and Politics* (Durham, NC: Duke University Press, 2010); Rosi Braidotti, *The Posthuman* (Cambridge: Polity, 2013); and Richard Grusin (ed.), *The Nonhuman Turn* (Minneapolis: University of Minnesota Press, 2015).

43 David Roden, *Posthuman Life: Philosophy at the Edge of the Human* (London: Routledge, 2015), p. 20.

44 Ibid., p. 23.
45 Veronika Hollinger, "Posthumanism and Cyborg Theory," in Mark Bould, Andrew Butler, Adam Roberts, and Sherryl Vint (eds), *The Routledge Companion to Science Fiction* (London: Routledge, 2009), p. 273; also quoted in Roden, *Posthuman Life*, p. 23.
46 For example, Hayles writes that "the posthuman does not really mean the end of humanity … It signals instead the end of a certain conception of the human [since] … [l]ocated within the dialectic of pattern/randomness and grounded in embodied actuality … the posthuman offers resources for rethinking the articulation of humans with intelligent machines" (Hayles, *How We Became Posthuman*, pp. 286–7). Or we can turn to Braidotti, who claims that the "posthuman knowing subject" is a "time continuum or a collective assemblage" that is best characterized as or through "co-presence," "that is to say the simultaneity of being in the world together" and that "defines the ethics of interaction with both human and non-human others" (Braidotti, *The Posthuman*, p. 169). Note also how in this kind of post-humanist thinking/writing, the non-human is still referred to as (an) other, presumably (an) other to what is remaining of the human/humanity.
47 For more on the metaphysics of substance (and its critique), see, for example, Judith Butler, *Gender Trouble: Feminism and the Subversion of Identity* (London: Routledge, 1990), p. 20. Butler traces the notion back to Nietzsche's criticism of philosophical discourse and of how (Western) philosophy seeks to make the world representative of some "true order of things," an order of things typically governed by and for a rational subject (Butler, *Gender Trouble*, p. 20).
48 Thacker, *In the Dust of this Planet*, p. 46.
49 Ibid., p. 8.
50 As Agamben puts it. Giorgio Agamben, *The Open: Man and Animal* (Stanford: Stanford University Press, 2004), p. 16.
51 In this way, horror may be reminiscent of Benjamin's notion of messianic time (and the violence that may come with it), a point I return to towards the end of Chapter 2. Walter Benjamin, "Theses on the Philosophy of History," in Walter Benjamin, *Illuminations: Essays and Reflections*, ed. Hannah Arendt (New York: Schocken, 1968), pp. 253–64.
52 Cavarero, *Horrorism*, p. 9.
53 Bennett, *Vibrant Matter*, pp. 2–3.

1

VULNERABLE BODIES

Rethinking camp-life and biopolitics

Thinking vulnerability topologically

An important debate in critical geography and spatial studies of late has led to a reevaluation not only of what space means but what it does. For some, this has entailed a move away from topography to look for new ways of understanding relations between space and bodies in a manner that instead privileges topology.[1] To look at space topologically is to emphasize "surfaces and their properties."[2] But to look and think topologically is also, and more crucially, to see space not as fixed, grounded, or stuck in place but rather as relational, connected, distributed, assembled, or supplemented. Topography seeks to identify, mark, demarcate, delineate, and represent, often by establishing a definite landscape or territory. Often, topography relies on the production of cartographic figures, drawings, and images that can enable us to "orient" ourselves. By contrast, topology does not wish to "map discreet [sic] locations or particular objects."[3] Topology points to a potentiality about spatial inscriptions or territorial markings: the potentiality of ascribed or inscribed space to extend its effects beyond its material and referential boundaries. Topology reveals that geographical markings and inscriptions are not given and that, instead, they are interventions (matters of geo-graphy and geo-graphing, of writing of, about, and on space) that seek to set limits to spatiality by privileging certain social, political, and economic relations among subjects and objects. Put differently, topology points to relations between objects and subjects that still take place in space and time but whose particular placing is often a forced and arbitrary ascription to and by representational power. As Paolo Giaccaria and Claudio Minca argue, a topographical representation is a "reduction of reality to the coordinates" privileged by a given spatial measure, structure, or scale. By contrast, a topological understanding of space points to what is always beyond the domain of "a strict and violently implemented regime of rational spatiality."[4] Thinking space topologically is thus a resistance to this forced or arbitrary inscription, to violent regimes of spatiality, and to geography as geo-graphing.[5] With topology, an open field of spatial relations becomes visible that can give us an understanding of the repressive but also, hopefully, expressive, destabilizing, and critical potentialities of power in/as space. Or, to put it differently, with topology, one may start to catch a glimpse of political possibilities that are emergent or potential for bodies-in-space.[6]

As many have noted, the camp has been a ubiquitous geographical as well as political space in modern and late-modern life.[7] Labor camps, youth camps, refugee camps, detention camps, concentration camps, and so on typically have been analyzed topographically. This means that they have been demarcated, closed off, identified, occupied, politically mobilized, territorially recognized, or mapped (sometimes, topographical renderings of the camp have been used to denounce their barbarity and inhumanity, too). Camps have been described as verifiable places and placements for geopolitical wrongs[8] and sometimes, although more rarely, for what may become geopolitically right to do.[9] Camps have also given power clear, localizable, and reproducible modes of political, cultural, and often racial legitimation. At times, power has been a function of the physical ability to put enemies, criminals, transgressors, or abnormal populations in places that can contain them.[10] The recognized territorial establishment of camps has helped political power to be authorized by yielding authority over and often by perpetuating violence on the variety of bodies placed in them.[11] Thus, the topographical function of most camps has also been, historically, closely linked to exercises of biopower (with the organization/arrangement of bodies and lives as one of the camp's primary modalities). Through what may be called a biopolitics of the camp, the sovereign state, often, has given itself the right to determine who or what goes where and who or what can be included and excluded through geographies that reproduce and at times multiply the logic of the camp through a series of related demarcations and oppositions (normal/abnormal, good/evil, safe/dangerous, here/there, inside/outside, friend/enemy, citizen/foreigner).[12] For (bio)political power (the power of the sovereign state and of many governmental agents/agencies, above all), the camp has topographically sanctioned human activities and biological attributes that have been kept under close watch, controlled, or regulated. It has also served (still topographically) to normalize the existence of other, perhaps more "acceptable" or "desirable," actions, conducts, and biophysical characteristics of populations and individual bodies that have been granted their "proper" place and allowed to "circulate" within the larger social and political domain. Put succinctly, as a modality of containment and demarcation, the camp has been a powerful topographical technique. The camp has been mobilized to express a "strict and violent spatial rationality":[13] the rationality of territorially inscribed geographical measures relied upon by the state, the sovereign, or various governmental agents and agencies to delineate biopolitical power and authority over certain people's bodies and lives. The camp has been commonly deployed as a preferred (although not unique) territorial technique—borders and walls are other examples—that has served to mark geo(bio)political locations of power. At the same time, the camp has given rise to many cartographical efforts so that, when needed, it could be found, known, or recognized for what, topographically, it could produce or reproduce. Mapped and cartographically located, the camp has been able to be recognized by the state/sovereign itself (for authorization and legitimation purposes), by the "good" or "normal" subjects of the state/sovereign (for what one may call an allegiance/legitimation effect), by the "bad" or "delinquent" subjects of the sovereign (who may thus see the camp as their likely fate, or what one might call a discipline and deterrence effect), and by other states/sovereigns (who might come to understand another state's camps as a matter of enmity or hostility, for example, or as a justified enforcement of humanitarian protection). Thus, biopolitics and representation have often come together as complementary dimensions of and justifications for topographical delineations of the camp, but also to ensure that, territorially as well as politically, a geography of camp-life could perpetuate itself and extend its effects in space and time. Indeed, modern political geographies, histories, and theories have insisted on the fact that we need to recognize and understand the camp for what topographically it can bring to political power, the state, sovereignty, or governmentality.[14] In a way, one could see the topographical space of the camp, the logic of representation, and biopolitical power as a key nexus at the heart of modern and late-modern geopolitics.

More recently, we have been encouraged to look at the spatiality of the camp and its biopolitical utility somewhat differently.[15] Beyond the camp's topographies and cartographies, we have been invited to think of the camp as a series of topological relations between the potentiality of certain "camp-like" configurations, realized or realizable, and the capacity of certain bodies/lives to be captured by regimes of power supported by conditions likely to turn some bodies/lives into potential "camp-dwellers." We have been offered the opportunity to consider the camp as a topological space—that is to say, as a spatiality that is "always potential—that is, both capable of becoming and *not* becoming."[16] I do not think that these suggestions that one might start to look at the space of the camp topologically rather than topographically are very new. As I suggested above, the apprehension of certain bodies and lives was always part of the topographical mission of the camp, and, more crucially, the potential for the camp's topographical effects to be extended beyond the enclosed spatiality of the camp's perimeter was present in some analyses of the camp too.

Still, I want to discuss in this chapter two complementary critical theorizations that have enabled us to think about the space of the camp in topological terms. Moreover, I want to suggest that, while topological theorizations enable us to better capture the biopolitical matrix of political/social/cultural organization and life (as well as death) that is the camp, these theorizations often leave us with the hope that, even if/when encamped, (some) human bodies and lives can survive, or remain intact, or at least be restored to human dignity (and, in some cases, remembered as such, too) and that, perhaps, human life can somehow be redeemed even in/with the camp and camp-life. As such, critical topological theorizations of camp-life never really seek to step beyond the threshold of life and death, beyond biopolitics and thanatopolitics, beyond the fact of the human, and beyond what is often horrifyingly done to humanity in the camps to start with (but, often, beyond them, too). Thus, as much as this chapter wishes to demonstrate the limitations and representational shortcomings of topographical rationalities and spatialities by introducing topological ways of rethinking the camp and camp-life, it also seeks to point out some of the biopolitical constraints, or limits, of critically and topologically thinking about space, bodies/life, and violence.

Recently deployed theories about the camp have tried to make us understand that what manifests itself topographically about the camp is often the product of a series of topological relations, dispositions, and configurations that mobilize subjects, bodies, and lives in spatial ways. Put differently, theories and theorists that read the camp topologically wish to make us aware not so much of the immateriality or ubiquity of the camp or camp-life (not every human body on the face of the earth is indeed a camp-dweller) but rather of the spatial but not necessarily territorial, cartographical, or representational arrangements that are always already in sight and crucial to the materialization of camps in specific contexts (when and where the potentiality of the camp is indeed actualized). In this chapter, I turn to the related yet distinct theories of the camp/camp-life offered by Giorgio Agamben and Judith Butler to examine how, in their respective work, what I call emergent topologies of camp-life manifest themselves. While I explore the critical potential of Butler's and Agamben's emergent topologies of camp-life, I also show how their theorizations remain tied to a commitment to biopolitical principles. Thus, they also display a reluctance to think the possibility of violence or annihilation beyond human life/humanity (or beyond what, in the Introduction to this volume, I called the metaphysics of substance).

Much has been written about Agamben and the camp. Much less has been said about Butler's take on the relation between space and camp-life. Agamben provides a perspective on camp topology that allows us to understand how it may be that biopolitical power, particularly the power manifested as a sovereign exception, is virtually everywhere. Butler importantly expands upon this Agambenian topological theorizing of the camp in ways that are intended to partially re-territorialize the camp, often in a hopeful or perhaps salutary manner. I take Butler's own topologies of the camp/camp-life to be a supplementation of Agamben's claim that the camp is virtually everywhere. As we shall see below, Butler never completely rejects this claim. Yet she also offers a way of envisioning space topologically in a manner that may be able to reshape certain topographical locations and certain geographical regimes of power, force, violence, and exception, sometimes by reintroducing some emancipatory possibilities, or what some have termed a more "positive" understanding of biopolitics.[17]

Agamben and the virtual camp

In his analysis of the camp as a prototypical space of exception, Agamben notes that "the camp is the most absolute biopolitical space that has ever been realized—a space in which power confronts nothing other than pure biological life without any mediation."[18] For Agamben, what characterizes the camp is not its physical and territorial demarcations and dimensions: where is it located, in or across sovereign territories? Where is it placed on a map? What are its material boundaries and how are they marked and identified (walls, barbed wires, fences, etc.)? What groups of people does it contain, how many, how are they transported to the camp, and how are they organized inside the camp? It is not that these questions are trivial for Agamben.[19] However, these considerations are secondary. They are the product of other, more urgent, concerns. What matters for Agamben (and what eventually may allow one to ask topographical questions such as those listed above) are the relations of power, violence, and utilization of bodies that the space of the camp both reflects and enables. The camp for Agamben occupies a key place in biopolitical designs because it operates as a topological matrix, one that potentially connects bodies in space to a range of operations of force, control, exception, and utility. This is what Agamben means when he declares that the camp is an "absolute" biopolitical space. Somewhat paradoxically given its topographical mandate to detain and contain, the camp is also an open modality, one that facilitates enclosure, foreclosure, and disclosure and has the management of life (including the possibility of death) as its primary target. In Agamben's language, the camp is "absolute" because there seem to be no clear spatial and political limitations to what the camp can be or can do (it can exterminate life, but it can also prevent bodies from being subjected to genocide), to where the camp may end up residing (it can be placed deep into the countryside or at the very heart of a metropolitan area,), and perhaps to who/what the camp's population may be (war prisoners, orphans, diseased bodies, economic refugees, unlawful combatants, etc.). Giaccaria and Minca use the concept of threshold (*soglia*) to make sense of Agamben's virtual non-placement or unlocalizability of the camp. *Soglia* or threshold "connotes a kind of spatiality, a realm of indistinction, in which the borders between the inside and the outside [of the camp] are blurred and un-mappable."[20] As Agamben further asserts, the camp as threshold works topologically, beyond and across spatial limits, because the goal of the camp is to make possible a range of biopolitical operations that are enabled when spatial conditions exist that have the potential to strip the camp dwellers "of every political status" and "reduce [them] completely to naked life."[21] Thus, for Agamben, the camp exists topologically before it exists topographically. The materiality of the camp (its shape, location, social/economic function, the nature and culture of its occupants) is important. For example, it can determine who, in a given context, has been "captured" by the violence of the exception. But it is not primordial in explaining why political power has chosen to represent itself territorially and, often, cartographically, too, in the form of a camp or through an investment in camp-life. This also means for Agamben that the camp is not unique. This is why Agamben writes that we are "facing a camp virtually every time that such a structure is created."[22]

Agamben wants us to understand what he calls the "structure" of the camp. He asks us to realize that the topography of the camp is representable and recognizable geopolitically because it is always already inscribed in multiple layers of topological relations in which bodies are potentially deprived of their "political status" (or what he calls "bare life" in *Homo Sacer*) and through which modalities of (bio)power that rely on what he calls practices of exception are deployed. Yet this topological figure of exception that is the camp, this threshold (*soglia*) between life and death, also resists simple, and perhaps convenient, representations. It is not just about identifying where this "structure" can be found or, for that matter, when it is more likely to emerge and in what kind of spatio-temporal contexts. Such spatial or temporal mappings are feasible, but only because camp-like conditions and relations of power have made them possible. Such mappings answer a need for referentiality: to demonstrate that political power, force, or violence does indeed have physical or material anchors. But, in a way, for Agamben, they give us only a glimpse of what the camp (and, through the camp, the exception) is and does. As Agamben suggests, it is the virtuality of the camp/camp-life that is of topological relevance because such virtuality captures the essentially undecidable or unlocalizable nature of a biopower that emerges by way of exception.[23]

In contrast to Giaccaria and Minca's claim,[24] the camp as a topological matrix or structure is not just a metaphor for Agamben. It is not simply an image that is meant to represent a reality. Rather, Agamben's camp is a reality-in-the-making, a reality-in-production. This is precisely what Agamben's notion of *potenza* tries to capture.[25] *Potenza*, or potentiality, is on the side of virtuality. Here, we need to understand virtuality not as a domain of cognition or representation parallel to the so-called real world but, rather, as a continuation of or even a fusion with reality. This Agambenian conception of the virtual, as expressed in his topology of the camp structure, is reminiscent of Gilles Deleuze's notion of the virtual as a condition, experience, or event that is always in a process of actualization (thus, reality is not so much opposed to virtuality but, rather, reality is the moment of actualization of something that is always already of the order of the virtual).[26] Thus, when Agamben states that camp-life is not simply localizable or not simply identifiable, he does not mean that the camp is imaginary, utopian, immaterial, or even metaphorical.[27] He also does not mean that camp-like conditions are topographically always and everywhere present or commonly distributed across the geopolitical landscape. Rather, the camp structure is both the condition of possibility for and, at times, the actualization of a modality of power/force/exception that is of the order of the virtual (or, as Agamben may prefer to put it, it is about *potenza*). For Agamben, the virtuality of the camp means that it operates topologically, in ways seen and unseen, through relations of power and exceptionality that can become and *not* become. This virtuality is the powerful potentiality (or *potenza*) of camp-life that a topological analysis allows us to be attentive to and that a topographical rendering often misses or simply occludes. From this perspective, it is hard to see how, as Giaccaria and Minca argue, "the topographical and the topological come together."[28] Indeed, there is a danger (one that, I believe, Agamben is concerned with too) of wanting to subsume topological potentialities under topographical materialities and rationalities since the topographical will to referentiality and representation often serves a desire for historical certainty or political truth that often insists on making the camp an exceptional space when, as some have noted, the exception has in fact already become the rule.[29]

Understanding the camp as a topological matrix (as a *potenza* to become and not become) helps us to see that virtual operations of power and violence are crucial to the deployment of a series of quite material political effects in both space and time (and it is perhaps only this way that it may appear that the topological and the topographical come together). The topology of Agamben's camp/camp-life has been criticized for flattening geopolitical topographies[30] and for rendering critically inspired and emancipatory political geographies somewhat "anemic"[31] —that is to say, deprived of actual bodies or blind to the differential exposure of bodies to various forms of suffering.[32] At some level (again, mostly a topographical level), Agamben's topology of the camp/camp-life may appear to place every single body or life on a single plane of geopolitical existence, with all equally vulnerable to the same operations of power and exceptionality, and all potentially confronting the precarious conditions of camp-life in the same way. However, to re-emphasize a point made above, to suggest that the camp is virtually or potentially everywhere, or that its spatial structure is not primarily topographical, is *not* to deny the fact that some bodies and lives will be differentially impacted by regimes of power/violence/exception. Undoubtedly, some bodies and lives are more likely to be captured in camps and harmed by camp-like conditions than others. A topological reading of the camp does not intend to deny such an obvious political and historical fact. Put simply, spatial configurations of power, whether topographical or topological, virtual or material, do target bodies and lives in different ways. But—and this is the key distinction—how bodies and lives are differentially impacted can be explained *not only* by referring to geographical materiality (that is to say, to some assumed nature or to some given condition, measure, or rationality about territory/space) but also by remaining attentive to the topological arrangements that often serve as conditions of possibility (and potentialities) for the geo(bio)political field.

Agamben's virtuality of the camp does not seek to revise the past, either. For example, as Agamben makes clear, a topological rendering of the camp does not at all wish to minimize what took place in the Nazi concentration camps.[33] But, crucially, it does not suppose that a body's capacity to be rendered vulnerable is *only* a function of one's particular geophysical location, position, or condition. It is not simply geography or, better yet, the encounter between geographical materiality and political power that can explain why certain bodies are more likely to be targeted by biopower and thus more likely to be affected by camp-like relations of force, violence, and exception. Or, rather, it is indeed a more complex, not merely topographically representational, geography that matters if one is to make sense of the differential exposure of bodies and lives to exceptionality, vulnerability, and the structure of the camp. Topology may thus help us to appreciate (but perhaps never to comprehend and certainly not to accept) the varying connections between configurations of power and bodies in space that, in some instances, appear to crystallize as peculiar geographical regimes of power, force, abandonment, capture, violence, terror, or death, all of which matter singularly, but none of which are fully—representationally or cartographically—similar to one another, despite the virtual reproducibility of the camp/camp-life.

The virtual distribution of bodies across violent structures of exceptionality is always open to (and perhaps serves as a condition for) the capacity of human life to be placed variably in camp-like situations. I believe that this is how Agamben explains differentials in the exposure of bodies to force and violence. This is also what I take Agamben to mean when he states that "the nexus between state of exception and concentration camp" offers the potentiality to be *and* not to be, to materialize *and* not to materialize.[34] For Agamben, the topological relations of possibility for the camp to manifest itself are always realizable, even if they are not always (often, fortunately) realized for all bodies and lives. This is precisely, in Agamben's perspective, what constitutes the horror of the camp/camp-life. Indeed, what is particularly horrifying about the camp, as revealed through a topological analysis, is that its virtual geography eschews any sense of topographical/representational certainty. Thus, virtually, potentially, nobody can ever claim to be safe from the camp/camp-life. At the same time, some bodies will have relations to spaces of exception that are better able to provide a buffer against the camp. And it is also undeniable that other bodies will continue to be organized, assembled, or distributed across space and in relation to power in ways that will increase their potential encounter with regimes of vulnerability. Once again, this is why the camp is virtual. Virtual, but not universal, immaterial, or undifferentiated.

If the camp is a topological matrix, its purpose is also not to reaffirm a dialectic of absence and presence, a space without the camp versus a space with or of the camp, or a life before the camp versus a now of camp-life, or even an emancipated body versus a body captured by the camp structure. These dichotomies are what topographical spatial representations of the camp tend to reproduce. By contrast, for Agamben, topological spatialities of camp-life are always operative across various politically effective registers of power. Because Agamben's camp is not a fixed locale nor a frozen moment in time (thus, the topological camp resists the idea of a unique historical experience, too), it is a *dispositif* of (bio)political power, violence, and exception that is always engaged, even if it invests bodies with great variety and flexibility, always mutable, always mobile, and always to be remobilized and reinvented (even after a particular camp has been dismantled). This Agambenian insight is reminiscent of another spatial structure of differentiation and containment, the structure of political borders and walls, that Wendy Brown has detailed and that has prompted her to wonder why walls keep on being erected, even by political agents who appear to object to such structures.[35] The materialization of the camp in a particular place cannot completely identify, represent, or explain what the camp is and does. Such a materialization matters. But the materialization of the camp as an event in space and time does not saturate the camp's field of virtual potency, its *potenza*.

Butler and the precariousness of camp-life

Interestingly, even when he theorizes the camp as a virtual condition and a topological matrix, Agamben still identifies specific locations and temporal configurations where and when the camp structure was, is, or will likely be actualized. Yet I believe that this is not so much because topology and topography are complementary. Rather, for Agamben, any topographical setting is derivative of the potentiality of camp-life to become or not to become. According to Agamben, one such actualization or materialization of camp-life was the Nazi concentration camp—Auschwitz, in particular (more on what Agamben had to say about life and horror at Auschwitz will be discussed in Chapter 4). Yet Auschwitz was always more than a calculated, delimited, or mapped space. First and foremost for Agamben, Auschwitz was the "site of an experiment . . . beyond life and death."[36] The site Auschwitz contained horrifying biopolitical experiments but also their proliferation. For Agamben, the biopolitical relations and distributions of power mobilized by the Nazi regime enabled the potential for Auschwitz to be actualized as a camp, as a space of horror. Topological arrangements did not universalize camp-life. Rather, their virtual deployment gave rise to a series of Nazi spatial topographies, one of which was the concentration and extermination camp.

Not unlike what Agamben claims about Auschwitz, for Butler, the camp tends to present itself through its physical manifestations and in ways that sometimes (should) make it hard to avoid or ignore. Differently from Agamben, for Butler, a primarily topographical encounter with the camp remains essential, because to not see the camp for what it is and does is precisely something that (bio)political power often hopes to achieve, particularly in contemporary geopolitical contexts. In contrast to Agamben and, in particular, to his topologically informed misgivings about the violence of representational geographies and rationalities, Butler seems to suggest that topological relations alone are not sufficient to critically engage the complex geography and biopolitics of camp-life. Thus, topography, for Butler, must remain a key part of topological theorizations, since to ignore the materiality of the camp, or to render such a materiality derivative of topology, could amount to allowing power and its "exceptional" force (including its force/power of representation) to remain unseen. According to Butler, the theoretical thrust is not to identify the violence of what is always potentially mobilized as the camp/camp-life: what needs to be urgently challenged is not the rationality of spatially representational regimes but rather the idea of who or what gets to be differentially represented or recognized by those regimes of referentiality and in what ways. As Katharyne Mitchell has argued, "spatial forms of contemporary sovereign power" are often involved in the determination of what she calls "surplus populations."[37] A similar sentiment seems to inform Butler's insistence that encounters with specific camp topographies still need to take place and cannot just be subsumed under a more general theorization about the virtual structure of topological spatialities.

In her work,[38] Butler's encounters with the physical topography of the camp have often been the result of her critical engagements with contemporary dominant practices and representations in the US-led global war on terror, with the proliferation of sites/sights such as Abu Ghraib, Guantanamo, detention zones in airports, rendition practices, and CIA "black sites" of interrogation and torture. Yet Abu Ghraib, Guantanamo, and other places of containment and exception are not just sites that can be geopolitically marked (or, at least, uncovered despite security practices of deception and occlusion), cartographically delineated (for some of them), or, in some cases, territorially recognized. They are actual lived-in locations and situations for certain bodies and populations that are intersected by various relations of force and power and by various possibilities for human life and, often, death (in this way, they are similar to some of the necropolitical spaces described by Achille Mbembe[39]). They are real spaces whose eventuality or materialization is related to complex connectivities between spatial arrangements of power and bodies. In this way, these sites/camps of terror are also reminiscent of what Ash Amin has characterized as "relational networks," whereby camps can be seen as "perforated entities with connections that stretch far back in time and space."[40] Another way of putting it would be to suggest that, for Butler, these camps and camp-like configurations are events whose often abhorrent manifestations still have to be represented, even if and when many dominant contemporary representational frames wish to negate or, at least, minimize their physical existence. Just as crucially, the camps also need to be positioned in a frame of vision that has the capacity to challenge the inevitability of the spatial and referential topographies of camp-life while remaining sensitive to the multitude of (geo)political dispositions that often have the capture of bodies and lives as their objectives. Thus, Butler's camps, in several of her post-9/11 texts,[41] are domains of topological *and* topographical analysis, and the two perspectives are often seen by her as complementary.

According to Butler, what provides today's camps with topological significance are relations of vulnerability and precariousness, or the multi-layered imbrication of bodies and lives in geo(bio)political discourses and representations of power, violence, terror, and death that establish or reinforce conceptual and ideological oppositions between who can live and who can die, whose death can be mourned and whose death is unworthy of remembrance, and who can be afforded the privilege to grieve for lost lives and who will not. More crucially than for Agamben, Butler's topological understanding of contemporary camp-life is about variable regimes of exposure to vulnerability as a result of the geopolitics of state-enforced exception in the context of the war on terror. Whereas Agamben's topology of the camp was often driven by the need to become aware of the potentiality of a somewhat ahistorical biopolitical "structure" of camp-life that is always virtually everywhere, thus evoking what some have referred to as Agamben's "negative biopolitics,"[42] Butler's approach to the spatiality of the camp/camp-life wishes to rediscover traces of life and the living within the multiply assembled political, cultural, ethical, and affective spaces of the camp. As Elizabeth Povinelli puts it (although not precisely about Butler's take on contemporary camp-life), the focus has to be put on "differentially distributed zones of vulnerability and abandonment as places in which, at least potentially, a new ethics of life and sociability could emerge."[43] In Butler's *Frames of War*, the camp figures as such a space, which, paradoxically but also potentially, despite its seemingly restrictive geography and its dark political materialities and rationalities, insists on the persistence of life.[44] Like Agamben, Butler's apprehension of space and places (space or places of terror, above all) is topologically informed. But, unlike Agamben, topology enables Butler to be on the lookout for specific topographies of terror as well as for new spaces of and for life in and through current modalities of representational power and violence. Butler's fused topology and topography of the camp hopes to enable a critical potentiality for a rekindled life or a rediscovered sociability (to use Povinelli's turn of phrase). In this way, Butler's camp-life may also offer some emancipatory outcome by trying to resist dominant brutal and often fatal topographies of detention, incarceration, torture, and disappearance in the post-9/11 era.

In particular, Butler opposes a topological reading of the US government's mobilization of Guantanamo Bay's Camp Delta, where post-9/11 enemy combatants, Al Qaeda members and sympathizers, terrorists, and Taliban fighters have been detained, as a space virtually open to exceptional power, sovereign violence, torture, and death, but also to a modality of life that stubbornly refuses to vanish, to go unnoticed, or to be stripped of the capacity to live a social/political life that Agamben often associates with the concept of bare life (a life deprived of any social/political qualities).[45] Among other things, Butler's topological reading of Camp Delta allows her to highlight the relevance of poems that have been written by the detainees there.[46] For Butler, the poems written by some of the inmates— leaked and finally made public despite US government censorship—open up a conceptual and political space that can usher in a different vision of and a different potential for the camp and camp-life, one that, hopefully, may also resist or refute the dominant topographical representations of biopower (here, the US state's power of life or death over the detainees). For Butler, the written fragments rescued from the hermetic space of the camp have the potential (*potenza?*) to reposition life topologically and, perhaps, to re-ignite life as survivability or over-living at a time when the camp increasingly seems to be a fateful generalized matrix of contemporary life. Thus, Butler's topological take on the Guantanamo detainees' poems helps her to question geopolitical frames and framings—the framing of the war, the framing of terror, perhaps the framing of life under conditions of torture—that dominant topographical discourses and representations about the war on terror have relied on and reproduced.[47]

The Guantanamo poems are about the virtuality of the camp/camp-life. They are what camp-life can become, Butler suggests. Camp-life is thus not only about topographically realized geopolitical power, force, or exceptionality. But neither is it only about multiple topological registers of biopolitical capture of life, as Agamben might claim. Here, revisiting the camp or camp-life through the Guantanamo detainees' textual traces offers a "how" (rather than a "what" and a "where") that "interrogate(s) the kinds of utterance possible at the limits of grief, humiliation, longing, and rage."[48] Still, for Butler, thinking and writing about a critical "how" of and about the camp/camp-life also seeks to make visible what appears to be a different, new, but most essential "what." These are some of the subversive potentialities that Butler's reading of the camp facilitates and that, for Butler, are urgently needed. As Butler puts it, the poems, as fragments of a life that the camp both limits and reveals, are "proof of stubborn life, vulnerable, overwhelmed, their own and not their own, dispossessed, enraged, and perspicacious."[49]

Thus, for Butler, the space of the camp is topological also in the sense that it carves out a domain of critical biopolitical possibility at the very moment when and at the very site where life seems to be doomed to disappearance. Butler's approach to camp-life is topological with regards to the future or the to-come (what may and may not become) as much as, if not more than, the past (what could have become). Among other virtualities of life, Butler's camp can become a place from which a critical plea and a political hope become visible, a place that, paradoxically (given its topographical delimitations), can also be open to a capacity for over-living/survivability through fragments of being that refuse to go away as well as through textual traces that conventional representations of (bio)political power, force, exception, and violence in contexts of emergency, war, and terror typically ignore.

The motif of survivability, or over-living,[50] highlighted by Butler in her theorization of post-9/11 camp-life seems to provide an alternative to Agamben's virtual camp. But Butler's camp possibilities for over-living are potential and virtual too. What may appear to allow Butler to surmount what some have considered to be Agamben's impasse with regards to the "everywhereness" of the topological camp[51] (even though, as I have argued above, such a reading is partial at best) is that her critical spatial and relational rendition of camp-life is meant to return us to topography, to representation, and to identifiable spaces, even if such a return to topography, representation, and identification is critically driven by political or emancipatory hope. Butler turns to a topological understanding of spatial relations to find there some critical inspiration to reframe geo(bio)political analysis and to offer political as well as ethical alternatives for human life. Thus, for Butler, to reconquer topography is a crucial political and ethical task, particularly when camp-life is at stake. In a more recent intervention on the thought of author and holocaust survivor Primo Levi, she reprises this critically politico-ethical posture by invoking not so much the camp (at least, not directly) but rather the notion of history and, in particular, what the language of history can do. Butler states that there is a "historical demand to produce a political practice and mode of engagement that respects and institutionalizes protection for the precariousness of life itself."[52]

At the same time, this attempt to re-appropriate topography for critical or emancipatory purposes (with regards to human life/over-living), this hope to steer topography towards different representational domains that may not have been allowed to be seen, is not without theoretical challenges and, at times, inconsistencies, too. Ironically, perhaps, Butler seems to forget some of her own lessons about the dangers of imposing or reinserting representational, referential, or topographical demarcations. In the name of a demand to "reconsider the way in which we conceptualize the body in the field of politics,"[53] Butler writes that

> we can think about demarcating the human body through identifying its boundary, or in what form it is bound, but that is to miss the crucial fact that the body is, in certain ways and even inevitably unbound—in its acting, its

receptivity, in its speech, desire, and mobility. It is outside itself, in the world of others, in a space and time it does not control, and it not only exists in the vector of these relations, but as this very vector.[54]

At first glance, such a conceptual reframing of the body in/and space seems to eschew topographical and representational thinking (and its limitations). It appears to reflect a topological understanding of relations and dispositions among spatialities and bodies. Moreover, as a result of this "not belonging to itself" of the body, or of an insistence on seeing the body as a "vector of relations," a new way of envisioning vulnerability may be illuminated, one that, from Butler's perspective, can only be beneficial. And again, with such a call for a de-anchoring, or unbounding, of the body vis-à-vis geopolitical demarcations and borders, a different form of social unity or solidarity about the human/humanity may be realized. Or, as Butler would have it, the lack of boundaries to the body leads to a necessary sense of survivability/over-living that can reflect what she calls the "constitutive sociability of the body," a constitutive sociability and survivability that perhaps will "minimize the conditions of precariousness in egalitarian ways."[55]

Butler's description of this unbound body—her opening of human life to virtual encounters with others or the outside on the ground of precariousness or vulnerability—seems to have the potential to operate topologically by creating conditions of life and being that can offer means to respond to power, violence, and the exception differently, even in the midst of a virtual condition of camp-life. By placing her analysis of the precariousness of life in a conceptual domain where the body is always already understood as having been displaced, othered, unbound, and possibly disseminated across space and time, Butler seeks to present a response to the geopolitical reality of biopolitical terror, a terror that, according to her, does not care for the life of some humans and some bodies. But the problem here is that Butler does not follow through on the promises that can be derived from her topological or critically topographical rethinking of space and the body. To put it differently, Butler still finds herself having to make references to a politics of life and the body that can be identifiable and localizable in particular places. This modality of biopolitics (although it may be "positive") needs to inscribe its political resurgence in topographical space, as indicated above. And so, while Butler argues that, as a result of encounters with an "outside" or an "other" that is impossible to plan for, certain "bodies will appear more precariously than others,"[56] she also explains that it is the case because it is a function of "which versions of the body, or of morphology in general, support or underwrite the idea of the human life that is worth protecting, sheltering, living, mourning."[57] Here, Butler's explanations as to why a given life or body is more likely to be precarious than another is not just about differential regimes of exposure to terror, exception, or violence. Rather, and somewhat strangely, the selective precariousness of life and the variability in the vulnerability of the body become the outcome of what she calls "morphology in general"—that is to say, the general, and often defining, shape, look, and context of the body. This puzzling choice to reassign the differentiality of human vulnerability to morphology takes Butler back to a rather conventional biological and political frame of representation and analysis,[58] but also to a more traditional and delimited mode of topographical thinking—an irony for a thinker so intent on resisting the "operations of the frame"[59]—whereby "frameworks establish in advance what kind of life will be a life worth living, what life will be a life worth preserving, and what life will become worthy of being mourned."[60] Equipped with her newly found critical perspective, made possible by her conceptual turn towards the topology of the camp/camp-life, Butler is eager to rediscover topography in order to re-anchor there a political and representational critique. She reintegrates geopolitical land-scapes where topographical representations, frames, maps, measures, rationalities, and indeed morphologies often tell stories about the opposition between a good life and an evil enemy existence (a rather traditional reframing of inside and outside, or of friend and enemy).

As we have seen, topography, for Butler, can never completely be left behind because too much of human life still resides there. The topological space of the camp (and the fragments of life it makes visible) matters because, for Butler, it is from there that the struggle to reconquer topographical representations can take place. Her argument remains critically compelling because, as Butler makes clear, it is still not supposed to be about rediscovering an essential truth about space, politics, or geopolitical relations that often crystallize in the form of the camp. Rather, it is about testifying to what has happened to precarious, vulnerable, and grieved bodies and lives, even if such a testimony is only a trace, an inaccurate remnant, or an imprecise recollection of what may have happened to humanity under camp-like conditions. Topography, rediscovered and perhaps critically re-energized through an appreciation for the topology of the camp/camp-life, can become another space of representation but hopefully a different form of representation that, as Butler clarifies in another text, would always be open to "fallibility or faltering."[61] Topographical space, then, would remain representational, referential, and real. But it would also be transformed into (and made meaningful as) a domain where rep-resentation takes the shape of a "testimony [that is] something other than securing a verifiable sequence of events."[62] Such a reinvested topography of the camp would thus retain, for the sake of life or over-living, traces of topological relations that, for Butler, are crucial in helping us to recognize not so much "what" the camp was, is, or will be, but rather "that" the camp has been and, probably, virtually, will continue to be.[63]

Thinking topologically for the sake of human life?

A topological understanding of the camp is an urgent necessity for both Butler and Agamben. As Agamben clarifies in *Remnants of Auschwitz*, the topological gaze can be the guarantee that camp-like conditions will not remain unspeakable and that we will not "contribute to the glory" of the camp (as he puts it) by treating it as an incommensurable topographical reality that, too often, we would prefer to leave untouched and perhaps unthought (for example, we know where it is located, we tell ourselves that we know what it was about, and we will forever leave it there, sacred, but also at bay).[64] Butler's own sense of urgency when partially leaving topographies of the camp behind (since, as we saw, she does not give up on topography altogether) seems to offer a complementary sentiment. For Butler, topology helps us to realize the importance of what she calls, in another work, "a place between life and death."[65] This place "between life and death" is also, for Butler, a "vacillating boundary" (since the potentiality for both life and death always remains).[66] Conditioned by dominant geo(bio)political representations and rationalities, this "vacillating boundary" must nonetheless remain in excess of them and their topographies. The "vacillating boundary" between life and death that Butler invokes is not exactly the same thing as Agamben's virtuality or *potenza* about camp-life. Yet, like Agamben's *potenza*, this boundary between life and death potentially affects all human bodies and lives, whether they are already physically captured by the camp or not.

Despite some important differences, Agamben and Butler believe that critical theorizing about the camp and its biopolitics requires one to think in terms of emergent topologies of camp-life. Both Agamben and Butler maintain, in their own ways, that emergent topologies of camp-life, as vacillating boundaries between survivability/over-living and disappearance/annihilation, can be guarantees that camps, human lives (as well as human deaths) in the camps, and vulnerable bodies will not be forgotten by being occluded by larger and supposedly more commanding geo(bio)political assumptions, justifications, and rationalities about power or violence. For Agamben and Butler, it is human life (in its specific modalities of living, dying, being made bare, being rendered vulnerable, being grieved, or over-lived) that is still very much at stake in and about the emergent topologies of camp-life they identify. Topologies of the camp/camp-life are for them still driven by biopolitical logics and considerations (not allowing the lives in the camps to become unknown, unspoken, or unthought, for Agamben; insisting on the stubborn presence of survivability even in the darkest recesses of the contemporary war on terror camps, for Butler), even if these logics and considerations insist on a crucial critical rethinking of the relationship between bodies and spaces of power. Ultimately, it seems that topological theorizations about the camp are urgent necessities for Agamben and Butler because, unlike topographical analyses, these topological ways of thinking will serve as reminders about certain spatial arrangements and dispositions that remain essential structures or matrices for modalities of (bio)power that have human bodies and lives as their main targets.

As Butler stresses, the "new configuration of power requires a new theoretical framework or, at least, a revision of the models for thinking power that we already have at our disposal."[67] As she and Agamben intimate, for scholars willing to think space and biopolitics critically, an emphasis on emergent topologies can offer, if not a new fully formed theoretical framework that can make sense of the relations between bodies and space, at least a constant call to pluralize, and to keep open, complex, and in excess of themselves, representational models, measures, and rationalities of geo(bio)political power, force, violence, and terror, often for the sake of the human/humanity. Such a move towards topological theorizing may not have to be hostile to certain (critical) topographies, as Butler once again has shown us. But such a move could also signal a refusal to place power, the state, sovereignty, or governmentalities and their geographical designs ahead of political practices from which a multitude of life possibilities may arise.

And yet, despite these theorizations' potentialities for human life, I wonder if a continued reliance on critical biopolitical perspectives in new theoretical frameworks such as those offered by Agamben's and Butler's topologies of camp-life can do justice to the forms of violence onto (human) bodies, as well as onto parts or even fragments of traces of bodies, in topological spaces like camps and their extensions. Put differently, can emergent topologies of camp-life make sense of what Butler calls "new configurations of power," including "configurations of power" (new or old) that do not have the life or death of humans—and probably not even over-living/survivability—as their objective or target, as we will see in Chapters 3 and 4? Encouraged by theoretical frameworks such as those presented by Agamben and Butler, the following chapters are on the lookout for supplementary theorizations that may be capable of thinking critically about a kind of power, force, destruction, or disappearance whose ties to biopolitics (the life or death of the human body, its possible survivability) are no longer crucial and, instead, having given itself over to horror, no longer appears to have as a primary concern the fate of humanity. The next chapter initiates the transition towards new theorizations reliant upon a horror beyond the human/humanity by examining the vulnerabilities that are tied to the dilemma of sovereign power/force (including its security), particularly as the life/body of the sovereign is confronted with the specter of the finitude of time.

Notes

1 See, for example, Sarah Whatmore, *Hybrid Geographies: Natures, Cultures, Spaces* (Thousand Oaks: Sage, 2001); Doreen Massey, *For Space* (Thousand Oaks: Sage, 2005); Jonathan Murdoch, *Post-Structuralist Geography: A Guide to Relational Space* (Thousand Oaks: Sage, 2005); or Martin Jones, "Phase Space: Geography, Relational Thinking, and Beyond," *Progress in Human Geography*, Vol. 33, No. 4 (2009), pp. 487–506.

2 Virginia Blum and Ana Secor, "Psychotopologies: Closing the Circuit between Psychic and Material Space," *Environment and Planning D: Society and Space*, Vol. 29, No. 6 (2011), p. 1034.

3 Oliver Belcher, Lisa Martin, Ana Secor, Stephanie Simon, and Tommy Wilson, "Everywhere and Nowhere: The Exception and the Topological Challenge of Geography," *Antipode*, Vol. 40, No. 4 (2008), p. 499.

4 Paolo Giaccaria and Claudio Minca, "Topographies/Topologies of the Camp: Auschwitz as a Spatial Threshold," *Political Geography*, Vol. 30, No. 1 (2011), p. 4.

5 See Gearóid Ó Tuathail, *Critical Geopolitics: The Politics of Writing Global Space* (Minneapolis: University of Minnesota Press, 1996); and Matthew Sparke, *In the Space of Theory: Postfoundational Geographies of the Nation-State* (Minneapolis: University of Minnesota Press, 2005).

6 The emergence of topological thinking in critical geography circles is partially the product of a reconceptualization of space and spatial units (place, region, nation, city, sovereign state, international relations, and so on) as a matter of relational networks.

See, for example, Ash Amin, "Regulating Economic Globalization," *Transactions of the Institute of British Geographers*,Vol. 29, No. 2 (2004), pp. 217–33; or Massey, *For Space*. The emphasis on the relational in and about space may have been spurred by the advent of globalization and, in particular, global networks of capital deploying what some have called "transformative spatial ontologies." See Ash Amin, "Spatialities of Globalization," *Environment and Planning A*,Vol. 34, No. 3 (2002), pp. 385–9; or John Urry, *Global Complexity* (Cambridge: Polity, 2003). Transformative spatial ontologies as topologies allow one to detect how modalities of governance (of space, of populations) have been able to proliferate their effects in non-traditional, non-referential, and relational ways (see Amin, "Regulating Economic Globalization," p. 229). Another important influence on the emergence of topological analysis among critical geographers has come from the discipline of philosophy and, in particular, the (phenomenologically) derived distinction between forms or modes of space and the concept of space as phenomenon. According to Jeff Malpas, this distinction alerts us to the importance of not treating space as a given but rather of studying space as spatialities, something that Malpas prefers to call a "philosophical topography." Jeff Malpas, "Putting Space in Place: Philosophical Topography and Relational Geography," *Environment and Planning D: Society and Space*, Vol. 30, No. 2 (2012), p. 227.

7 See, for example, Jenny Edkins, "Sovereign Power, Zones of Indistinction, and the Camp," *Alternatives*, Vol. 25, No. 1 (2000), pp. 3–25; Derek Gregory, *The Colonial Present: Afghanistan, Palestine, Iraq* (London: Blackwell, 2004); Bülent Diken and Carsten Laustsen, *The Culture of Exception: Sociology Facing the Camp* (London: Routledge, 2005); and Claudio Minca, "The Return of the Camp," *Progress in Human Geography*, Vol. 29, No. 4 (2005), pp. 405–12.

8 Hannah Arendt, *Eichmann in Jerusalem: A Report on the Banality of Evil* (New York: Penguin, 2006).

9 See, for example, Michel Agier, *On the Margins of the World: The Refugee Experience Today* (Cambridge: Polity, 2008).

10 Michel Foucault, *Discipline and Punish: The Birth of the Prison* (New York: Vintage Books, 1979).

11 Hannah Arendt, *The Origins of Totalitarianism* (New York: Harcourt, Brace, Jovanovich, 1973).

12 On this topic, see, for example, R. B. J. Walker, *Inside/Outside: International Relations as Political Theory* (Cambridge: Cambridge University Press, 1992); Roxanne Doty, *Imperial Encounters: The Politics of Representation in North-South Relations* (Minneapolis: University of Minnesota Press, 1996); or, more recently, Wendy Brown, *Walled States, Waning Sovereignty* (New York: Zone Books, 2010).

13 Giaccaria and Minca, "Topographies/Topologies of the Camp," p. 4.

14 On the topographical uses of the camp for political power—state sovereignty, in particular—see, for example, Wolfgang Sofsky, *The Order of Terror: The Concentration Camp* (Princeton: Princeton University Press, 1999); Mitchell Dean, "Demonic Societies: Liberalism, Biopolitics, and Sovereignty," in Thomas Blom Hansen and Finn Stepputat (eds), *States of Imagination: Ethnographic Explorations of the Postcolonial State* (Durham: Duke University Press, 2001), pp. 41–64; and Patricia Owens, "Humanity, Sovereignty, and the Camps," *International Politics*, Vol. 45, No. 4 (2008), pp. 522–30.

15 Among the relevant studies here are: Giorgio Agamben, *Homo Sacer: Sovereign Power and Bare Life* (Stanford: Stanford University Press, 1998); Diken and Laustsen, *The Culture of Exception*; Minca, "The Return of the Camp"; Claudio Minca, "Giorgio Agamben and the New Biopolitical Nomos," *Geografiska Annaler*, Vol. 88, No. 4 (2006), pp. 387–403; Derek Gregory, "The Black Flag: Guantanamo Bay and the Space of Exception," *Geografiska Annaler*, Vol. 88, No. (4) (2006), pp. 405–27; Mathew Coleman, "Review: State of Exception," *Environment and Planning D: Society and Space*,Vol. 25, No. 1 (2007), pp. 187–90; François Debrix, "The Virtual Nomos?" in Stephen Legg (ed.), *Spatiality, Sovereignty, and Carl Schmitt* (London: Routledge, 2011), pp. 220–6; and Giaccaria and Minca, "Topographies/Topologies of the Camp."

16 Belcher *et al.*, "Everywhere and Nowhere," p. 502.
17 Janell Watson, "Butler's Biopolitics," *Theory & Event*, Vol. 15, No. 2 (2012), available at: https://muse.jhu.edu/article/478357.
18 Giorgio Agamben, *Means without End: Notes on Politics* (Minneapolis: University of Minnesota Press, 2000), p. 41.
19 Giaccaria and Minca, "Topographies/Topologies of the Camp," p. 7.
20 Ibid., p. 5.
21 Agamben, *Means without End*, p. 41.
22 Ibid., p. 41.
23 Agamben, *Homo Sacer*, p. 19.
24 Giaccaria and Minca, "Topographies/Topologies of the Camp," p. 5.
25 For more on Agamben's notion of potentiality or *potenza*, see Giorgio Agamben, *Potentialities: Collected Essays in Philosophy* (Stanford: Stanford University Press, 1999). See also Minca, "The Return of the Camp."
26 On Deleuze's notion of the virtual, see Gilles Deleuze, *Difference and Repetition* (New York: Columbia University Press, 1994); and Miguel De Landa, *Intensive Science and Virtual Philosophy* (London: Continuum, 2002).
27 For further clarification on this question, see Nick Vaughan-Williams, "The UK Border Security Continuum: Virtual Biopolitics and the Simulation of the Sovereign Ban," *Environment and Planning D: Society and Space*, Vol. 28, No. 6 (2010), pp. 1071–83; and François Debrix and Alexander Barder, *Beyond Biopolitics: Theory, Violence, and Horror in World Politics* (London: Routledge, 2012), pp. 69–74.
28 Giaccaria and Minca, "Topographies/Topologies of the Camp," p. 5.
29 See Walter Benjamin, "Theses on the Philosophy of History," in Walter Benjamin, *Illuminations: Essays and Reflections*, ed. Hannah Arendt (New York: Schocken, 1968), pp. 253–64; Agamben, *Homo Sacer*; and Michael Hardt and Antonio Negri, *Multitude: War and Democracy in the Age of Empire* (New York: Penguin, 2004).
30 Mitch Rose and John Wylie, "Animating Landscape," *Environment and Planning D: Society and Space*, Vol. 24, No. 4 (2006), pp. 475–479.
31 Mathew Coleman and Kevin Grove, "Biopolitics, Biopower, and the Return of Sovereignty," *Environment and Planning D: Society and Space*, Vol. 27, No. 3 (2009), pp. 489–507.
32 On "anemic" geographies, see also Sparke, *In the Space of Theory*.
33 Giorgio Agamben, *Remnants of Auschwitz: The Witness and the Archive* (New York: Zone Books, 1999).
34 Agamben, *Means without End*, p. 39.
35 Brown, *Walled States, Waning Sovereignty*.
36 Agamben, *Remnants of Auschwitz*, p. 52.
37 Katharyne Mitchell, "Pre-Black Futures," *Antipode*, Vol. 41, No.1 (2009), p. 241.
38 Primarily, her post-9/11 books *Precarious Life: The Powers of Mourning and Violence* (London: Verso, 2004) and *Frames of War: When Is Life Grievable?* (London: Verso, 2009).
39 Achille Mbembe, "Necropolitics," *Public Culture*, Vol. 15, No. 1 (2003), pp. 11–40.
40 Amin, "Regulating Economic Globalization," p. 234.
41 Again, *Precarious Life* and *Frames of War*, primarily.
42 See, for example, Roberto Esposito, *Bios: Biopolitics and Philosophy* (Minneapolis: University of Minnesota Press, 2008); Lorenzo Chiesa, "Giorgio Agamben's Franciscan Ontology," *Cosmos and History: The Journal of Natural and Social Philosophy*, Vol. 5, No 1 (2009), no page given (online journal); and Watson, "Butler's Biopolitics," available at: http://cosmosandhistory.org/index.php/journal/article/view/130.
43 Elizabeth Povinelli, *Economies of Abandonment: Social Belonging and Endurance in Late Liberalism* (Durham: Duke University Press, 2011), p. 109.
44 Butler, *Frames of War*, p. 59.
45 Agamben, *Homo Sacer*.
46 Butler, *Frames of War*, pp. 55–62.
47 See, for example, Thomas Barnett, *The Pentagon's New Map: War and Peace in the Twenty-First Century* (New York: Berkley Trade, 2005); Robert Kaplan, *Imperial Grunts: On the*

Ground with the American Military, from Mongolia to the Philippines to Iraq and Beyond (New York:Vintage, 2006); or Robert Kaplan, *The Revenge of Geography:What the Map Tells Us about Coming Conflicts and the Battle against Fate* (NewYork: Random House, 2012).

48 Butler, *Frames of War*, p. 59.

49 Ibid., p. 62.

50 On over-living, see also Bonnie Honig, *Emergency Politics: Paradox, Law, Democracy* (Princeton: Princeton University Press, 2009), p. 11.

51 See, for example, Coleman and Grove, "Biopolitics, Biopower, and the Return of Sovereignty."

52 Judith Butler, *Parting Ways: Jewishness and the Critique of Zionism* (New York: Columbia University Press, 2012), p. 201.

53 Butler, *Frames of War*, p. 52.

54 Ibid., p. 53.

55 Ibid., p. 54.

56 Ibid., p. 53.

57 Ibid., p. 53.

58 For more on this reading, see François Debrix, "Rethinking Democracy's Emergence: Towards New Spaces of Grief and Survivability," *Environment and Planning D: Society and Space*,Vol. 29, No. 2 (2009), pp. 369–74.

59 As Butler puts it. Butler, *Frames of War*, pp. 8–12.

60 Ibid., p. 53.

61 Butler, *Parting Ways*, p. 183.

62 Ibid., p. 183.

63 Ibid., p. 183.

64 Agamben, *Remnants of Auschwitz*, pp. 32–3.

65 Judith Butler, *Antigone's Claim: Kinship between Life and Death* (New York: Columbia University Press, 2000), p. 78.

66 Ibid., p. 78.

67 Butler, *Precarious Life*, p. 92.

2

TIME AND THE SOVEREIGN BODY

How security politics confronts the horror of finitude

Introduction

At its core, the politics of security is obsessed with the survival of the sovereign.[1] Security tends to envision the sovereign as a vulnerable body/subject,[2] one whose existence is always at the mercy of all sorts of forces or agents whose purpose is to challenge the life of the sovereign and, in particular, the continuity of the sovereign order from one embodiment (a king, a political system, a regime, a body politic) to the next (the next king, the next regime, the next political system, etc.). In this chapter, I turn to theological concepts, and to the historico-philosophical linkages of these concepts to sovereignty and security, to shed light on the existential dimensions of the idea of the life and duration of the sovereign and on the politics of (sovereign) survival defined as security. More crucially, I mobilize theological concepts to rethink the relationship between sovereignty and security. I wish to make sense of the place that the question of life versus death, the fact of sovereign violence, and the problem of temporality for the sovereign occupy in modalities of security.

The notion of sovereign restraint, a notion captured by the theological concept of *katechon*,[3] is introduced to suggest that the politics of security, geared towards survival as it may be, is dependent upon a fundamentally violent, exclusive, uncompromising, and often terrorizing objective: to keep at bay forces of finitude. Thus, sovereign restraint or, if one prefers, katechontic sovereignty, placed in the hands of security agents, is often about the making of death worlds[4] in order to enable the sovereign order/body to exist permanently, perhaps eternally. This katechontic logic of overwhelmingly violent and aggressive restraint in the face of finitude or life termination, as I suggest in this chapter, may be better captured by confronting the notion of *katechon* (the dimension of sovereignty designed to hold off finite ends) with the concept of *eschaton*. The *eschaton* is a figure/agent that ends time/the temporal order or refuses to abide by the belief in infinity or eternity.[5] Put some-what differently, the securitizing work of the *katechon*, or restrainer, assumes that the sovereign's existence is always fragile and that, as such, eschatological time (the revelation that life—including the life of the sovereign—is finite and that human activities have this-worldly ends) must be opposed. Thus, I argue, katechontic sovereignty is a modality of power/force/violence/terror that calls in or, in fact, invents security and security practices to fend off the *eschaton*, or, at least, to cast away all the uncertain, temporal, finite, or non-eternal possibilities for (human as well as sovereign) life that eschatological time represents.

The theoretical context of this study is informed by the suggestion that the theologico-political confrontation between *eschaton* and *katechon* involves decisions over life and death, matters of biopolitics and necropolitics, and encounters between security and terror that have their origins in the precarious positioning of the sovereign order/body, always on the cusp of permanence and disappearance. The notion of katechontic sovereignty, as explained in this chapter, can make sense of the seeming paradox between order and restraint, on the one hand, and chaos and boundless violence, on the other, a paradox that is generative of much of security politics today. Indeed, katechontic sovereignty requires that operations of security incessantly and intensely be performed so that material and concrete instances of violence, force, or terror may remain within the purview of the sovereign's power, order, or body. In this way, katechontic sovereignty reveals that security and terror cannot be thought as antagonistic concepts and practices (as so many security or terror/terrorism studies experts claim). Rather, security and terror form a contin-uum of actions, decisions, and political representations, often actions, decisions, and representations over life and death.

My intimation that theological concepts are needed to make sense of sover-eignty, security, and the violence/terror that security often brings is not meant to be an answer to the call made by many international relations or geopolitics scholars of late that "religious actors, institutions, and practices need to assume their proper role in international political theory and practice" (something that, for example, Elizabeth Shakman Hurd has deplored[6]). It is not just about bringing religion or theology into the international relations or even political theory realm. It is also not primarily about explaining international politics or political theoretical issues by way of theology. Rather, and somewhat in line with a post-secular trend in political theorizing,[7] it is a recognition that the so-called rupture of modern political forms and ideas from the religious or spiritually metaphysical[8] was always a forced and arbitrary move, one that often betrayed (and, to some extent, still does) a desire to affirm political origins or foundations on novel, self-sufficient, and secular grounds that were attempts at "killing God" in order for humanistico-political notions (man, the state, reason, etc.) to take over the ontological core once occupied by the divine. I do not claim that religion or theology is a "variable" in an otherwise permanent domain of international political theoretical life.[9] Rather, the close kinship, then and now, between the existence and maintenance of sovereign order/life and the perpetuation of violent security practices evokes the inseparability, in pre-modern as well as (late) modern contexts, of theology and theory, or of the sacred and the secular. This sentiment about the inseparability of theology and theory is reminiscent of Wendy Brown's reflections on the contemporary condition of sovereignty. As Brown notes, contemporary "nation-state sovereignty becomes openly and aggressively rather than passively theological."[10] While I agree with Brown's observation, she nonetheless errs in seeing the complicity between theology and theory on the matter of sovereignty as mainly a contemporary phenomenon. Carl Schmitt was closer to capturing the kinship when he declared that "all significant concepts of the modern theory of the state are secularized theological concepts."[11] Although the present chapter is not about Schmitt, and although it is not interested in postulating a view of the relationship between politics and religion that is uniquely Schmittian, it does recognize that, over the past century, Schmitt may have come closest to expressing the katechontic dimensions of modern sovereign power.

The first part of this chapter explores the modality of katechontic sovereignty, and it explains how the sovereign, although seen as eternal, must nonetheless be perceived as constantly vulnerable and threatened in order for the work of the *katechon* to gain meaning and force. A second section introduces the linkage between the work of the *katechon* and security politics. It develops the argument about the confrontation between katechontic sovereignty and the *eschaton* of time, and it reveals that, perversely perhaps, the *katechon* must always mobilize the *eschaton* (or agents of disorder and finitude). Indeed, without eschatological figures or agents to be antagonized and, in some cases, eradicated, the precarious order of the sovereign (and the power/terror of the *katechon*) would be purposeless. The third section of this chapter pushes further the point about the need for the constant presence as threat of the *eschaton* in security politics and policies, and it investigates the possibility that the work of katechontic violence vis-à-vis the *eschaton* may be primarily a compensatory mechanism, one that, among other things, may seek to hide the material temporal vulnerabilities of the sovereign body. The conclusion of this chapter offers a provocative call to reclaim the finitude of time and, to some extent, to recall the presence of the *eschaton*, horrifying as it may be from the perspective of sovereignty, security, and terror, in a way that may try to challenge enduring forms of overwhelmingly violent sovereign restraint. In so doing, the concluding section starts to evoke the possibility of offering a different understanding of horror, one that may recognize some of the radically subversive and, perhaps, oddly liberating, powers of horror, particularly once horror is dissociated from the security–terror continuum.

The sovereign power to restrain

Sovereignty is premised upon a power to withhold or restrain. In so doing, modern sovereignty is heir to pre-modern religious—primarily Christian—forms of power and order. Sovereign power—the power of the divine, the king, the emperor, the general will, the state—is a matter of holding out, keeping at bay, or postponing that which cannot or should not be imagined or thought. This holding out—or katechontism—can be seen as the terrestrial or this-worldly mission of sovereign power. This is also the preoccupation from which the power of the sovereign appears to derive its force and violence.[12] The sovereign katechontic quest to restrain is also an activity that helps to carve out sovereignty as a sacred space, a sacred space whose existence is both of this world (temporal and terrestrial) and transcendent (eternal and universal). Thus, what is sacred about sovereignty or the sovereign body is an imagined core (a sacred form of life, perhaps) presumed to be in need of protection/preservation. This further suggests that the power to restrain or withhold—the power of the *katechon*—needs to cast away that which, once again, cannot be imagined or thought and yet, paradoxically, must still be envisioned or anticipated in order for the sacred order to be realized or, at least, justified.[13] That which cannot be imagined or thought, as I clarify below, is the finitude of sovereign life, its temporal ending(s), or what Mick Dillon has called the "time of the *eschaton.*"[14]

Modern sovereign power, like pre-modern religious power (of the Christian kind, in particular), is theological. It is politically theological in the dual sense that, on the one hand, it manifests "the expansion of the reach of religious meanings and values into the sphere of political life" while, on the other hand, it represents "a contraction of the domain of religious life and practices" that seemingly displaces religion, but only to "elevate politics" through the presence of "theological values and concepts."[15] More crucially, it is theological in the way that modalities of sovereign power/order, as constructions of a sacred body/life, are katechontic. As Schmitt argued, the power of the medieval Christian Empire as well as the decisive power of the modern sovereign were premised on "the belief that a restrainer [*katechon*] holds back the end of the world."[16] This is not just a Schmittian perspective (although, as we shall see below, Schmitt's thought plays an important part in the contemporary formulation of katechontic sovereignty). To hold back the finitude of time and to ensure the perpetuity of the sacred sovereign order is the task assigned to the *katechon*. Put differently, the sovereign must be *katechon* if it is to exist and remain in the face of time and history. The split nature of sovereign power as both that which is sacred and that which maintains the sacred order is geared towards the ever present struggle to ward off the materiality of time and history, the fact of finitude, or the temporality of life—in other words, physical death. The idea and practice of sovereign restraint—an ironic use of the notion of restraint, to be sure, since the katechontic sovereign can and must employ all available terrestrial and non-terrestrial means to push back this unimaginable finitude—are ways of conjuring away the material powers of time, history, and life. They are about combatting earthly finitude in the name of a perpetual teleology incarnated by a sacred sovereign order/body as a form of rule and life that can only be comprehended and judged through its capacity to transcend temporal/historical (that is to say, human) endpoints. This is why sovereign teleology is inevitably faced with eschatology, with the question of how to end things (life, the world, power). This is why the sovereign *katechon* is invariably faced with "the *eschaton* of time conceived as factical finitude."[17]

To succeed in its quest "to interrupt the interruption,"[18] this sacred/sovereign power to restrain must be equipped with an arsenal commensurate with its mission of performing this endless combat not just to the death but beyond death, towards and in the name of immortality. The *katechon* must own force and violence to block and defeat the *eschaton*. Thus, katechontic sovereignty both *has* and *is* a power to combat what it takes to be eschatological "terror"—the terrestrial, material, or this-worldly "terror" of the *eschaton*—since this so-called terror seeks to impose a limit—an endpoint—to earthly and non-earthly matters. The "terror" of the *eschaton* is thus presented as a constant threat to the sacred/sovereign order/life, not because the *eschaton* seeks to occupy the sovereign's place or wishes to usurp the sovereign's role, but rather because it fundamentally undermines the idea of such a sacred space/rule/life/body. The *eschaton* "shatters an established horizon" of sacred law and power, Jacob Taubes writes (thus, it also tends to be described, in the language of the katechontic sovereign, as an "apocalyptic wave").[19] As Dillon puts it, the terror of the *eschaton* presents itself "as an open horizon of temporal possibility" that calls for "finite things, happenings, and events" to relinquish their "infinite becomings."[20] This is what terror must be made to look like from the perspective of the katechontic sovereign. Or perhaps, as we will see below, this is what or where the sovereign would like terror to be: on the side of the *eschaton*. Eschatological "terror" and its shattering insecurity represent the fear that the immortality of the sacred sovereign order/life/body could be doubted, or, to put it differently, that time could be thought of as other than what it is proclaimed and ordained to be by the sovereign. Thus, the eschatological "terror" that the *katechon* must confront is also the sovereign's own anxiety that time or history could be more than one (more than the one and only time—immortal, permanent—of the sovereign). In a way, it is an anxiety about sharing history, a fear that a thought could entertain the possibility that, on the one hand, there may be the sacred or infinite time of the sovereign's life but also, on the other hand, a somewhat profane, or perhaps fragmented, delimited, and finite, time of human/earthly activities and lives (lives that also may not owe their "being" to or may not derive their meaning from the sovereign's own existence). Any possibility about a dual perspective on time/history is anathema to the rule of the sovereign and the work of the *katechon*. Even though or, better yet, because the sovereign must indeed maintain two bodies—one that has an earthly and finite life, and another that runs through such a life, endows it with meaning, and forever "exists"—time cannot be shared. The time/history of eschatological "terror" is thus a threat to the eternity and universality of the sacred sovereign order, even when such a sacred order must be temporally (and temporarily) embodied. As Ernst Kantorowicz revealed, the king lives (on) at the very moment that the king's earthly body expires (*le Roi est mort, vive le Roi!*).[21]

Katechontic power, the power to restrain or hold back that the sovereign must be and must have in order to "live," is thus not only a sovereign power that preserves and protects (a sacred order/body) and redeems (by bringing the subjects of the sovereign into a united community or communion, such as the state or the Church).[22] It is also a power that, as intimated above, must turn to force and violence to combat the "evil" of finitude. Katechontic sovereignty is thus sovereignty at work—and when the katechontic sovereign is at work, it seeks to fight and destroy through all means possible (material and immaterial, earthly and transcendent) anything that appears to threaten the course of perpetuity or universal dispositions. This is why Dillon remarks that "[k]eeping the *eschaton* out of the question demands relentless political and ideological work."[23] It demands that the time of the sovereign on earth (a time that, once again, cannot be shared with human history) be occupied by political struggles against terrorizing and de-securitizing eschatological figures that embody a different (but unacceptable, unimaginable) infinity, the "infinity of finite possibilities."[24] These material political struggles (what I will refer to below as matters of security politics) that the *katechon* is involved in and, in fact, initiates do not mark a rupture in the sovereign order. Rather, as Schmitt understood well, they are the manifestations of a theologico-political order of things and of the need for such a sovereign order to remain perpetually secure or unchallenged. This is why, from the perspective of the sovereign, all political concepts are indeed "secularized theological concepts"[25]—that is to say, they are concepts whose presence and application in the state and by the sovereign necessarily reflect the struggle of the *katechon* against forces of eschatological insecurity that seek to pluralize the sacred order/body/life of the sovereign. This is also the reason why any forceful and apparently paradoxical finite political decision and intervention by the katechontic sovereign against insecurity and "terror"—including the launching of crusades and wars to fight back and repel the threat of "infinite finite possibilities"— is the equivalent of a miracle for Schmitt.[26] The exceptional decision by the katechontic sovereign to combat the "terror" that threatens the permanence of the sacred order is undoubtedly finite in its execution. Yet it is finite only in appearance, since, in the greater and indeed eternal scheme of things, it is actually miraculous. The exceptional intervention to fight back eschatological finitude is only finite to the extent that a miracle may appear to be finite—that is to say, as if it is coming out of nowhere, unexpected, and yet redeeming or salving. For Schmitt, then, the image of a finite political exception by the sovereign in earthly state matters is merely a glimpse of the miracle that the katechontic sovereign is capable of when it fends off eschatological time.[27] Here, the political finitude of the miraculous sovereign exception and, likewise for Schmitt, the finite instances of confrontation and war between friend and enemy that define the political domain,[28] are *not* proof of the surrender to the *eschaton* of time (after all, the concrete enemy has a "providential" quality, according to Schmitt[29]). The Schmittian sovereign, even when it makes decisions *in concreto*, is not the anti-Christ. Rather, the miracle of the ever present and everlasting sacred sovereign order is what takes the form of finite time or concrete happening in order to try to defeat the *eschaton* on its own terrain and through its own so-called terror.[30]

The miracle of security in katechontic sovereignty

Roberto Esposito poses the following question: "Who is the *katechon* of our time?"[31] However, instead of attempting to provide a name for today's *katechon*, Esposito reverts back to a Schmittian explanation: "the categorical epicenter of the *katechon* is located precisely at the point of intersection between politics and religion in the horizon defined as 'political theology'."[32] Here, for Esposito, the *katechon* appears to reproduce what may be called the "double duality" of the sovereign: the sovereign is both this-worldly and other-worldly; but it is also the sacred order or core and the enforcing agent of this sacred core. For Esposito, the *katechon* is both the sovereign and of the sovereign: it is the agent that withholds and restrains in the concrete circumstances and history of "our time," but it is also the "categorical epicenter" as a point of intersection between the political and the theological. As some scholars have shown, this ambivalently double "agent" that is both a part of the sovereign core and acts on behalf of the sovereign resembles what security is and does for the modern (sovereign) state.[33] Security is at the heart of the sovereign's being. It breathes everlasting life into the sovereign order, rendering the space/order of the sovereign a domain where one wants to be and safely remain, a cradle of order that becomes the mark of the sacred and that security makes permanent.[34] It is, perhaps, in this way that sovereign restraint is understood classically.[35] The sovereign appears to show restraint (or magnanimity, perhaps) towards its subjects by protecting them from social chaos or anarchy. Outside of the sovereign order, while restraint may be pragmatically recommended between sovereigns (diplomatic restraint), such a quality can be brushed aside and, when the life of the sovereign and the sovereign order are at stake, ignored altogether. Thus, as Dillon explains, security has "always been concerned with securing the very grounds of what the political [sovereign] itself is, specifying what the essence of politics is thought to be."[36] But security is also what cordons off the sacred domain/body of the sovereign, what makes it impermeable and impenetrable from the outside, preserved, protected, and indeed secure. Security in this second complementary configuration is a borderline, a buffer, and a perimeter necessary for the so-called core to stay intact, pure, and permanent. Security is the sovereign's border or wall because, in Brown's words, it recognizes that "political sovereignty, . . . like God, is finished as soon as it is broken apart."[37] In a certain fashion, security always operates at the limits of sovereign restraint.

The sovereign *katechon* is endowed with security and, in turn, it endows "life" with a need for security, particularly in the face of the *eschaton*'s presumed "terror." The sacred space/order/body of the katechontic sovereign is thus a political domain of and for security and of and for security practices. This means that the space of the sovereign, as seen from the perspective of the *katechon*, is always a reactive and insecure space in need of defense, one that is inevitably defined by what can constantly threaten its perpetual existence or immortality. Thus, the security performed by katechontic sovereignty also defines the sacred order of the sovereign in a negative manner as that order or life whose survival is always at risk. Katechontic sovereignty and the miraculous task of keeping the sovereign secure and sacred must invent the notion of political *survival*—and must position it at the very heart of sovereign political designs—so it can function as the defensive embodiment of what the order of the sovereign must be like under conditions of repeated confrontations with eschatological agents of finitude, disorder, anarchy, or evil. As Esposito notes, philosopher

Henri Bergson understood well that Judeo-Christian religions, in a context of katechontic thinking, primarily operated as instrumentalities of and for security, as
ways of providing believers and followers with the security that they were told they
craved through an always reconstructed existential angst about survival. Esposito
suggests that, for Bergson, religion worked by "opening up a salvific space of survival [for God, for God's sacred domain, for the Church, and for the members of
the Church] beyond the natural boundaries of life."[38] In more general terms, it
could be said that the miracle of security gifted to the world by the katechontic
sovereign—for the sovereign's own glory but also for the salvation of the sovereign's
followers/believers—introduces the notion of survival as a defensive principle that
stands in for the needs and attributes of the sovereign's body in this world and in
this time, a world and a time in which the sovereign and its agents are constantly on
the lookout for forces of temporal/historical finitude that allegedly seek to shatter
the certainty of the sacred order and the promise of the sovereign's eternal life.

Like the *katechon*, which it embodies and serves, security—and security's
requirement to permanently enable sovereignty as a "salvific space of survival"—
works (theologically, politically, ideologically, militarily) with and through limits.[39]
Security operates in liminal spaces and border zones where the (in)distinction
between finitude and infinity is at stake. Security performs its duty to hold back,
preserve, protect, and react in times when the perpetual life of the sovereign is
threatened by the possibility of a multitude of other, finite ways of living/being
that derive their historical legitimacy from the claim that they, unlike the sovereign, cannot hope to last forever because, for them, physical death is a definite
endpoint. This is the reason why Dillon believes that the politics of security is
always eschatological.[40] It is eschatological because it is always concerned with
mobilizing survival, with not ending, with endlessly deferring the fatal outcome.
Security fights on behalf of the katechontic sovereign in the frontlines of the
katechon's wars against the *eschaton*'s "terror." Thus, it may not be an exaggeration
to state that the politics of security is the katechontic sovereign's own permanent
war on terror or its endless crusade against insecurity and enmity. Security's mission indeed can never stop. As Dillon puts it,

> it is from the catastrophic threat of the dissolution of the order of things that
> the politics of security not only derives its very warrant to secure ... [but is
> also mobilized] to supply the governing technologies by which the political
> order [of the sovereign] is regulated to be 'fit' for war ... [and] to resist the
> same catastrophic threat-event.[41]

Thus, security is not just the sovereign *katechon* operating at the limits (between
death and eternal life, order and anarchy, glory and evil, infinity and history, or
God's ordained world and human events in this world). Rather, security is the very
condition of possibility for thinking the limit (or boundary/border) as a founda-
tional but always reinvented or reproduced duality that renders the sovereign order,
space, and time meaningful and permanent. This is perhaps the miracle that security

is called to perform throughout its involvements with eschatological matters. The miracle that the katechontic sovereign orders security to perform, over and over again (and yet, every time, as if it came from nowhere), consists in producing instances of danger, terror, and insecurity in which, concretely, the survival of the sovereign order is said to be at stake. Put in yet another way, security's miracle, derived from and taking place in this world on behalf of katechontic sovereignty, is to reproduce an infinite amount of limit situations or conditions through which threatening eschatological others (impure, profane, and terrorizing) are discovered, confronted, pushed back, and defeated. Without security's capacity to always reinvent the limit or border, without security's miraculous task of always reimagining a finite outside, and without security's awesome katechontic violence to bring eschatological others into apocalyptic struggles and wars on and against terror, sovereignty may not have anything to defend itself from. More crucially, without security's power to restrain or withhold—a power granted to security by virtue of the fact that it is of and for the sovereign, once again—sovereignty may not even have a sacred core to perpetually preserve. Thus, the ontological necessity of the katechontic sovereign is once again indistinguishable from security[42] and from security's capacity to always rethink, reinvent, and reproduce spatial and temporal limits (or what many political and international relations thinkers of sovereignty and national security have argued for decades determines the survival of the sovereign).

Yet what if the finite, de-securitizing, evil, or terrorizing eschatological other were in fact *not* positioned on the other side of the border, on the outside, or beyond the line or limit?[43] What if the limit, always reimagined by the miracle of security's intervention in this world, were not on the perimeter of sovereignty, as if it were a buffer for its sacred core or an advanced line of defense for its survival? What if security, so intimately tied to the katechontic sovereign, were not just *of* and *for* the sovereign, but indeed *in* the sovereign, in its very essence? What if security's liminal points of contact with the *anomos* (through security's wars against the "terror" of the *eschaton*) were already inside the sovereign *nomos*?[44] Moreover, what if the dual life of the sovereign could never be guaranteed, and what if the sovereign power to restrain, hold back, and ward off was all there could ever be to the sovereign order? What if what was sacred about sovereignty or the sovereign body was the sacrilegious secret that it did not and, in fact, never had a glorious core that had to be preserved in the first place?[45] What if the *katechon* were primarily a tool of sovereign deception?

Esposito's own analysis of katechontic power in the context of his reassessment of political theology in an age of immunitary biopolitics (or how life is enjoined to turn on itself in order to be saved/secured) prompts this critical interrogation of the limits of security.[46] Esposito's purpose is not to abandon the categories of *katechon* and *eschaton* to arrive at an understanding of the nexus power–security–life. Rather, what Esposito seeks to show is that these politico-theological categories need to be closely re-examined if one is to apprehend contemporary forms of power for which the threshold of life and death, the dilemma of finitude and infinity, and the opposition between eternal order and concrete human events are crucial operating modalities.

Esposito recognizes that the work of the *katechon* is driven by security. The *katechon*, in Esposito's words, is a "force of order" that stops the "plunge into the abyss" and "blocks the *anomos*, the principle of disorder, the rebellion [against the sovereign order]."[47] The *katechon* secures the sovereign domain, as we saw above. But it also does so "by containing [evil], by keeping it, [and] by holding it within itself."[48] Thus, Esposito clarifies, the katechontic sovereign's politics of security is as much geared towards holding or keeping within as it is to holding back. Esposito adds an important element to the notion of *katechon*. Katechontism, Esposito intimates, is unable to distinguish withholding from holding with or within. Thus, Esposito's reading offers a theoretical (and critical) supplement. It suggests that security operations do ensure that the *katechon* with-holds—that is to say, that it holds and keeps *with*, *in*, and, ultimately, *for* the sovereign itself. Esposito adds that security, according to the katechontic sovereign's designs, is about "hosting ... and welcoming" the outside or the other within oneself so that, in fact, security ends up "binding [the sovereign's] own necessity to the presence of evil."[49] This necessary internalization of otherness or of the so-called outside by means of security is not just about preserving the sovereign and sacred order/body/space but also about producing and cultivating the outside, the foreign, the other—in other words, the so-called terror of the *eschaton* of time. For the *katechon*, the outside (where the time and "terror" of the *eschaton* are said to reside) is perhaps "not another space," as Giorgio Agamben also implies, but rather a "passage," a connection, or an opening to the sovereign "inside."[50] Thus, security must always accommodate the *eschaton*. Security must give the *eschaton*'s terminal/terrestrial "terror" a home and a target within the sovereign domain, at the very heart of what is supposedly sacred, so that the sacred can indeed be secured. If security were to fail to position the other or outside not just in relation to but indeed *within* the space of the sovereign, security would effectively "eliminate itself," render itself purposeless, and undermine the always threatened glory of the katechontic sovereign. Indeed, what would remain in this world of the sacredness of a sovereign order/life that faces no ontological threat? Consequently, security must safeguard by de-securitizing; it must fend off the finitudinal "terror" of the eschatological "outside" by making terror, violence, and antagonism a part of the sovereign's own being, of its sacrosanct inside.[51] As was suggested above, the repeated miracle that is security does give life and meaning to the sovereign. But, as Esposito helps us to clarify, it does so in a manner that invents or mobilizes the so-called terror of the *eschaton* of time to justify the katechontic sovereign's own awesome terror (do we not rediscover here precisely the Hobbesian formula about sovereign power?)—that is to say, to validate the sovereign's own ways of terrestrially mobilizing the powers to keep alive and to put to death (and, further, to decide who is worthy of being redeemed and kept safe and, on the contrary, who will have to be sacrificed and eliminated). In this manner, in the way security turns the *katechon*'s war on or against terror into sovereignty's own wars of and for terror, the *katechon* inevitably ushers sovereignty into the sphere of biopolitics, through the deployment of biological, corporeal, or even carnal regimes of power, rule, and force that place the management of life and death (and the organization of secure or vulnerable bodies in time and space) at the very center of the sovereign's political edifice. Or, to return to Esposito's language, the investment of katechontic security into this-worldly biopolitical matters makes sovereignty a paradigm of immunity since the sacred order/life of the sovereign "is nurtured by the antidote [the *eschaton*] necessary to its *survival*."[52]

Sovereign vulnerability and katechontic terror as compensation

Mick Dillon and Julian Reid have remarked that "biohumanity is . . . conceived as a continuous and contingent becoming-dangerous to itself."[53] They go on to suggest that, in our (biohuman) age, "every kind of threat from pandemics to systemic failures of critical national infrastructure now yields its own 'war'"—that is to say, it provides security with biopolitical opportunities to "violently polemicize all aspects of the social body."[54] This reflection is a recognition of the relevance of Esposito's immunitary paradigm in contemporary political life. It offers a current and concrete demonstration of how the miracle of security is able to turn eschatological time and its alleged insecurity into katechontic sovereignty's own weapons of violence, war, and holy terror. Contemporary bio-geo-politico-theological topographies and topologies (as I put it in Chapter 1), particularly in the current context of a never-to-end global war on terror, or of "our" universal confrontation against the evils of terror(ism), thus seem to confirm what Esposito theorized. Instead of an antagonism between the *katechon*'s forces of universal order and eternal life and the *eschaton*'s finite, pluralizing, and destabilizing "terror," the sovereign's reliance on security seeks to establish a continuum from what is said to render insecure and must be cast away to what must be preserved or protected at all costs. Chaotic disorder or rebellion from the so-called outside of the state/sovereign and the survival of the sovereign order/rule are not binary opposites. Rather, they operate on the same politico-theological plane and they partake of the same modality of terror and security. As Agamben might put it, a principle of indistinction is in place between operations of sovereign power and activities or even thoughts said to be threats to the sovereign's life.[55] Consequently, the sacred space of the katechontic sovereign is simultaneously enforced or made safe *and* challenged or rendered insecure. The paradox of sovereign restraint calls in the paradox of security.

Put in yet another way, by welcoming the "terror" of the *eschaton* on the inside, within the realm of the sovereign itself, as Esposito claims, the *katechon* and its security politics undermine the dual existence of the sovereign (the "King's two bodies"). This immanent de-securitization of the sovereign achieved through security's quest in the very name of the sovereign's survival is what Eric Santner has theorized as the sovereign's own "ontological vulnerability." While Santner first developed the notion of ontological vulnerability in relation to the investment of human beings' bodies in biopolitical contexts,[56] he recently extended it to the dilemmas attached to the idea/imagery of the body of the sovereign.[57] For Santner, ontological vulnerability is an exposure to finitude and mortality. It is an implicit recognition on the part of the vulnerable sovereign body that the supposedly guaranteed passage from one temporal dimension (historical, terrestrial, physical, this-worldly, corporeal, human) to another (transcendent, immemorial, immaterial, infinite, other-worldly, theological) can no longer be assured. Sovereign ontological vulnerability (my turn of phrase) is the realization that insecurity inevitably "permeates human being as that being whose essence it is to exist in forms of life that are, in turn, contingent, fragile, susceptible to breakdown."[58] Sovereign ontological vulnerability is the manifest or repressed recognition by the sovereign of the powerlessness of the *katechon* in the face of the *eschaton* at the very moment that the *katechon*'s power is called forth to fend off (but also to hold within) eschatological finitude. It is the revelation of the sovereign's always complicit participation in its own uncertainty or frailty at the very same time that it deploys its powerful arsenal of security, violence, and terror. Here again, we rediscover the paradox, and perhaps futility, of security practices and security apparatuses. Or, as I would rather put it, the *eschaton* is revealed as the *katechon*'s own paradox. The "terror" initially and purposefully attributed to the time of the *eschaton* is in fact an always ardent desire for katechontic sovereignty's own terror. Thus, katechontic sovereignty's paradox is that the more the sovereign seeks to secure its immortality, the more it exposes its vulnerability to finitude and decay. Or, as Santner argues, "[t]he paradox … is that the defense mechanisms cultures [or implements of sovereignty] used to protect against a primordial exposure—to 'cover' our nudity—serve in the end to redouble this exposure."[59] Sovereign ontological vulnerability, both reliant on and bedeviled by this paradox, is the *katechon*'s fateful realization that "self-preservation" is always "a form of mortification."[60]

Yet this sovereign vulnerability both conjured away and expressed by the *katechon*'s securitizing work comes at a hefty price for everything and everyone encapsulated by the sovereign's order, in this world and perhaps in the imagined beyond, too. The subjects of katechontic sovereignty (that is to say, those who have pledged allegiance to the sovereign body—whether they know it or not—and, as such, are the subjects of its sacred rule/order/life) often pay for the sovereign's ontological vulnerability through the exposure of their own (physical, finite) bodies to the *katechon*'s security practices, strategies, policies, and technologies, as we saw in Chapter 1. This is, once again, where biopolitical considerations come into play, or why biopolitics—the inclusion of the "vital processes of the living subjects" in power configurations[61]—is the outcome of the *katechon*'s always ambivalent and unsatisfactory confrontation with and mobilization of the *eschaton*. In other words, the katechontic sovereign's wars on terror taking place in this world through the use and abuse of the sovereign's subjects' physical bodies and earthly lives are tools of terror against finite eschatological and de-securitizing "other" bodies or agents (enemies, terrorists, rebels, outsiders, evil-doers, etc.) who, as we saw above, can never be clearly distinguished from the sovereign's own subjects (since the *eschaton*'s "terror" is always held or produced inside the sovereign and thus becomes a vital part of it). This explains why, as the *eschaton*'s threat of insecurity or disorder becomes the *katechon*'s own terror, any subject of the sovereign can be terrorized by the sovereign itself. Anybody subjected to the rule of the katechontic sovereign can be "killed yet not sacrificed."[62]

The task of security through the designs of katechontic sovereignty is thus also to search for, identify, and weed out agents and bodies of imagined eschatological "terror" that "live within" or "are among" us, as many of our contemporary political security enforcers like to remind us. This is, once again, what the immunitary paradigm of katechontic sovereignty requires (as contemporary instances of counter-terrorism often confirm). But since eschatological agents to be found and expelled are always produced by and within the sovereign, security's apparent search for evil or terrorizing others on the outside is relentlessly a crusade to create physical and bodily targets for the *katechon*'s own terror on the inside (since the outside, in fact, is primarily required as an excuse or a justification). The outside or others that are said to embody the *eschaton* are often alibis for the constant work performed by the sovereign's security operatives to make some of the sovereign's subjects vulnerable and superfluous (might we not interpret recent efforts by the contemporary katechontic sovereign and its security agents to go after national security practices' whistle-blowers as an example of such a blurring between the so-called terror of the eschatological outside and the desire of the sovereign to proliferate its own biopolitical terror?). The katechontic sovereign's security operations can never be anything but a series of punctual interventions to terrorize (literally, to impose a terrestrial, earthly, physical, visceral fear of death and destruction) the sovereign's "own" subjects, people, or populations. As Judith Butler might argue, the precariousness of individual subjects and bodies is thus intimately tied to the precarious and unsure ways that the sovereign and the sovereign's security agents cope with their own vulnerability and incommensurability (or perhaps with their inability to "grieve" for the sovereign's own mortality).[63] The *eschaton*, then, is also what must be established as the other of the katechontic sovereign so that the struggle with eschatological time can try to mask the fact that the sovereign is never anything more than a relentlessly ideological, political, and military machine of terror.[64]

Reclaiming the horror of the *eschaton?*

In a recent study, Hurd argues against the view that (late) modern political institutions and processes need to be seen as secular modalities of organization, preservation, or even devastation of social and political life. "Secularism is not the absence of religion," she writes. Rather, secularism "enacts a particular kind of presence. It appropriates religion: defining, shaping, and even transforming it."[65] Looking back at the ancestral, yet always active, practice of sovereign restraint and its close ties to security and security practices, Hurd's assessment has to be revised. As I have shown in this chapter, because sovereignty must always be katechontic, because the sovereign must always define its survival in terms of security and by way of security operations geared towards agents or figures of finitude (seen as disorder or, indeed, "terror"), sovereignty is never a fully secular notion. Sovereignty is always obsessed with eschatological questions and with the quest to live and remain in power perpetually. Thus, not only the body of the sovereign, but the very principle of sovereignty itself, guarded by security, must seek to maintain its two "lives"— that is to say, its this-worldly (and security-driven or terror-removing) attributes as well as its other-worldly or eternal existence, from which its claims about making or securing universal political meaning, rule, and order can be derived. Katechontism, I suggest, allows one to recognize the obsession with immortality and permanence that, in a way, dooms sovereignty always to seek out forces of finitude in an effort to oppose them (or, indeed, to make them other). It also helps to clarify how and why security is the main theologico-political practice for the sovereign and its agents. The specter of eschatological time and finite ends explains why the sovereign's order/body and, just as crucially, how the sovereign's subjects (whether they agree with this or not) must be mobilized and perhaps made into "subjects of security."[66]

Yet, perhaps, the *eschaton* could be rescued or redeemed. Perhaps we need to remove the *eschaton* from the clutches of the sovereign's practices of restraint. Perhaps we can extirpate the *eschaton* from the sovereign order/body, and from its insecurities, not so much to recreate an outside or to reinvent an other (nor even to hope to form a new dialectic of power) but rather to encourage the possibility of an "infinity of finite possibilities" (as Dillon, once again, puts it) in a more open domain that would not be defined by the ontological vulnerability of the sovereign. Perhaps we need to confront the actual terror, the terror brought on by the *katechon* and security politics (and a terror falsely attributed to the *eschaton* of time, once again), with the vision, specter, or even horror of finite time.

The time of the *eschaton* promises different ends than the sovereign hopes to see. The time of the *eschaton*, or the "infinity of finite possibilities," foretells of situations and events (including violent conflicts or security operations, many of them initiated in the name of the life of the sovereign) that may render the image of the sovereign unrecognizable or indistinguishable from human history and finitude. Put another way, the specter of the *eschaton* haunts the ontological security of the sovereign by presenting a multitude of ways of putting the sovereign to political death and, perhaps more crucially, of continuing the proliferation of the sovereign's remains beyond the point of the sovereign's physical extermination.[67] Perhaps better read as a figure of horror than of terror (since the finitude of the *eschaton* targets the sovereign beyond its physical collapse, the *eschaton* never allows a certainty about the eternity of the sovereign's life to be reasserted), the *eschaton* may matter as a principle of demolition or undoing that takes advantage of the sovereign's ontological vulnerability, insecurity, or fear of fragmentation.[68] Indeed, the temporal/terrestrial finitude of the *eschaton* transforms the terrorizing biopolitical and thanatopolitical force of the sovereign and its security agents into a horrific violence— often from within the sovereign order itself—for which the threshold of life and death or of the human and the inhuman may no longer matter (this confusion of the human and the inhuman or, better yet, the non-human in or by horror is key to the theorizations offered in Chapters 3 and 4 and the Epilogue).

Perhaps, then, it is time to reclaim eschatological finitude or ends (horrifying as they may be from the perspective of sovereignty and security). But I would argue that they need to be reclaimed not because the *eschaton* (or what it may represent through its haunting work) is a positive force of salvation or, on the contrary, an evil presence or deed, but because the horrifying presence/deed of the *eschaton* is neither good nor evil. It is neither good nor evil because, even when its "infinity of finite ends" pulverizes the power/order/life of the sovereign, it does not seek to impose a new order or permanence to life in return. It does not seek good or evil because, politically or ethically, it does not need to position itself in relation to an other (sacred or profane). Precisely because it is beyond good and evil, eschatological horror can offer a space of solace away from sovereign violence and the politics of security and terror. This is what I take Dillon to mean when, gesturing towards Walter Benjamin's thought on the irruptive violence of history, he writes that one way of dealing with end-of-time questions without submitting to forces of kate-chontic power is "to side with the order of the repressed subjected to the rule of truth and the truth of rule of ... [the sovereign's] temporal order."[69] Put another way, eschatological horror has no place for the sovereign's miraculous intervention and, in total indifference to the religious/sacred foundations of the katechontic sovereign, it offers events and bodies a series of messianic possibilities for a more open and perhaps more just here and now to-come. This, I think, would be the kind of messianism that Jacques Derrida, for example, had in mind, particularly in his reading of Marx's work and "spirit".[70] Derrida did not call for a notion of escha-tological horror but rather for what he referred to as a "messianic eschatology," or the idea of "a certain experience of the emancipatory promise ... a messianism without religion, even a messianic without messianism, an idea of justice ... and an idea of democracy."[71]

I would like to suggest that what I call eschatological horror can be such a messianic idea. It can operate as a punctual force that shatters boundaries and limits and refuses to settle or to inflict eternity or universality (or the inevitability of a certain mode of sovereign immortality). Only through its dismantling work can this form of horror be left to encounter an "infinity of finite possibilities" or be put in contact with the this-worldly to come, here and now, of other (non-sovereign) possibilities, including possibilities for freedom and justice, but also, since nothing is preordained anymore with eschatological horror, for equally plausible encounters in this time and in this world with coercion and injustice. Only by recognizing the "messianic opening" provided by the *eschaton* can we perhaps try to incant an "eschatological relation to the to-come of an event *and* of a singularity, of an alterity that cannot be anticipated."[72]

The messianic character of the *eschaton* and its horror may also take us away from discourses, justifications, and beliefs about the absolute necessity (for the sake of the sovereign's own life and of a humanity allegedly dependent upon it) of the *katechon's* many wars on and of terror. Again, this does not mean that eschatological horror, if it is to-come, may arrive without its own extreme force or destruction. The messianic violence of eschatological horror can indeed be devastating. Horror undoubtedly emerges as a destructive force. But this destructive force does not seek to "kill but not sacrifice" (to use Agamben's turn of phrase), unlike the sovereign's own biopolitical as well as thanatopolitical designs. It may be more accurate and just to see eschatological horror as an interruptive and transgressive force. Like the messiah, it emerges suddenly, unexpectedly. Yet, unlike the katechontic sovereign's miracle (by way of security), it represents or embodies nothing. Thus, eschatological horror is perhaps messianic in relation to time in the way that Benjamin understood the time of the messiah or the emergence of messianic violence.[73] As Butler has argued, the time of the messiah for Benjamin was a "now time" that, as Benjamin stated, was "shot through with chips."[74] Butler goes on to suggest that Benjamin's time of the messiah is as if something had "broken off" from a repressed past and "shot through" the homogeneity of a dominant/hegemonic history or a continuous temporal order (such as the time of the sovereign, or the time of katechontic terror).[75] Messianic time is fragmentary ("chips of time"), a shrapnel, something fleeting, made of some fleshy bits of dismembered but also, perhaps, remembered bodies or lives.

I would argue that messianic time is the punctual emergence or "flashing up" (as Butler puts it) of eschatological horror. Like horror or, rather, as horror, messianic time pops up in the now of time and history, and it "interrupts [a] homogeneity."[76] It pulverizes the temporality, order, life, and duration of the katechontic sovereign, but it also disappears or moves on as quickly as it arrived. Its horrifying violence is an attack on anything that seeks or claims "uniformity and progress."[77] With regard to universality and eternal life, it is merciless and does not appear to make sense. Yet it is characterized as much by what it dismantles as by what it gives a glimpse or a flash of. Thus, the messianic time of eschatological horror is not simply destructive or avenging. It can be liberating, too (although not salvific or redemptive in the same immemorial and immortal ways that the time of the sovereign seeks salvation or redemption). But what may be liberating about the horror of messianic violence/time can never be guaranteed. Thus, Butler adds that the "messianic is always of the order of the 'might enter'."[78] Perhaps only this way (sudden, unexpected, unsure, and, indeed, insecure) can the horror of eschatological or messianic time offer us a glimpse/flash of justice and, perhaps, of a justice on behalf of "the forgotten history of the oppressed," as Butler suggests (reprising Benjamin's phrasing).[79]

We might do well to not rush to cast away the *eschaton* of time and its messianic horror. This, I suggest, would be a non-sovereign and non-katechontic wager. It would perhaps start not so much with an apprehension—if not a comprehension—of horror (for horror is never meant to be comprehended) but with a recognized dissatisfaction with, and perhaps rejection of, the insecurity and terror that regimes of sovereign security invariably bring. Once such a dissatisfaction with or rejection of security and the *katechon* is affirmed, the possibility of a different time, a time to-come, may be envisioned, if only fleetingly. As political theorist James Martel has noted, there probably would be nothing grandiose about this to-come of a different time and its encounter with sovereignty.[80] If nothing else, at this point, and in a manner inspired by Benjamin's thought, one might see a flashing image, horrifying as it may appear to be to start with, of "what it might be to have the history of the oppressed enter ... the time of the present otherwise understood as a kind of marching on,"[81] often a marching on of the infinite temporal order of the sovereign and its security practices and politics.

Notes

1 See, for example, Hans Morgenthau, "Another 'Great Debate': The National Interest of the United States," *American Political Science Review*, Vol. 46, No. 4 (1952), pp. 961–88; R. B. J. Walker, "Security, Sovereignty, and the Challenge of World Politics," *Alternatives*, Vol. 15, No. 1 (1990), pp. 3–27; or Michael Dillon, *Politics of Security: Towards a Political Philosophy of Continental Thought* (New York: Routledge, 1996).
2 Mark Neocleous, *Critique of Security* (Montreal: McGill-Queen's University Press, 2008).
3 On the notion of the *katechon*, see, for example, Carl Schmitt, *The* Nomos *of the Earth* (New York: Telos, 2003); Michael Dillon, "Specters of Biopolitics: Finitude, *Eschaton*, and *Katechon*," *The South Atlantic Quarterly*, Vol. 110, No. 3 (2011), pp. 780–92; Roberto Esposito, *Immunitas: The Protection and Negation of Life* (Cambridge: Polity, 2011).
4 As Mbembe and Dillon and Reid put it. Achille Mbembe, "Necropolitics," *Public Culture*, Vol. 15, No. 1 (2003), pp. 11–40; and Michael Dillon and Julian Reid, *The Liberal Way of War: Killing to Make Life Live* (New York: Routledge, 2009).
5 See Donald McKim, *Westminster Dictionary of Theological Terms* (London: Westminster John Knox Press, 1996); and Jacob Taubes, *Occidental Eschatology* (Stanford: Stanford University Press, 2009).
6 Elizabeth Shakman Hurd, "International Politics after Secularism," *Review of International Studies*, Vol. 38, No. 5 (2012), p. 944. See also Elizabeth Shakman Hurd, "The Political Authority of Secularism in International Relations," *European Journal of International Relations*, Vol. 10, No. 2 (2004), pp. 235–62.
7 On the post-secularism debate, see, for example, Philip Blond, *Post-Secular Philosophy: Between Philosophy and Theology* (New York: Routledge, 1998); Dillon, "Specters of Biopolitics"; or Eric Santner, *The Royal Remains: The People's Two Bodies and the Endgames of Sovereignty* (Chicago: University of Chicago Press, 2011).
8 On this topic, see Stephen Collins, *From Divine Cosmos to Sovereign State* (Oxford: Oxford University Press, 1989).
9 As Philpott does, for example. Daniel Philpott, "The Religious Roots of Modern International Relations," *World Politics*, Vol. 52, No. 2 (2000), pp. 206–45.
10 Wendy Brown, *Walled States, Waning Sovereignty* (New York: Zone Books, 2010), p. 62.
11 Carl Schmitt, *Political Theology* (Chicago: University of Chicago Press, 2005), p. 36.
12 Max Weber, "Politics as a Vocation," in Max Weber, *The Vocation Lectures* (Indianapolis: Hackett Publishing, 2004), pp. 32–94.
13 Esposito, *Immunitas*, p. 63.
14 Dillon, "Specters of Biopolitics," p. 780.
15 As Santner puts it. Santner, *The Royal Remains*, p. xii.
16 Schmitt, *The* Nomos *of the Earth*, p. 60.
17 Dillon, "Specters of Biopolitics," p. 781.
18 To use Esposito's turn of phrase. Esposito, *Immunitas*, p. 58.
19 Taubes, *Occidental Eschatology*, p. 85.
20 Dillon, "Specters of Biopolitics," p. 781.
21 Ernst Kantorowicz, *The King's Two Bodies: A Study in Mediaeval Political Theology* (Princeton: Princeton University Press, 1997). See also Michel Foucault, *Discipline and Punish: The Birth of the Prison* (New York: Vintage, 1979), pp. 28–9; Giorgio Agamben, *Homo Sacer: Sovereign Power and Bare Life* (Stanford: Stanford University Press, 1998), p. 92; and Santner, *The Royal Remains*, pp. 35–6.

22 Esposito, *Immunitas*, p. 66.

23 Dillon, "Specters of Biopolitics," p. 783.

24 As Dillon puts it. Ibid., p. 781.

25 Schmitt, *Political Theology*, p. 36.

26 Ibid., p. 36.

27 See also Dillon, "Specters of Biopolitics," p. 790.

28 On the friend-versus-enemy distinction, see Carl Schmitt, *The Concept of the Political* (Chicago: University of Chicago Press, 1996).

29 Heinrich Meier, *The Lesson of Carl Schmitt: Four Chapters on the Distinction between Political Theology and Political Philosophy* (Chicago: University of Chicago Press, 1998), pp. 59–60.

30 This may also explain why, for Schmitt, the danger of a *nomos*-less global political order driven by earthly powers intent on "democratizing" all of humanity and on deploying endless wars to achieve international peace is a threat to the political order of states and to sovereignty. For Schmitt, it is a threat to katechontic sovereignty because such a model of global order misunderstands the nature of the miracle and, instead, replaces the sovereign miracle with an ideological messianism on the part of this-worldly crusaders for democracy, human rights, liberty, the free market, or peace on a global scale that operate as *dei ex machina* and, in so doing, seek to impose their own secular religion of liberal universalism in lieu of the political and theological sovereign order. Schmitt, *The* Nomos *of the Earth*.

31 Esposito, *Immunitas*, p. 66.

32 Ibid., p. 66.

33 See, for example, Dillon, *Politics of Security*; R. B. J. Walker, *Inside/Outside: International Relations as Political Theory* (Cambridge: Cambridge University Press, 1992); R. B. J. Walker, "The Subject of Security," in Keith Krause and Michael C. Williams (eds), *Critical Security Studies* (Minneapolis: University of Minnesota Press, 1997), pp. 61–81; Brent Steele, *Ontological Security in International Relations: Self Identity and the IR State* (New York: Routledge, 2008); Larry N. George, "American Insecurities and the Ontopolitics of US Pharmacotic Wars," in François Debrix and Mark Lacy (eds), *The Geopolitics of American Insecurity: Terror, Power, and Foreign Policy* (New York: Routledge, 2009), pp. 34–53.

34 For a classical formulation of the relationship between security and the sovereign, see Thomas Hobbes, *Leviathan* (New York: Penguin, 1995); and Neocleous, *Critique of Security*.

35 For more on classical formulations of restraint in international politics, see, for example, Barry Posen, *Restraint: A New Foundation for US Grand Strategy* (Ithaca, NY: Cornell University Press, 2015).

36 See Dillon, *Politics of Security*, p. 13.

37 Brown, *Walled States, Waning Sovereignty*, p. 70.

38 Esposito, *Immunitas*, p. 58. See also Henri Bergson, *The Two Sources of Morality and Religion* (South Bend: University of Notre Dame Press, 1991).

39 Dillon, "Specters of Biopolitics," p. 781.

40 Ibid., p. 782.

41 Ibid., p. 782; my inserts.

42 Others have mentioned this point as well. See, for example, Dillon, *Politics of Security*; David Campbell, *Writing Security: United States Foreign Policy and the Politics of Identity* (Minneapolis: University of Minnesota Press, 1998); or Neocleous, *Critique of Security*.

43 For further critical thinking on the border/boundary/line, see Brown, *Walled States, Waning Sovereignty*; R. B. J. Walker, *After the Globe, before the World* (New York: Routledge, 2010); and Nick Vaughan-Williams, *Border Politics: The Limits of Sovereign Power* (Edinburgh: Edinburgh University Press, 2012).

44 As Esposito intimates. Esposito, *Immunitas*, p. 63.

45 Among some of the thinkers who suggest this possibility are Jean Baudrillard, *Forget Foucault* (New York: Semiotext(e), 1987); Claude Lefort, *Democracy and Political Theory*

(Cambridge: Polity, 1991); and Giorgio Agamben, *The Kingdom and the Glory: For a Theological Genealogy of Economy and Government* (Stanford: Stanford University Press, 2011).

46 See Roberto Esposito, *Bios: Biopolitics and Philosophy* (Minneapolis: University of Minnesota Press, 2008); and Esposito, *Immunitas*.
47 Esposito, *Immunitas*, p. 63; my inserts.
48 Ibid., p. 63.
49 Ibid., p. 63.
50 Giorgio Agamben, *The Coming Community* (Minneapolis: University of Minnesota Press, 1993), p. 67.
51 On how security relies on and (re)produces terror, see François Debrix, *Tabloid Terror: War, Culture, and Geopolitics* (New York: Routledge, 2008), pp. 112–17.
52 Esposito, *Immunitas*, p. 64; Esposito, *Bios*, p. 52.
53 Dillon and Reid, *The Liberal Way of War*, p. 108.
54 Ibid., p. 108.
55 Agamben, *Homo Sacer*, p. 110.
56 Eric Santner, *On Creaturely Life: Rilke, Benjamin, Sebald* (Chicago: University of Chicago Press, 2006).
57 Santner, *The Royal Remains*.
58 Ibid., p. 6.
59 Ibid., p. 6; my inserts.
60 Ibid., p. 7.
61 Nikolas Rose, *The Politics of Life Itself: Biomedicine, Power, and Subjectivity in the Twenty-First Century* (Princeton: Princeton University Press, 2007), p. 53.
62 As Agamben famously puts it. Agamben, *Homo Sacer*, p. 8.
63 See Judith Butler, *Precarious Life: The Powers of Mourning and Violence* (New York: Verso, 2004) and Judith Butler, *Frames of War: When Is Life Grievable?* (New York: Verso, 2009). On precariousness/vulnerability, see also Julian Reid, "The Vulnerable Subject of Liberal War," *The South Atlantic Quarterly*, Vol. 110, No. 3 (2011), pp. 770–9.
64 Similar sentiments about sovereignty, security, and the state and their imbrication in contemporary instances of terror have been offered by Debrix, *Tabloid Terror*; Dillon and Reid, *The Liberal Way of War*; Brad Evans, "The Liberal War Thesis: Introducing the Ten Key Principles of Twenty-First Century Biopolitical Warfare," *The South Atlantic Quarterly*, Vol. 110, No. 3 (2011), pp. 747–56; François Debrix and Alexander Barder, *Beyond Biopolitics: Theory, Violence, and Horror in World Politics* (New York: Routledge, 2012); and Brad Evans, *Liberal Terror* (Cambridge: Polity, 2013).
65 Hurd, "International Politics after Secularism," p. 955.
66 On the subject(s) of security, see Michel Foucault, *"Society Must Be Defended": Lectures at the Collège de France, 1975–1976* (New York: Picador, 2003); and *Security, Territory, Population: Lectures at the Collège de France, 1977–1978* (New York: Picador, 2007). See also Walker, "The Subject of Security."
67 As Santner suggests. Santner, *The Royal Remains*, p. 12.
68 On horror as the undoing, fragmentation, or even pulverization of the body, see Talal Asad, *On Suicide Bombing* (New York: Columbia University Press, 2007); and Adriana Cavarero, *Horrorism: Naming Contemporary Violence* (New York: Columbia University Press, 2009). See also Chapters 3 and 4 in this volume.
69 Dillon, "Specters of Biopolitics," p. 784.
70 Jacques Derrida, *Specters of Marx: The State of the Debt, the Work of Mourning, and the New International* (New York: Routledge, 1994).
71 Ibid., p. 59.
72 Ibid., p. 65.
73 Walter Benjamin, "Theses on the Philosophy of History," in Walter Benjamin, *Illuminations*, ed. Hannah Arendt (New York: Schocken Books, 1968), pp. 243–64.
74 Ibid., p. 263. See also Judith Butler, *Parting Ways: Jewishness and the Critique of Zionism* (New York: Columbia University Press, 2012), pp. 99–113.

75 Butler, *Parting Ways*, p. 103.
76 As Butler puts it. See ibid., p. 103.
77 Ibid., p. 102.
78 Ibid., p. 103.
79 Ibid., p. 104.
80 James Martel, *Divine Violence: Walter Benjamin and the Eschatology of Sovereignty* (New York: Routledge, 2012), pp. 44–5.
81 See Butler, *Parting Ways*, p. 104.

3

BODY PARTS OF TERROR

Rethinking security politics through the disseminated body

Fallen man

On April 15, 2013, at the finish of the annual Boston Marathon, two pressure-cooker bombs were detonated within seconds of each other, leaving three people dead and scores of runners, their family members, and spectators gravely injured. A few days later, a manhunt in the Boston area resulted in the death and arrest of the two immediate perpetrators, Tamerlan Tzarnaev (killed during a chase and shooting with the police) and Dzhokhar Tzarnaev (caught by the police and suffering from multiple wounds), two brothers originally from the Central Asian nation of Dagestan, holding Russian passports, and granted refugee status in the United States in 2002–3.[1] The Boston Marathon bombing quickly resurrected the specter of terrorism on US soil. Within a matter of minutes, US media drew connections between "Terror at the Marathon" and the 9/11 attacks,[2] no matter how different these two events might have been in their execution, points of origin, and immediate effects. In the minds of many Americans, the terrorist attacks on 9/11/2001 and now on 4/15/2013, both occurring in highly populated and historically significant East Coast urban centers, were the source of deep shocks at the heart of the nation. On April 15, 2013, media images showcased plumes of smoke, torn structures, and scattered artifacts against a background of city streets and high-rise buildings, inevitably prompting somatic, psychological, and symbolic linkages to the 9/11 attacks.

Among the many images of the Boston Marathon bombing, one kept coming back over and over on TV screens, online, through social media, and in newspapers/magazines a few days later: the image of one of the marathon runners, 78-year-old Bill Iffrig, forced to the ground by the blast within a few feet of the finish line, falling to his knees, and later helped across the line by marathon officials. Undoubtedly, this image was very powerful. It showed how fierce the bomb's blast had been, and how powerless human beings, running or watching the race, were in that precise instant. It also was quite graphic and potentially traumatic without, however, displaying gruesome injuries, dismembered bodies, or dead people. In its symbolism (how impotent innocent beings are in the face of terror) as well as its visual representation, this image of the Boston Marathon "Fallen Man" (as some media networks and journalists called him[3]) recalled two similarly tragic, awe-provoking, yet relatively "clean" images from 9/11, images that also would be shown over and over: that of one of the planes impaling itself into one of the Twin Towers, and that of the towers collapsing in a cloud of dust, smoke, and debris. In those two infamous images from 9/11, no human beings were immediately visible (although other snapshots and films from 9/11 would show bodies jumping from the skyscrapers). In the Boston bombing episode, by contrast, human beings and bodies were back in the picture as the blast—clean, antiseptic, and implacable as it was—brought human victims to their knees, even if many of them, this time, would get up again.

I do not think that the visual insistence on the Boston Marathon bombing's "Fallen Man" is innocent, incidental, or trivial. In fact, I want to argue in this chapter that the sight of fallen or falling bodies and, in some instances, the representational or narrative emphasis on the particular body parts that lead bodies to fall (reports liked to repeat that Iffrig fell down because "his knees buckled" under him) have something to tell us about the status of the war on terror today, some 15 years or so after 9/11, and about the contemporary deployment of security politics and policies designed to "keep us free from terror." More broadly, I want to suggest that "our" late Western modernity has become quite adept at dealing with falling or fallen bodies, at seeking them out, in fact, and at highlighting their presence and purpose—symbolic, aesthetic, political, moral—in societies allegedly in need of security, protection, or moral reassurance. The falling bodies of hapless victims of terrorism in the West (like Iffrig's in Boston); the fallen bodies of soldiers or government officials turned heroes when returning (some of them dead) from "our" wars against terror in Iraq, Afghanistan, Libya, Pakistan, Somalia, and so on; the felled and often barely visible (although still seen thanks to online and digital media) killed and, sometimes, partially mutilated bodies of some of "our" biggest villains and enemies (Saddam Hussein, Osama bin Laden, Muhammad Ghadafi): these are all ubiquitous sights and scenes of "our" security politics and wars in the last decade. At some level, these images seem to tell us that, as the war on terror goes on, bodies slowly but surely are allowed back into the picture (again, we did not see many bodies in the 9/11 photos and videos, other than those of the rescuers; and we certainly were not allowed to see fallen bodies in the early years of the wars in Iraq and Afghanistan). Bodies do matter more and more, it appears, in the representations "we" give or the stories "we" want to tell about "our" ongoing need for security in an always insecure world.

Fallen or falling bodies may now serve to humanize "our" wars on terror and "our" security politics, while continuing to dehumanize "our" enemies. This is more or less how official and media discourse has tried to make sense of the Boston Marathon bombing's "Fallen Man" images: resilience, courage, compassion, and collective moral uplift in the face of terror, all centered around the sight of the body that falls but, sometimes, rises or is propped up thanks to fellow human beings. But this interpretation, comforting as it may be for "us" to believe, is not satisfactory. After all, the emphasis on some fallen or falling bodies, such as those mentioned above, should not blind us to the fact that there are many more fallen/falling bodies that we are still not allowed to see, think of, or, indeed, as Judith Butler intimates, grieve for.[4] Even the images of the dehumanized fallen bodies of our greatest enemies perform a similar task: the killed body or dead face of a terrorist or terrorizing figure seems to justify, after the fact—after the long wars and endless security operations and tracking missions—the fall of "our" heroes (Western troops, above all) but also the invisibility of the hundreds of thousands of bodies that "our" wars and security campaigns have forced to the ground, never to rise again.

Bringing the human back into the picture in the form of a body that is shown to be vulnerable to insecurity and terror, as is the case with the Boston Marathon "Fallen Man," but resilient, too (or victorious and vengeful, as the images of the fallen bodies of "our" enemies seem to imply as well), is no guarantee that humanity is restored or, at least, sought after in "our" most common representations of terror and "our" responses to it. In this chapter, I seek to show that the visual presence of the falling/fallen body in images/representations of the ongoing war on terror corresponds to a different logic, one for which humanity and humanization are mere afterthoughts. Indeed, I believe that the insistence on the image of the falling/fallen body is the assurance that the threat of terror/terrorism that anchors our contemporary politics of security (as I suggested in Chapter 2) will not go away and thus will remain productive of security policies and politics. Put differently, theories and practices of security, at home and abroad, must remain essential to the missions and workings of the (Western) state and state sovereignty (as we saw, once again, in the previous chapter) because "we" are repeatedly told that it is through them, and perhaps only through them, that "Fallen Man" can stand up again.

Here, I want to challenge the representational logic that links the moment/event of terror to the so-called humanity of "Fallen Man." Moreover, I want to problematize the biopolitical uses that are made of fallen/falling bodies in the long afterglow of a never-to-end war on terror. I want to do so by suggesting that "Fallen Man" never falls naturally, normally, or inevitably. "Fallen Man" falls and, in some cases, never gets up because, as commentaries about the Boston Marathon bombing already suggested, specific body parts—not the whole body, not the body in its entirety or integrity—are targeted, victimized, and, in fact, take center stage. As these body parts are being hit (and, sometimes, visually highlighted, too), the unity of the body is challenged in the moment/event of terror. The body loses its balance; it is toppled over. Knees no longer provide bodily stability. Limbs, in some cases, are torn apart. Faces are disfigured. Body parts and bits and pieces of things are all blown by the blast, merged together, unrecognizable, unidentifiable. If I am right that the iconography of the humanity of "Fallen Man" is challenged by the presence and sight of body parts no longer serving the function of uniting the body or making it whole again, then different questions (perhaps reflecting a different sense of critical urgency) can and, perhaps, must be asked. For example, what if the sight of falling or fallen man matters, not because of the singular human body or being who drops to the ground and may or may not get up again, but because it reveals that contemporary security politics as well as the logic of terror it supposedly confronts can only conceive of the body as an amalgamation of parts or bits that can be dismantled, dismembered, or disseminated in some cases (for example, when looking at enemy or terrorist bodies) but never when "our" own (Western) bodies and their assumed integrity/unity is at stake? What if the iconography of "Fallen Man" counts primarily as a visual, narrative, or representational cover not only for what the war on terror and the contemporary politics of security do to bodies (fallen, falling, felled, or possibly fallible bodies, including sovereign bodies) and, indeed, to body parts, but also for the impossibility of the human(ized) body to stand up as one again, even "our" Western body in need of security? Or what if the incommensurability of human/bodily dismantling—that is to say, the dismantling and pulverization of our enemies' body parts reduced to particles and dust (for example, as a result of "our" drone attacks) but also of "our own" bodies and body parts—can never be allegorized by the image, representation, or narrative of "Fallen Man" and, in fact, is meant to be conjured away by its irruption? These questions may well put us in the presence of or face to face with a horrific vision, the "vision of the unthinkable" or the "unrepresentable," as Jacques Rancière puts it.[5] But this "unrepresentable" still is something, some event, that demands to be dealt with and no longer can be deferred by allegories or iconographies of the humanity of the body when what I call "body parts of terror" take center stage. Before turning to the questions raised by the incommensurability or unrepresentability of body parts, the first section of this chapter offers a critique of the role played by the image of the fallen/falling body in prevalent interpretations of terror and security politics.

Falling for terror

The image of the falling/fallen body victimized by the act of terror is central to "our" ways of understanding terror/terrorism, of dealing with the endless insecurity and fear it brings on, of making sense of "our" responses to terror attacks through war and various security strategies, and of keeping terror/terrorism alive. Thus, the sight of the fallen body has become our late modern iconography of terror. Iconography, as Julia Kristeva has explained, is primarily an invention of medieval Christian faith that enables the image/representation of God.[6] It is, Kristeva adds, an "economy of the visual" that ensures that the invisible or unrepresentable becomes visible or is represented.[7] An icon "inscribes" a transcendental idea or ideal into everyday life. Thus, it also "provides the conditions for the possibility of discourse on God" in this world.[8] The icon enables a "space of representation," Kristeva further clarifies,[9] one that pushes the visible or the image (what is to be seen) towards the guaranteed presence of something or someone (a transcendent being, an essence) that may not be materially present and yet orders or organizes all of human/political life. As I will argue below, iconography always points to the metaphysics of substance.

As an iconography of terror, the image of "Fallen Man" crystallizes what terror means for societies that have geared their politics of security towards its prevention. This icon of terror serves as a reminder of what "our" politics and policies stand for: resilience, perseverance, unity, victory, superiority, and, last but not least, a triumphant humanity. The ideals or values that "we" attach to those human sentiments or qualities and that, often, "we" deploy to justify "our" wars, campaigns, strategies, policies, or measures—democracy, human rights, freedom, equality—are colorful excuses that seemingly justify "our" quest for security in the face of endless terror threats. "Fallen Man" as "our" contemporary icon of terror also clarifies and simplifies what is at stake in security politics, on a daily basis, at home and abroad, even if "we" do not immediately see or understand it (it is, once again, the force of its "visual economy"). Just as importantly, the glaring and glorious vision of "Fallen Man" blinds us, too. Indeed, the iconography of terror hides as much as it illuminates. It occludes much of what takes place in the war on terror and in "our" security operations. To start with, as I intimated above, it removes a lot of bodies, other fallen or falling bodies and lives, from "our" field of vision and domain of understanding.

But the image/icon of "Fallen Man" has a pedagogical function, too. It teaches "us," citizens of the state/sovereign and subjects of security politics, how to behave in an age of terror and terrorism, what to expect in a security emergency, and what "our" motivations, as human bodies, should be in a context of terror-induced generalized insecurity. In this way, "Fallen Man" has an interpellating function, too.[10] "Fallen Man" tells us that bodies will indeed fall, and that, perhaps, it is impossible *not* to fall when assaulted by terror. More crucially, perhaps, it reveals that falling does not have to be a permanent condition (for "us," at least), that it may only be a painful, dramatic, and traumatic phase—perhaps a necessary one—leading to recovery, response, retaliation, resilience, reaffirmation, and, possibly, resurrection (thus, the icon of terror serves a theodicean mission, too). All these concepts and beliefs were famously invoked by George W. Bush during his first address to the nation after the 9/11 attacks.[11] But they may be better allegorized by the icon of "Fallen Man" today, whether it is the image of Bill Iffrig getting up again to finish the marathon in Boston or the eulogies recalling the courage and abnegation of "our" fallen troops, whose dead (but supposedly not forgotten) bodies are returned to "us" from the various hot zones of the war on terror (or, perhaps, in the commentaries that followed the killing of US Ambassador Christopher Stevens during the 9/12/2012 attack on the US Consulate in Benghazi, Libya[12]).

Even if terror is what forces us to fall to the ground—even if terror is, as Adriana Cavarero suggests, a force that pushes us to flee, to run (away)[13]—terror always allows the body—at least, the surviving or resilient body—to come back, or to rise again, in one way or another (it seems that the theology of terror and its iconography allow for the possibility of resurrection, as we saw above). Contemporary security politics relies on this conditioned belief in human resilience, on an allegorized power (that of the state, the sovereign, the nation as a whole, each of "us") to run away only to better return, more united and, possibly, more resolute and powerful. This, I think, is what the iconography of "Fallen Man" tells "us." It explains that terror is a dynamic force or, again, as Cavarero argues, that it has a movement or, in fact, *is* the very definition of movement and motion. Yes, terror forces movement; it leaves us with no choice but to escape and run (thus, ironically, a marathon was always going to be a prime site for an iconography of terror). But terror enables a dynamic opening or outcome, too, a physics of response and return. We run away, and we may well fall as we try to escape, but it is only to better regroup or restart. "Our" contemporary security politics actively rely on this expectation to regroup, return, and respond that, as Cavarero puts it, is part of the dynamics/physics of terror.[14] In fact, contemporary security politics and policies are premised upon the expectation that terror attacks and terrorist actions will occur and will demand a response, often an anticipated reaction. Even when an attack takes place, the techniques and technologies mobilized in the act of terror, innovative as they may appear to be, present security politics with an opportunity to reorganize itself, to rearrange its *dispositifs*, and, indeed, to re-securitize aspects of social life that were always potential targets of terror, even if they had not been prioritized in previous security strategies and designs. Put differently, terror does not prevent or stop security from deploying its modalities of action. Rather, terror provides security with a chance to be reassessed, recalibrated, or redirected. In the process, terror also gives security systems new ways to reinvest bodies (soldiers, government officials, and security forces but also, and more crucially, the bodies of the state's citizens). This probably explains why, for many individuals working for the state's various security agencies today, dealing with terror/terrorism amounts to being involved in a constant play or game where guessing, anticipating, preempting, reacting, and retaliating are key. In other words, terror and security are part of the same motion, of the same physics of movement, of the same dynamic and fluid domain where falling, rising, falling again, and rising again (and so on and so forth) are normal occurrences.

It is such an acceptance of terror as part of the processes of everyday security (or, perhaps, the acceptance of security as part of everyday terror) that the iconography of "Fallen Man" helps "us" to understand. That "Fallen Man" indeed falls should not and cannot prevent bodies from rising again and, more importantly, perhaps, from stopping the course or movement of security politics. In fact, it is mainly through security politics, as we saw above, that human bodies are today enabled or encouraged to get up and stand tall again. "We" can get up and stand tall thanks to "our" wars (that also make some of "our" fallen bodies into the nation's heroes), thanks to "our" security operations overseas (that ensure that the felled bodies of "our" dehumanized enemies will never rise again), and thanks to an array of security and safety procedures and technologies "at home" (that guarantee that the vast majority of the state's or the nation's human bodies will be ready to get up and move along even if an attack is to take place on home soil again).

Thus, one could say that the politics of security in an age of terror has fallen or falling bodies as its primary object. This point should not only be taken to mean that both terror and security politics target bodies, individual and collective, through many of their operations and executions. This is undoubtedly the case, and many contemporary studies emphasizing the relevance of biopower/biopolitics in security configurations have covered much of this terrain (as I discussed in Chapters 1 and 2),[15] but biopolitically informed perspectives may not be sufficient here. Or, rather, their analytical logic may need to be pushed further.[16] To say that contemporary regimes of security have the icon of "Fallen Man" as their main object or objective also means that security politics and terror, together, as part of their endlessly dynamic encounter or play, want to make sure that questions about the unity or integrity of the (human) body are not raised. That a body brought to its knees by a terrorist bombing must get up and walk or run again (and live to tell us about it), or that a body's disappearance as a result of an improvised explosive device must never be a vain loss, speaks to the ideas or values of human resilience, continuity, or unity that are expected of the human body in security politics and, even, in what security politics understands terror to be and do. Put differently, security politics and its understanding of what terror is and does to human bodies insist on maintaining a metaphysics of substance at the very heart of both terror/terrorism and its security challenges.

Simply stated, and as I started to discuss in the Introduction to this volume, the metaphysics of substance guarantees that there is always an image of the human body, a representation of an embodied humanity, that can be found in both terror and security politics. As Elizabeth Povinelli explains, the metaphysics of substance has served to anchor the body to the idea of the unity or identity of being throughout Western modernity.[17] One could say that the metaphysics of substance goes back to Aristotle's discovery of "social man," whereby the main characteristic of being alive and human is associated with the capacity of the human body to exhibit individual qualities that give it a political/social presence (or identity). Povinelli writes that substance, attached to a human body, reflects "a hierarchy of being in which being has a primary sense (substance) and a secondary sense (qualities, quantities, relations, and modalities of substances)."[18] Thus, each substance represents some being, or essence, or life; yet each embodied substance also has fundamental characteristics derived from its primary being. For human beings, the primary substance is to live (zoe), but this being/life is qualified as having or representing a humanity, which becomes essential to the meaning of having/being a human body ($bios$).[19] The quality of humanity, the metaphysics of substance stipulates, demands that beings and bodies (characterized as selves, subjects, individuals, agents, citizens, and so on) be prioritized as what or, rather, as who must be preserved, who must continue to live, and whose existence and bodily integrity/permanence cannot be questioned, let alone interrupted. The humanity in and of beings and bodies must be immutable. And moral, political, and cultural institutions must elevate it as such since it embodies or represents the primary (human) substance as the "singular, stable, independent, and ultimate referent." Thus, humanity marks the presence of (or, indeed, re-presents) "an immovable and unmoving being."[20]

Once again, the iconography of "Fallen Man," this prevalent and perhaps primordial image of terror and security, helps to re-ground the metaphysics of substance in contemporary representations, visions, and narratives of late-modern Western society, politics, and culture. In this way, it is not unlike another common late twentieth- and early twenty-first-century iconography, that of the "suffering victim." Susan Sontag intimates that the "iconography of suffering" is part and parcel of Western civilization.[21] It traces its origins to Biblical writings, Sontag suggests (Elaine Scarry also hints at the fact that the Christian iconography of suffering starts with the image of the body of Jesus[22]). Contemporary icons of suffering cannot fail to show the human body in pain, struggling to live, asking for compassion, pity, support, and fellow feeling from humankind. In fact, the "iconography of suffering" is often designed to rally humanity (the so-called fellowship of "mankind") behind the fallen/falling body, a suffering human body that will not be allowed to be forgotten or die in vain (suffering "as the place of the subject," Kristeva writes[23]). One can note in passing that contemporary security and terror politics are still very adept at making use of this "iconography of suffering," as we saw, for example, in the Obama administration's attempt in 2013 to mobilize images of sarin-gas victims in Syria to try to justify military action against the Bashar Al-Assad regime. Similar to the iconography of "Fallen Man"—one might say that "Fallen Man" is a reprise of the image of suffering in a context of terror/terrorism—the iconography of suffering recalls and demands the priority of the metaphysics of substance. In this way, iconographies of suffering and terror seem to capture the essential unity or formal integrity of the human body for the sake of humanity. But, more than this, the preserved unity and resilient continuity of the body of "Fallen Man" (as an icon of terror and suffering) sustains the requirement in the contemporary politics of security and terror for the continued dominant presence of the metaphysics of substance. Thus, we may say that security politics represents "our" last line of defense, not so much against terror *per se* but against the possible loss of the metaphysics of substance.

To lose the metaphysics of substance would *not* be terrorizing, since terror, as we saw above, does not problematize the integrity of the body and humanity. Rather, to lose the metaphysics of substance would be horrifying. The horror provoked by the possible disappearance of the metaphysics of substance is far more unbearable to the idea of humanity than the concept or reality of terror. Whereas terror remains "in line" with security, horror is what "our" politics of security cannot confront and must representationally cast away (as we saw towards the end of Chapter 2, with the horror of eschatological time). Yet, perhaps, such a horror is already announced by the targeting of and focus on body parts in the iconography of suffering and terror.

An iconoclastic parody of terror?

I want to turn to the relationship between the targeting of body parts and the confrontation with horror, a horror that may well be on display already in some images of terror(ism). But to start to perceive the horror already at work in the sight of terror, we need to defamiliarize ourselves to the iconography of "Fallen Man" and the promises it appears to offer to political, moral, and cultural regimes of representation that are still dependent upon a metaphysics of substance. Before introducing the horror conveyed by the dissemination of the body parts of terror/terrorism, I wish to take a deconstructive detour, one enabled by another vision of "Fallen Man." This deconstructive detour is provided by Don DeLillo's post-9/11 novel, *Falling Man*, which recounts the disjointedness of a few New Yorkers' lives in the days that followed the September 11, 2001 attacks in Lower Manhattan.[24]

What DeLillo's novel provides is a counter-scene or, perhaps, a counter-iconography of terror. In *Falling Man*, there is no humanity that responds or stands up again in the wake of the trauma. As "Fallen Man" falls, and falls again, DeLillo's characters are faced with a blank screen, a void, a boundless but also banal incomprehension. The survivors go on living their lives with the paralyzing images of the fallen (for example, the images of those who jumped to their death from the burning Twin Towers), of the dead, and of the never-to-be-found-again, forever engraved in daily routines, in one's sense of normalcy. DeLillo's fallen or falling bodies have a contagious effect. But instead of uplifting, reviving, or resurrecting, this image or counter-icon of "Fallen Man" contaminates "us" and condemns "us" to a blunt realization: humanity, the so-called unity of humankind, is always "beyond reach." This is perhaps not so much what the 9/11 event reveals (for there is little place for 9/11 as an event in DeLillo's text). Rather, what the languishing hours, days, and weeks after 9/11 convey is that there is not and perhaps never was such a thing as a human community, human communication, or human communion organized and united against terror, or possibly against "evil," or against anything that causes harm to the human body. All there ever was is an "inoperative community,"[25] or an incomplete mode of communicability among bodies and lives, which, far from bearing witness to a metaphysics of substance, incarnate an existential or melancholic aimlessness, meaninglessness, and vulnerability.

A particular moment in DeLillo's *Falling Man* poignantly illustrates this inoperativeness of the iconography of "Fallen Man." In the days that followed the 9/11 attacks, a stuntman/street performer, simply referred to by people as Falling Man, had become famous for faking his own fall (and death) by jumping from tall structures in the city (buildings, bridges, subway platforms, etc.). The act typically took place in front of huge crowds of terrified New Yorkers, who were left to wonder about the meaning and apparent visual cruelty of the performance. One afternoon, on one of her walks through the city, Lianne (one of the protagonists of the novel, often simply referred to by DeLillo as "she") comes upon what seems to be Falling Man. The following are excerpts from DeLillo's rendition of this encounter:

> It took a moment for him to come into view, upper body only, a man on the other side of the protective fence that bordered the tracks. He wasn't a track worker in a blaze orange vest. She saw that much. She saw him from the chest up ... He seemed to be coming out of nowhere. There was no station stop here, no ticket office or platform for passengers, and she had no idea how he'd

managed to gain access to the track area. White male, she thought. White shirt, dark jacket ... The man had affixed the safety harness to the rail of the platform ... She moved back. She moved the other way, backing into a building that stood on the corner. Then she looked around for someone, just to exchange a glance ... She wished she could believe this was some kind of street theater, an absurdist drama that provokes onlookers to share a comic understanding of what is irrational in the great schemes of being or in the next small footstep ... This was too near and deep, too personal. All she wanted to share was a look, catch someone's eye, see what herself was feeling. She did not think of walking away. He was right above her but she wasn't watching and wasn't walking away ... Lianne tried to understand why he was here and not somewhere else. These were strictly local circumstances, people in windows, some kids in a schoolyard. Falling Man was known to appear among crowds or at sites where crowds might quickly form. Here was an old derelict rolling a wheel down the street. Here was a woman in a window, having to ask who he was ... He stood balanced on the rail of the platform. The rail had a broad flat top and he stood there, blue suit, white shirt, blue tie, black shoes. He loomed over the sidewalk, legs spread slightly, arms out from his body and bent at the elbows, asymmetrically, man in fear, looking out of some deep pool of concentration into lost space, dead space ... She slipped around the corner of the building. It was a senseless gesture of flight, adding only a couple of yards to the distance between them ... She watched him, her shoulder jammed to the brick wall of the building. She did not think of turning and leaving ... They all waited. But he did not fall. He stood poised on the rail for a full minute, then another ... Then she began to understand ... he wasn't here to perform for those at street level or in the high windows. He was situated where he was ... waiting for a train to come, northbound, that is what he wanted, an audience in motion, passing scant yards from his standing figure ... The man stared into the brickwork of the corner building but did not see it. There was blankness in his face, but deep, a kind of lost gaze ... The train comes slamming through and he turns his head and looks into it (into his death by fire) and then brings his head back around and jumps ... Jumps or falls. He keels forward, body rigid, and falls full-length, headfirst, drawing a rustle of awe from the schoolyard ... She felt her body go limp. But the fall was not the worst of it. The jolting end of the fall left him upside-down, secured to the harness, twenty feet above the pavement. The jolt, the sort of midair impact and bounce, the recoil, and now the stillness, arms at his sides, one leg bent at the knee. There was something awful about the stylized pose, body and limbs, his signature stroke ... She could have spoken to him but that was another plane of being, beyond reach.[26]

DeLillo's depiction of the scene at times evokes the image or sensation of the planes bursting into the Twin Towers. Perhaps it can be read as an allegory of it, albeit one deprived of the meanings and categories "we" have tried to attribute to the event, after the fact (attack on the homeland, America versus terror, the "evil" of terrorism, threatened US security, a justified war on terror, and so on). But Falling Man's act is a very strange allegory of terror/terrorism and its meanings for the US nation, its people, and its government. First, the fall (or jump) of Falling Man is carefully planned, stylishly performed, and meticulously choreographed. It may mimic the terror/terrorist attacks this way. But it also renders them commonplace (by reproducing the performance of falling/fallen bodies throughout the city). Perhaps it is the choreographed replay of the 9/11 images and story, the meanings "we" are supposed to get out of this iconography of terror, that this Falling Man's fall/jump towards a suspension of both life and death (he does not die, but his body remains lifelessly suspended) wishes to mimic and parody. In this way—critically, perhaps—it aims to achieve maximal effects of awe and incomprehension, not so much about the terror attacks themselves but about their discourses and representations, about the political and ideological justifications they enable, and about their rationalizations.

Second, as Lianne's bodily expressions betray, Falling Man does not provoke terror among the onlookers. Instead, Falling Man freezes the body of the spectator in horror. Lianne attempts a half-hearted movement away from the scene, but she cannot walk or run away (to gather herself, to call the police, to ask for help). She is tethered to it. She looks on, petrified both by the sight of this soon to be falling human form and by the apparent meaninglessness of the scene. She cannot grasp what she is witnessing, but she also cannot prevent herself from staring at it (the "absurdist drama," the irrationality in "the great schemes of being"). Falling Man does not seem to have any grand scheme either ("a blankness in his face" and "kind of a lost gaze"), other than to fall/jump in front of an "audience in motion," who may or may not be able to capture his fall. In fact, falling in front of a moving audience may be the act's only objective: to force some onlookers to stop running, to block their movement/motion, to compel them *not* to get up and stand tall by turning their backs to the moment/sight of trauma, to transform their fear and terror into horror.

Third, Falling Man is never presented to Lianne, or to the reader, as a fully human body, an entirely human form, a human being, with a clear, perhaps recognizable, identity. Nothing about his appearance reveals substantial human traits or a unity/integrity about his body. Lianne can only describe him by the clothes he is wearing. His choreographed gestures and postures are those of a lifeless puppet, an automaton. His shape merges with the surroundings (the rail, the platform, the train, the "lost and dead space" around). More tellingly, perhaps, what appears to be his body is depicted as a loose collection of body parts: his "upper body" is the only thing Lianne sees for a while; his legs, arms, and elbows are displayed "asymmetrically"; his face is blank; his limbs are jolted and evoke an "awful stylized pose." Faced with this amalgamation of parts, Lianne's body too is rendered purposeless, almost lifeless: she wants to walk away but cannot; she hopes to catch someone else's eyes or "share a look" to see "what she is feeling," but she does not manage to do so; she could have tried to speak to him, but that was always "beyond reach." She, like

Falling Man, becomes completely anonymous (fused and confused with the brick wall her shoulder and back lean against as she stares at the scene). Falling Man's body fragmentation and its resistance to identity, human unity/integrity, and, indeed, substance seem to produce similar effects to other bodies and forms around. This is also why Falling Man's performance is *not* about offering an allegory of terror. Rather, I would argue that Falling Man—the stylized performance, the dismembered and upside-down dangling body, and the novel's narrative itself—is a vision of horror.

DeLillo's *Falling Man* is an iconoclastic moment. It confronts the ideology of substance and human presence/resilience represented by the icon of terror with a deconstructive vision and narrative about the human body and life in a seemingly endless aftermath of terror/terrorism, war, and prevention performed through security politics. DeLillo's *Falling Man* does not really antagonize the icon of "Fallen Man"—the body who is blown by the bomb or the planes, falls down, but may rise again and sometimes even "makes it across the line." Rather, in its form and performance, Falling Man's act parodies this icon of terror. Eventually, it de-centers it, too, by revealing that the visual representation of terror has no core, no essential substance, no identity, and perhaps no body. What sustains and maintains the appearance of the body captured by the icon of "Fallen Man" is a loose and fragile agglomeration of body parts that, when terror's violence hits, are likely to "buckle" under the pressure, collapse the unity/integrity of the human body, and eventually become undistinguishable from non-human matter. What "Fallen Man" as an icon of terror must not reveal is the fragility or accident that is the configuration, form, or idea of the body as one or whole, as a human unity, or as an image of human continuity, integrity, or completeness. But this is precisely what DeLillo's Falling Man's performance shows us: the appearance of the unity of the human body, and human life, is always propped up and maintained by an arrangement of autonomous, frail, and vulnerable body parts, a plurality of precarious bits that we are faced with during or as a result of the terror event.

Thus, what is not acceptable for the human body and which, in their own ways, terror and security strive to occlude is the incongruity or incommensurability of the vulnerable body, the looseness or disconnectedness of the body's parts, and, sometimes, the rawness of exposed and mangled flesh that not even "our" politics and policies of security can prevent (in fact, "our" security politics and policies, by continuing their association with terror, perversely add to such vulnerability or rawness). Even in the moment of terror, the reunited, recomposed, or, indeed, re-securitized body must never give way to the sight of the disconnected and scattered body parts. Security's body of terror ("Fallen Man" as the icon of terror) cannot become a body of horror—that is to say, a frozen, paralyzed, or immovable body that is already in excess of its so-called human unity, integrity, or completeness. And yet one must also wonder why, if this is the case—if occluding the sight of the body of horror has become humanity's categorical imperative—so many of "our" contemporary images and sights of terror (starting with the image of "Fallen Man" at the Boston Marathon bombing) seem to refuse to do away with a certain fascination with the horrifyingly disjointed or dismembered body parts that cause human bodies (just like material structures) to collapse and human lives to vanish in a cloud of dust, debris, and other remains of things and objects. The next section starts to explore this seemingly perverse fascination with the disseminated body parts of terror. It shows that horror cannot be disentangled from the representation of terror and security.

The horror that befalls the human body

Even if one feels one has become immune to the often gruesome details found in media reports of terrorist attacks, civilian mass shootings, torture scenes, or war kill-ings, one may still be taken aback by the large amount of insistent descriptions of wounded, destroyed, or disappeared body parts, limbs, and other bodily attributes in the aftermath of the Boston Marathon bombing. After the bombs exploded and after some bodies tried to recover from their injuries, a wide array of news and social media posted witness accounts of what had happened that day and in the days that followed to people and to their bodies (primarily, to figure out why or how they fell, and how they later tried to stand up again). Here are a few telling examples from a *Washington Post* open blog called "Battling Back," created on April 23, 2013 (and prompting victims to "share their story"):[27]

> (Heather) Abbott, 38, had taken the train up from her home in Rhode Island for … [a] Red Sox game. The Sox had all but defeated Tampa Bay when Abbott and her friends left Fenway Park to hit the nearby bars. She was the last of her friends waiting to get into Forum on Boylston Street when she heard the first blast. "I heard a big bang and saw people screaming and panicked," Abbott said Friday [four days after the bombing], **when she still hoped her left foot might be saved.** Abbott saw smoke swirling and peo-ple rushing into the bar – but she didn't make it inside. The second bomb exploded, **and a piece of shrapnel hit her foot. "Who would help me now?" she remembers thinking.** But a woman came to Abbott's aid, dragging her inside the bar. Abbott's friends crowded around her. One used his belt as a tourniquet for her leg, and she was carried to an ambulance on a makeshift cardboard stretcher. "I saw blood trailing behind me," she said. "My friends kept saying, 'We won't leave you.'" She finally made it to the hospital. **Her left foot was shattered, with damage to the bones, tendons, and nerves.**
>
> In a photograph relayed around the world, Jeffrey Bauman became the face of the Boston Marathon bombing — a 27-year-old man in a wheelchair, **rushed away from the wreckage with his legs sheared by shrapnel.** Bauman was a bystander to the blast that day, a big-hearted guy who plays guitar and works at Costco and had joined crowds near the finish line to cheer on his girlfriend. He survived **but lost both legs near the knee** …

Since April 15, Bauman has become an inspiration to a growing circle of friends and strangers who admire his strong spirit and positive view of the world, **even as the bombing changed his life.**

Kaitlynn Cates went to the Boston Marathon to cheer on her friends in the race. She was about 50 feet from the finish line when the first bomb went off, **throwing her to the ground and injuring her leg.** She was there with Leo Fonseca, 41. "Leo tried to hook his body around me," Cates, 25, recalled in a statement released by Massachusetts General Hospital, where she was taken for her injuries. "He literally straddled me and said 'Stay down. Stay down' because I was trying to get up and he didn't know if there was going to be another bomb," she continued. **"Bodies had fallen back on us and I started to crawl under them to get away."** Fonseca wrapped Cates's **injured leg in a blanket and his sweatshirt, picked her up and carried her to the alley where he had parked his car . . .** Cates and Fonseca met President Obama when he visited Boston in the wake of the attack. According to a website created to raise money for Cates's recovery, **her leg has been saved.** "I'm definitely going to rise above this," she told Fox News. **"It's always going to be a scar,** but I'm not going to let them win . . ."

J.P. Craven was watching for his dad to finish what was expected to be his final Boston Marathon when the first explosion knocked him to the ground. **He got up, confused, ears ringing, intensely dizzy, and thought: "I must have walked into a pole." Then he tore off his sweatshirt, which was on fire, and his shirt, which was wet with blood, and he ran. He didn't feel any pain in those first moments — doctors were surprised, later, that he was able to walk away, let alone run . . .** His parents said they are incredibly grateful [to the hospital's doctors and nurses]. . . **especially after waiting in the intensive care unit that night as doctors operated on his head, repairing his ear and nose and worried about brain damage.** "The doctors said there's really no medical explanation why he's not more injured," Joe Craven said. "He was so close" to the bomb, his mother Nancy Craven said. **"All the other victims that close lost legs." Her son, in contrast, took ball bearings in the head, but none of them pierced his skull . . . On Tuesday, when they took out the breathing tube and Craven came to and was able to talk, his family really knew he was going to be all right. He had another four- or five-hour surgery on Wednesday to reconnect some of the nerves on his forehead.**

Adrianne Haslet-Davis' first thought after the explosion was whether she would survive. Her second: **"If I do make it, how will I dance again?"** Adrianne, a dance instructor, had been walking along the Boston Marathon sidelines enjoying the day with her husband U.S. Air Force Capt. Adam Davis, who had just gotten home from a deployment in Afghanistan, when they heard the first blast. The second bomb went off four feet away . . . **She dragged**

herself with her elbows into a nearby bar, where Adam pulled his belt off to use as a tourniquet. Others nearby tried, too. "The pain was excruciating," she said. "There aren't words for it." Then a man came through the crowd and said he was a doctor, **"and he pulled on the tourniquet so incredibly hard I couldn't feel my leg anymore. That was a wonderful moment."** When people were helping her get on a stretcher, they told Adam, "You're in bad shape, buddy, don't move, we're going to put a tourniquet on you as well." **He had been so worried about her that he hadn't realized how much he was bleeding, with shrapnel all through his legs, torn nerves in the arch of one foot, and broken bones in the other.** At first she was only aware of the two of them, as they both cried and said they loved one another. But when she was getting carried to the ambulance, she saw how many people were hurt, images she wishes she could forget. **She closed her eyes and pleaded for painkillers: Knock me out.** When she woke up from surgery, her mom was there and told her Adam was in another hospital and would be OK. **And she told Adrianne that her foot was gone.**

The gaping shrapnel wound from the second bomb blast at the Boston Marathon that cut deep into 11-year-old Aaron Hern's left thighbone is healing. After nine days, a rough patch in intensive care, two surgeries, and well-wishing visits from no less than First Lady Michelle Obama and players from the Oakland Athletics baseball team, Hern was released from Boston Children's Hospital . . . **Aaron happened to be standing at the finish-line barricades next to eight-year-old Martin Richard. The boys didn't know each other. But the same explosion that shredded Aaron's leg tore through Martin and killed him. For several terrifying minutes after the blast, Aaron lay alone on the sidewalk, blood seeping from his leg, staring at the small boy's body** . . . In the chaos after the explosion, Alan Hern [Aaron's father], a high school football coach, grabbed Aaron's younger sister and bolted to a nearby restaurant. When Alan realized Aaron wasn't with them, he fought the crowd, raced back and found his son, frightened and in pain, **his left thighbone exposed. "It looked like a war wound,"** Alan Hern, a Naval Academy graduate, like Katherine [Aaron's mom], and former naval officer who had deployed to the Persian Gulf, told NBC's Today Show. A passerby stripped off his belt for a makeshift tourniquet to stem the flow of blood, and others helped load the child onto an ambulance bound for Children's Hospital. **What followed were long vigils in ICU, breathing tubes, IVs, fear of infection setting in and worry that the child would never again jump around the backyard with a Star Wars light saber with the same joyful abandon.**

It probably does not come as a surprise that many of these accounts, filtered by the *Washington Post*'s own blog editors, want to highlight the spirit of recovery and resilience of the human beings and bodies that suffered such horrible wounds that day. Many of these stories are about standing up again, even though standing is physically impossible now for quite a few of these wounded bodies. Still, most of these accounts partake of what I suggested above is an expected iconography of terror. In a way, all these victimized and terrorized human bodies (most of them got to walk away, escape the scene of terror, one way or another) are replicas of "Fallen Man." Like Iffrig, whose knees buckled underneath him but was soon helped to walk again, these figures or bodily forms were able to retain their human unity or dignity thanks to the support of fellow human beings and bodies (other marathon spectators or runners, passers-by, local store patrons and owners, first-aid providers, doctors and nurses, family members, loved ones, and even the President of the United States and the First Lady). Their stories, it seems, are stories of and about humanity that are anchored to the image of the human body, hurt, damaged, maimed, dismembered, but somehow resolutely put back together, reunited, reconstructed, and, possibly, re-secured.

Yet it is also obvious that these accounts are telling us something else, or pointing us to another object from which our eye may not be able to disengage itself so easily. In each of these narrative vignettes, incompleteness or disconnection are fateful elements of the bombing and its aftermath. Bodies have been left unable to walk or stand; if they can stand or walk again, it is at the cost of great pain or sacrifice. Lives, careers, pastimes, well-beings, futures have been made discontinuous, uncertain, insecure, unpredictable. In some cases, all these are simply gone. Traumas, wounds, scars have been forced open onto bodies, mundane things and objects, daily routines and habits, and relationships, perhaps indefinitely. And all this because, as these accounts clearly point out, all sorts of body parts have been exposed, targeted, detached from the rest of the body, exploded, dispersed, lost, or fused with other parts, other bodies' parts, other bits of flesh, or other bits of stuff and things, organic or not, neither alive nor dead. Body parts, it is clear, were not able to support and sustain the human body in these bombings (indeed, multiple reports noted that the Boston Marathon terror attacks were particularly harmful to the body because the pressure-cooker bombs had been placed at ground level, thus ensuring maximal damage to lower limbs and extremities[28]). This realization became particularly visible. Indeed, whereas much narrative and visual insistence was placed on the image of human unity, renewal, and resilience in the face of terror and insecurity—the image/idea conveyed by the icon of terror, once again—a parallel image and narrative representation was also at play in the Boston Marathon bombing accounts and reports. Not unlike DeLillo's Falling Man's deconstructive and iconoclastic performance, some of the visions and narrations of "Terror at the Marathon" offered deconstructive and iconoclastic moments, or possibilities for their own representational undoing. By focusing so much attention (and anxiety and uncertainty) on the body parts of terror, they inserted or, better yet, exposed horror in an otherwise "safe" or, at least, more comforting and comfortable scene and iconography of terror and insecurity.

This apparently perverse, horrifying, and deconstructive emergence of dissociated or disseminated body parts into the representational logic of terror and security is unsettling but perhaps not unusual. Perhaps we are less likely to want to see it in moments of rekindled unity and humanity such as those allegorized by the icon of Fallen Man. Perhaps we would be more comfortable with it if it were to remain confined to "other" scenes of terror, particularly to those scenes and sights of terror that are not "here," with "us," at the heart of "our" late Western modernity (or at the heart of "our" cities). Perhaps this is also why "we" are more likely to associate horror—particularly as it manifests itself through bodies and body parts— with suicide bombings and suicide bombers "over there," and not with terror/ terrorist attacks "in here" (in the West and its many transnational extensions—a four star hotel in Mumbai, an upscale shopping mall in Nairobi, a Starbucks coffee shop in Jakarta, for example). But perhaps we need to pay closer attention to the place horror occupies in visions and representations of suicide bombing allegedly "over there" if it is indeed the case that the representational guarantees supposedly provided by "our" iconographies of terror and security cannot be maintained when body parts take center stage.

In his book *On Suicide Bombing*, Talal Asad brings horror to the forefront of "our" narratives, representations, and, indeed, understandings of what suicide bombings and bombers are and do. Suicide bombing is marked by horror because suicide bombings and bombers have "no object."[29] By suggesting that suicide bombing and horror have no object, Asad intimates that, by contrast, terror still has an objective, a design, a purpose, or, indeed, a motive. In other words, terror/terrorism intends to secure or maintain certain meanings (political, ideological, moral, theological, etc.). To say that the horror that emerges through suicide bombing has "no object" is not precise enough, however. I think what Asad wants to say is that horror has "no object" *in relation to* human life, the human body, or humanity. This is why Asad partly derives his understanding of horror, which, he argues, becomes visible in and as a result of suicide bombing attacks, from the work of Stanley Cavell, for whom horror is a confrontation with "the perception of the precariousness of human identity."[30] Thus, Asad is, in my view, more on target when he adds that horror is "intransitive."[31] The adjective "intransitive" is apt here because, as I have argued elsewhere, horror impedes any sort of transmission of meaning, any form of interpretation and, perhaps, representation as well.[32] Horror's images confound meaning and established certainties, including those that relate to the identity or substance of human life. This is why horror, like the suicide bomber, has the unity of the human body, the metaphysics of substance invoked by the integrity or wholeness of the body, in its sights, as its target—perhaps not the body as horror's object of representation or reference but the body as horror's object of demolition or pulverization (and, here, horror shows us as well that, as Rey Chow has encouraged us to do, we may need to revisit the notion of object as something that is always meant to be targeted, often for destruction or decomposition[33]). Asad gestures towards this reading of horror (via suicide bombing) when he writes that it "explodes the imaginary, the space within which the flexible persona demonstrates to itself its identity."[34]

Thus, unlike terror that, once again, allows the body to flee, run away, get up, or stand tall (as we saw above, terror and security work in concert to "emancipate" the human body as an integral and dynamic unity), horror leaves "no alternative" to what occurs in the instant of the attack/bombing.[35] This is again why, for Cavarero, horror blocks any movement of the body towards escape or survival. This is also why the horror visible in suicide bombings does not aim at causing death but, instead, reaches into a non-human domain that is beyond the biopolitical threshold of life or death. What takes central stage in the horror of, for example, suicide bombing (and what may be its main target) is the "body undone," the body that "loses its individuality."[36] What Cavarero calls the "scraps of the bodies of the victims,"[37] or what Asad refers to as the "sudden shattering and mingling of physical objects and human bodies," are what render the scene of horror unwatchable or unrepresentable.[38] Or, as I put it above, these are the images and understandings that the iconography of terror must protect the human body/humanity from, because, unlike terror, horror directly "offends the ontological dignity that the human figure possesses."[39]

Here, both Asad and Cavarero seem to imply that two apparently divergent moments or logics—one of diffusion or dissemination, the other of merging and confusion—manage to complement each other in the act/scene/instance of horror. Indeed, what appears to be especially unbearable to the idea of the human and of the unity/integrity of the body is both the decomposition of the body down to the level of body parts and bits of flesh *and* the reformation or reconfiguration of those parts into something monstrous, non-human, and supposedly unrepresentable when bits of human flesh, organs, tissues, and bones are fused by the violence of the explosion/destruction with fragments of other things and objects or parts of formerly human or, perhaps, animal bodies. Both moments—and logics—are horrible to consider, let alone witness. But we are really not in the presence of two different moments or logics since diffusion/dissemination and refiguration/confusion take place instantaneously. This is what, I believe, Asad has in mind when he writes about the "confounding of the body's shapes."[40] Such a confounding of the form/figure of the body is far beyond any sense of humanity or, indeed, any ontological dignity. Rather, it is the revelation (not representation since, once again, horror is "intransitive") of the simultaneous dismantling of the human, the pulverization of its parts, and the recomposition of a material shape/form that is evidently no longer human and yet does retain some traces of formerly human parts, flesh, and tissues in its making ("so mutilated that it might be the body of a pig," Cavarero—via Virginia Woolf—writes[41]). I believe that horror *is* the name one may be able to give to this revelation.

After recalling a journalistic account of a suicide bombing attack in Jerusalem in 2003, Asad finds particularly striking the way the reporting witness refers to certain body parts of victims dispersed throughout the bombing site. A woman's "bloody hand is described as an alien thing"; the loose head of the suicide bomber in the street is now "a fright mask"; a man's burning head looks like a piece of coal to the transfixed onlooker; a young girl's arm is no longer a "natural limb."[42] Body parts, Asad suggests, play a crucial role in the revelation and unfolding of the horrific scene. They mark the decomposition and dissemination of the body and, by extension, of the metaphysics of substance that has grafted itself onto the belief in the unity/integrity/identity of the human body/being. In a way, body parts are agents of horror because they participate in the confounding of shapes that prevents a return to the idea/image of the human body. Body parts are what enable the human to be morphed into alien things, fright masks, fossilized rocks, or disfigured animals. And yet body parts of horror are not totally inorganic or non-human. Perhaps this is the most horrifyingly disturbing part (at least, for the human body and the sense of ontological integrity). The body parts or remnants of human flesh and tissue that merge with non-human things and objects to become something else altogether (a newly configured shape) still contain organic traces of a matter that once was human. Thus, it is as if the body parts of and in horror bear responsibility for the surrendering of human matter/life to this something else, to this new form, to a "machinic vitality" (as Rosi Braidotti has suggested),[43] or to a new species of matter, perhaps (more on this in the Epilogue to this volume), which, like things/objects, but also more than them, is forever suspended in a state/condition where life and death have new purposes and have become indistinguishable from one another.[44] Perhaps this is why the "confounding of the body's shapes" generated by dismembered body parts is so horrible and, possibly, unrepresentable. It is horrible because it reveals a new matter or vibrancy/vitality[45]—dare we say a "substance"?— that is "born" out of complete and unremitting human devastation and disintegration and yet compels those who see it (or, rather, cannot run away from it in terror) to perceive a few flashes of something that appears to have been human or to have belonged to a human body in it. In other words, this horrible newly fused shape or matter that emerges through the horror of suicide bombing (and perhaps of other bombing attacks that target body parts) may force us to catch a glimpse of what may be in store for the human body, human life, human substance, and, indeed, human forms when fragile and always artificial "boundaries" between so-called species or types of matter "are breached."[46]

Thus, what cannot be seen in the image of terror—a terror unleashed by a suicide bomber or by cowardly terrorists who have placed devices designed to explode after they themselves have had a chance to run away—is this horrific revelation that body parts are not just the weak or soft spots of the human body's defense, resilience, or security but also, and more disturbingly, the vectors of a vulnerable humanity's own opening onto confusion, recomposition, or merger with other types of matter and material. What should not be seen or represented (because it is not acceptable) is that body parts, liberated from the organic unity of the body and the ontological priority given to the human, lead us (humans?) towards a "confounding of shapes" in which human substance is but one of many remaining traces. This is why the iconography of terror is so crucial to security designs and operations that claim to have the protection or preservation of a certain idea of the human as their main goal. Once again, such an iconography/idea of terror (and the movement of still alive or alert human bodies that terror encourages) serves as a buffer against this post-ontological, post-anthropomorphic, or, simply, more-than-human breach or recomposition that the horror of body parts appears to announce. Yet scenes of terror and terrorism (the suicide bombing attack in Jerusalem in 2003 recounted by Asad, the many victims' accounts of the Boston Marathon bombing, the photos of the collapse of the Twin Towers, etc.) can never completely manage to remove the body parts from the picture. Some images of terror—in particular, many suicide-bombing sights—are left with no representational safeguards in the face of horror. Others—for example, many images and narratives from terrorist attacks "in here," at the heart of late Western urban modernity—try to muster as much representational, iconographic, and allegorical purpose and force as they can in order to maintain the belief that security (and, by extension, humanity) can still have a chance in the face of horror, even if this means that horror must continue to be presented as nothing more or nothing less than terror/terrorism.

And yet, as we saw in the Boston Marathon-bombing witness accounts, even this representational economy of terror in the West does not fully succeed in keeping the horror of body parts at bay. Despite what appears to be a representational urgency to ward off the sight of horror behind the veil offered by the icon of "Fallen Man," body parts keep on re-emerging, and bodies have a hard time getting up or standing tall again. Why, then, does the horror of the dissemination and recomposition of body parts revealed in suicide bombings also seem to be invoked through many accounts and images of falling bodies in recent Western instances of terror/terrorism? Are falling bodies not able to fulfill the representational task they seem to have been assigned? How might one explain this ongoing fascination with the "unrepresentable," or, indeed, to use Rancière's phrase, with the "visually unthinkable" in contemporary scenes of terror/terrorism taking place not just "over there" but "in here," too?

Representing the unrepresentable

In a brief reflection on what appears credible and what does not in narrative and cinematographic accounts of the concentration camps, Rancière seeks to address a seemingly simple question: are some things unrepresentable—particularly, in a visual sense?[47] In this short text, Rancière takes issue with, among other concepts, Jean-François Lyotard's notion of the sublime.[48] Rancière suggests that Lyotard's understanding of the sublime reintroduces the idea that certain forms of art, or certain modalities of vision, cannot achieve representation. Instead, these artistic/visual forms evoke its impossibility, and they gesture towards something incommensurable. Rancière initially appears to adopt this binary understanding of representation versus unrepresentation by indicating that "two regimes of art" are at play.[49] One, the representational mode, remains subject to the ideas of speech, language, signification, and narrative continuity: art or visual forms that represent succumb to the "adjustment of the visibility of speech," Rancière writes.[50] Put differently, speech is rendered visible and (ever) present by some forms of art/visual aesthetics. Meaning/signification as what humans—and humans only—do is boosted by this modality of artistic/visual representation. In this manner, to represent is to put human thought into language, and art/visual aesthetics remain wedded to this logocentric postulate.

But another regime of art/aesthetics—visual aesthetics, particularly—appears to be based upon the impossibility of logocentric affirmation or reassurance. In this way, the unrepresentable (perhaps what is "sublime" in art, according to Lyotard) is art or the visible freed from speech. As Rancière puts it, art/the visual is "no longer subject to the identification of the process of signification with the construction of a story."[51] The unrepresentable in art/vision thus severs the ties to language/narrativity. By no longer readily making sense or signifying, this form of art/vision appears to reverse the logical order since speech and language now become subject to the whims of the artistic or the visible. Horror, as I have theorized it above, seems to be akin to this modality of art/vision as unrepresentable, since, as both Cavarero and Asad have intimated, horror renders one speechless and shatters regimes of signification/meaning.

Rancière is somewhat sympathetic to this binary opposition between representation and unrepresentation, meaning and non-sense, and logocentrism and horror. And yet he is also not totally satisfied with it either. Turning to some of the introductory scenes of Claude Lanzmann's film *Shoah*, scenes of the holocaust that seem too shocking, too inhuman for some to believe or face, Rancière refutes the alleged unrepresentability of these images. Note that Rancière does not deny the horror these scenes reveal. Rather, Rancière argues that the "elimination of the Jews and the elimination of the traces of their elimination" are "perfectly representable."[52] But they are representable according to a non-linguistic, non-speech-dominated, non-narrative, and non-logocentric logic of exhibition or action. For Rancière, they are representable as what he calls "the form of a specific dramatic action."[53] This "specific dramatic action" is the form of representation—or, perhaps, of revelation, as I called it above—taken by that which is no longer contained in language or subjected to speech. It is not simply an excess or surplus of speech or language, however, but something else altogether. Although it is something other than language and meaning, it still can be represented, Rancière insists. In fact, such an "unrepresentable representation" (my term, not Rancière's) is approachable or seductive because of its alluring resemblance to narrative modalities of representation. Indeed, this form or art/vision is not altogether unfamiliar to the viewer, the witness, the spectator, or the one gazing in horror. The point of departure or anchor for this image or artistic experience can be a common sight or experience: a human form or expression, a familiar surrounding, a colorful scene, an enticing sound or voice, even a body that falls. Viewers may thus be initially tempted to draw connections and correspondences between, on the one hand, the "unrepresentable" artistic, aesthetic, or visual and, on the other, everyday life, common understandings, or even stories we tell or are told about our lives. Indeed, we appear to want to make sense of the "unrepresentable representation," as we do of what makes linguistic sense. This is what language/speech and the demands of representation have conditioned us to do and expect. But, as Rancière argues, any resemblance or correspondence with language/signification is faulty. Instead, this "other" representation "lays bare the radical dissemblance, the impossibility of adjusting today's tranquility to yesterday's."[54]

If we read the scene of horror—and the pulverization /dissemination/recompo-
sition of the body or matter that it exposes—through Rancière's false opposition
between the representable and the unrepresentable, it becomes possible to suggest
that horror is *not* visually unthinkable. Rather, the reconfigured more-than-human
body/form/substance that emerges through horror still represents. But it represents
through the specific dramatic action that is the horrific scene/image. There is no
language, no narrative, and no meaning for what it represents or, better yet, exhibits
(signification is disempowered to bridge the gap with the logic of action/exhibition).
And there is no longer any human subject or body at the heart of this display either.
If nothing else, if we insist on trying to put the scene of bodily horror into
language—which, to some extent, I am doing here, theoretically speaking—we are
left with the impression that the human, or what is left of it, is but "a miniscule
figure in the middle of the enormous clearing."[55] Although horror's exhibition of
post-anthropomorphic fusions is beyond language and speech, Rancière seems to
want to give it a name. He is tempted to call it a "logic of extermination."[56] Yet one
also senses that calling the "unrepresentable representation" that is the scene of horror
"extermination" is yet another of those faulty and fragile resemblances or correspondences, one that our desperately logocentric cravings for meaning and narrative coherence may force upon us, no matter how pointless such an exercise is in
the face of horror.

Following Rancière's intimations about the "unrepresentable," one might wonder if "our" ongoing fascination with horror—the horror of disseminated body
parts of terror/terrorism, in particular—is not a secret or disavowed craving for an
altogether different representation, a representation that "we" cannot make sense of
or that has no place in language. Perhaps what "we" are craving in the horror of
images of disseminated bodies, limbs, and their reconfiguration as something else, as
something no longer just human, is the possibility of abandoning "Fallen Man" as
the icon of terror and what it linguistically represents—that is to say, the desire to
make sense of and give meaning to all things according to "our" human substance/
presence, through "our" human bodies seen as one: integral, complete, or continuous. This "secret wish" of humanity to lose itself in the scene of horror recalls Jean
Baudrillard's reading of the 9/11 terror attacks.[57]

Perhaps, then, what is fascinating about this "other" representation that is horror
is the possibility to pluralize the ontology of the human through the idea/image of
the "body undone," and, in so doing, to free oneself from the metaphysics of substance, terror, security, and their politics of humanity and identity. Perhaps what
Rancière refers to as an "impossibility of adequate correspondence" between the
"place" of the body and the "speech" of and about the body is what "we" are perversely seeking in and through the image of terror,[58] an image that can reveal more
and more loose body parts and more and more recomposed bits of matter and
things. Perhaps "we" never really intend to abject the fragility or frailty of "our"
body parts even when, in the instance of terror, they no longer appear to fulfill their
essential function of propping up the entire body, of keeping it whole. Instead, perhaps, "we" want to embrace this total volatility of body parts since it manifests a

wish/dream to remain open to another representation—indeed, to horror itself. This possibility of leaving language/meaning behind, of burying "our" metaphysics of substance and of letting "ourselves" ("our" bodies, "our" body parts, "our" human—all too human—flesh) be exposed to horror as that which pulverizes but also radically liberates bodies and things from the weight of the one or the subject, from the priority given to what is represented as ontologically human, and from the powerful logic of terror and security, is something worth pondering (this is also reminiscent of what, towards the end of Chapter 2, with the help of Benjamin's thought on the messianic, I asked with regard to the possibility of reclaiming something about horror).

As we saw above, Rancière's reflections on the "unrepresentable" do not reject the possibility of representation in horror. Rather, they encourage us to reclaim representation from language, speech, and meaning, from logocentrism and the metaphysics of substance, from the weight of the human. A representation reattached to action and exhibition (even if, in doing so, this representation also detaches bits and parts from the unity of the human body) may bring back a certain immediacy of things, actions, or events, along with horrific traumas and incomprehensions for the human. In a way, Rancière offers us a choice about what to do with representation (Rancière wants to return representation to a matter of aesthetic choice[59]). Either one adopts the comfort or security seemingly offered by placing visual representation and art under the control of language and human speech, or one dispossesses oneself of language and signification and lets the exhibitory logic of action, the image, and horror do its work of demolition but also of liberation and reformation of matter (even if this matter is no longer just human). Although I am far from certain that what Rancière presents as a second option with regard to representation is indeed an option or a choice (in my view, like horror, this representation just happens or takes place; it is not about being chosen or decided), the second perspective according to Rancière is the only one from which any form of critique can be recovered. Rancière is eager to reassign a critical role to aesthetic/visual representation. Or, to put it slightly differently, the demolition or extermination revealed by the "unrepresentable representation" can be valuable because it also performs an important task of ontological *and* epistemological critique.

The critical potential that Rancière still insists on seeing in representation as action, exhibition, elimination, and, indeed, horror may offer additional clues regarding the seemingly unrelenting fascination with the sight of body parts of terror today. Simply, are "we" not fascinated by the body parts of terror and the horror they confront or indeed confound "us" with because of the critical potential they invoke? Indeed, whereas the iconography of terror always seeks to return "us" to the logic of the one, to the belief in a resilient and reunited humanity (which, as we saw above, also justifies the destruction of "other" bodies that, "we" like to affirm, caused "us" to fall in the first place), and to a principled submission to a generalized politics of security, images of horror destabilize without re-stabilizing, without bringing back any meaning or signification. Their refusal to make narrative sense invites the possibility of other representations and, in particular, of representations that have not already been filtered through systems of conceptual resemblance or correspondence supported by "our" politics of security and terror. In other words, the horror of the sight of disseminated body parts, somewhat reminiscent of what DeLillo's Falling Man tried to perform, may help "us" (if it still must be about "us") to problematize that which is never meant to be problematized in the imagery of terror: namely, the shady collaboration between the human body, the idea of a resilient humanity, the politics of security, and the act of terror/terrorism. I want to conclude this chapter by mobilizing another visual/artistic representation, a representation that some may well think of as "unrepresentable," that precisely seeks to place body parts at the center of reflections on human identity, power, and terror, and that appears to do so in order to allow the critical potential of the image to be closely linked to action, exhibition, and, perhaps, demolition.

Conclusion: *Valery's Ankle*

Canadian documentary filmmaker, author, and performance artist Brett Kashmere's film *Valery's Ankle* is not about horror, at least not evidently so.[60] *Valery's Ankle* is Kashmere's critique of the violence that lies at the heart of Canadian national identity as filtered/mediated through the sport of hockey, Canada's national pastime, or, indeed, secular religion. By placing center stage Canadian hockey hero Bobby Clarke's purposeful breaking of Russian opponent (and star) Valery Kharlamov's ankle during the 1972 Summit Series between Canada and the Soviet Union (a series of hockey matches between the two nations meant to initiate a slow return to normalized diplomatic relations after years of Cold War antagonism), Kashmere seeks to force a visual rupture in discourses and representations of "Canadian nationalism, identity, and masculinity."[61] *Valery's Ankle* pushes viewers to revisit the nexus identity–humanity–security–terror (then, during the Cold War, and now, some 40 years later) from the visual perspective of a "moment of violence,"[62] a moment or event that "explodes the spectacle of hockey violence" by putting the fractured body part of the Soviet player on display.[63] I should clarify, however, that Kharlamov's broken ankle is never shown. What is shown, or, better yet, what is dissected over and over again, through replays, close-ups, blurred shots, and discolored shots (accompanied by harsh/acute sounds and music), is the act/action—or exhibition, perhaps—of Clarke's stick brandished like an axe, smashed in a single blow onto Kharlamov's ankle and then splintering into pieces as a result of the sheer force of the blow (and then, of course, we see Kharlamov's falling body, contorted on the ice, incapable of standing up). The becoming-loose of Clarke's slashed hockey stick as a result of its crushing of Valery's ankle is vivid. Kashmere's blurred and discolored close-ups of it add to the surreality of the scene (and further slow down the moment and movement of the act of fracture to a crawl, thus allowing it to be fully and graphically showcased and inescapable). What Kashmere achieves in this shot and through its many replays is a total confusion for the viewer between the Russian's fractured body part and the loose shreds of the Canadian player's stick. Canadian hockey violence is thus revealed as gruesome, extended, and horrific—a violence that is aimed at body parts, cuts players/bodies loose but does not allow them to skate away, and leaves flying bits of stuff (a human ankle, a helmet, a broken stick, crushed ice, etc.) for all to see in the frozen exhibitory moment of the violent action.

While part of Kashmere's intention with *Valery's Ankle* is to "uncover the disturbing history of unforetold and abject Canadian behavior,"[64] both through Canada's national pastime and through its geopolitical aspirations (the linkages between "hockey diplomacy" and Cold War fears/terrors are made obvious in the film), I would suggest that one might also benefit from understanding *Valery's Ankle* as a vision of horror, as an "unrepresentable representation" in which disjointed and disseminated body parts cannot be ignored. In fact, it is possible to read *Valery's Ankle* not as an iconography of Cold War terror but rather as a visual statement about the horror that is always contained in Canadian national identity and security politics and that, inevitably, also befalls any sense of a united Canadian national body. As suggested above, *Valery's Ankle* exhibits the moment of horror that is Canada's "explosion of violence" but also the equally horrifying revelation of the confusion, unsettling, or disjoining that this abrupt pulverization of body parts causes for any sense of Canadian national security or comfort. While it is not the Canadian player's ankle that is targeted or "exploded," it is, perhaps, worse for Canada and its sense of national certainty that it is the Canadian human body that causes the horror and dismantles other bodies in plain sight. Thus, Kashmere's scene of hockey horror does not just disseminate body parts, hockey sticks, and meanings and certainties about the national Canadian body: it reconfigures or recomposes Canada's national identity and its sense of humanity (as well as the dignity/integrity of Canadian bodies) as something that is always suspect, always uncertain, always open to wielding violence and terror (onto others and itself), and, perhaps, always prone to elimination and extermination, too. As Kashmere notes, the horror of Valery's fracture "disrupts self-identification."[65] But *Valery's Ankle*, through the disjoining/recomposition achieved by way of the image of the loose parts, also denounces the complicity between "our" dignity, identity, and humanity (the "good" Canadians who learned to play hockey with their friends on a small-town ice-rink when they were kids) and the logic of war, violence, and terror. It refigures hockey's violence or terror (hockey's own Cold War) as a succession of moments, scenes, events, or actions in which a different horrific representation—one that does not explain much but exhibits a lot—sets in and exposes Canada's national body (and the bodies of its citizens) as inhuman, vengeful, and, perhaps, driven by a principle of "extermination" of bodies.

In light of Rancière's understanding of representation, I would suggest that Kashmere's film marks "the predicament of recording 'the trace of the unthinkable'."[66] It is an "unthinkable" whose visual horror must nonetheless be introduced, seen, and gazed at with intensity. Kashmere's replayed/revisited scene of Canadian horror shows falling bodies, and falling bodies (human, political) whose parts or components have been so damaged, so disseminated, rendered so unrecognizable, and so recomposed that they resist any belief that those (and perhaps other) bodies will soon be able to rise and stand tall again. Here, I argue, we have another counter-image, a perverse and deconstructive exhibition, perhaps, of the Boston Marathon bombing's "Fallen Man." The icon of terror has been turned into a figure of horror. And an aesthetic of pulverization and grotesque recombination of bodies, forms, and matter has taken the place of "our" human iconographies of suffering, terror, security, and human resilience/unity. Baudrillard had already indicated that we may be better off distrusting icons and iconographies.[67] We may want to distrust them, Baudrillard ventured, not because they were hiding another, more pressing, more genuine reality behind the image, but because all there ever was to iconographic representation was endless possible manipulation, or a manifold of the fake. The fake in the icon was a simulacrum, a way of presenting and imposing an image and making it stand for and appear as reality (when the so-called real object or subject of iconography was long gone). In this way, the icon could be about an indefinite number of things. It could encapsulate endless meanings and significations, each more fantastic and (in)credible than the next.

This "fakeness" of the icon of terror, of "our" sacrosanct image of "Fallen Man," is today confounded by a surplus of the visual and representation, a "repertory of horror" (as Cavarero puts it) that concentrates the gaze on the sight of disseminated body parts, sometimes recombined to form a new or different matter, one with only a few traces of the human left in it. "Our" security politics, in their representational but also ideological complicity with terror, are powerless in the face of this violence that targets but also liberates body parts. Worse yet, security's desperate insistence on presenting horror as a matter of terror—that is to say, as something security claims it can protect "us" from by enabling "our" fallen bodies to stand up again—renders horror more focused and determined and makes the incommensurability of the scattered human body even more fatal. Perhaps it is time to recognize that we can only deal with horror—and perhaps learn to live with it, even "here" in the West—if we finally give up on wanting to reaffirm and reimpose the kind of metaphysical beliefs about humanity and human substance that insist on telling "us," often in an all too familiar language, that security is the human body's only path to salvation. I pursue this line of investigation in Chapter 4, a chapter in which recent encounters with severed heads confront us yet again with the powers and radical possibilities of horror.

Notes

1 *Boston Globe*, "102 hours in pursuit of Marathon suspects," April 28, 2013, available at www.bostonglobe.com/metro/2013/04/28/bombreconstruct/VbSZhzHm35yR88EVm-VdbDM/story.html.

2 See, for example, *Telegraph*, "Boston Marathon bombings victim: It reminded me of 9/11," October 21, 2013, available at www.telegraph.co.uk/news/worldnews/northamerica/usa/10020061/Boston-Marathon-bombings-victim-it-reminded-me-of-911.html; and *CNN online*, "Boston Marathon terror attack," April 22, 2013, available at www.cnn.com/interactive/2013/04/us/boston-marathon-terror-attack/.

3 See, for example, Matilda Battersby, "Image of terror: 78-year-old runner knocked over by second Boston Marathon blast," *Independent*, April 16, 2013, available at

www.independent.co.uk/news/world/americas/image-of-terror-78yearold-runner-knocked-over-by-second-boston-marathon-blast-8574515.html; and Marc Tracy, "The Fallen Man: Marathons push ordinary people to be extraordinary. One photo from Monday's bombing made that clear," April 15, 2013, *New Republic*, available at www.newrepublic.com/article/112927/boston-marathon-bombing-fallen-man-photo.

4 Judith Butler, *Frames of War: When Is Life Grievable?* (London: Verso, 2009).

5 Jacques Rancière, *The Future of the Image* (London: Verso, 2007).

6 Julia Kristeva, *The Severed Head: Capital Visions* (New York: Columbia University Press, 2012), pp. 48–51.

7 Ibid., p. 51.

8 Ibid., p. 52.

9 Ibid., p. 55.

10 On interpellation, see Louis Althusser, "Ideology and Ideological State Apparatuses," in Louis Althusser, *Lenin and Philosophy, and Other Essays* (New York: Monthly Review Press, 1971), pp. 170–6.

11 George W. Bush, "Address to the Nation on the Terrorist Attacks," September 11, 2001, available at The American Presidency Project, www.presidency.ucsb.edu/ws/?pid=58057#axzz2iJMceZ4F.

12 See, for example, Scott Johnson, "Family, friends, dignitaries pay tribute to Ambassador Stevens," written for the *Oakland Tribune* and reported in the *San Jose Mercury News*, October 16, 2012, available at www.mercurynews.com/top-stories/ci_21786355/memorial-services-start-ambassador-christopher-stevens.

13 Adriana Cavarero, *Horrorism: Naming Contemporary Violence* (New York: Columbia University Press, 2009), pp. 4–5.

14 Ibid., p. 4.

15 See, for example, Achille Mbembe, "Necropolitics," *Public Culture*, Vol. 15, No. 1 (2003), pp. 11–40; Jenny Edkins, Veronique Pin-Fat, and Michael Shapiro (eds), *Sovereign Lives: Power in Global Politics* (London: Routledge, 2004); Elizabeth Dauphinee and Cristina Masters (eds), *The Logics of Biopower and the War on Terror: Living, Dying, Surviving* (London: Palgrave, 2006); Michael Dillon, "Governing Terror: The State of Emergency of Biopolitical Emergence," *International Political Sociology*, Vol. 1, No. 1 (2007), pp. 7–28; Butler, *Frames of War*; Julian Reid, *The Biopolitics of the War on Terror: Life Struggles, Liberal Modernity and the Defence of Logistical Societies* (Manchester: Manchester University Press, 2009); François Debrix and Mark Lacy (eds), *The Geopolitics of American Insecurity: Terror, Power and Foreign Policy* (London: Routledge, 2009); Luis Lobo-Guerrero, *Insuring Security: Biopolitics, Security and Risk* (London: Routledge, 2012); Brad Evans, *Liberal Terror* (Cambridge: Polity, 2013); and Michael Dillon, *Biopolitics of Security: A Political Analytic of Finitude* (London: Routledge, 2015).

16 François Debrix and Alexander Barder, *Beyond Biopolitics: Theory, Violence, and Horror in World Politics* (London: Routledge, 2012).

17 Elizabeth Povinelli, *Economies of Abandonment: Social Belonging and Endurance in Late Liberalism* (Durham: Duke University Press, 2011), pp. 106–7.

18 Ibid., p. 106.

19 I draw this distinction between *zoē* and *bios* from Agamben. Giorgio Agamben, *Homo Sacer: Sovereign Power and Bare Life* (Stanford: Stanford University Press, 1998).

20 Povinelli, *Economies of Abandonment*, p. 106.

21 Susan Sontag, *Regarding the Pain of Others* (New York: Farrar, Straus and Giroux, 2003), pp. 40–3. See also David Campbell, "The Iconography of Famine," in Geoffrey Batchen, Mick Gidley, Nancy Miller, and Jay Prosser (eds), *Picturing Atrocity: Photography in Crisis* (London: Reaktion Books, 2012), pp. 79–91.

22 Elaine Scarry, *The Body in Pain: The Making and Unmaking of the World* (Oxford: Oxford University Press, 1985), p. 216.

23 Julia Kristeva, *Powers of Horror: An Essay on Abjection* (New York: Columbia University Press, 1982), p. 140.

24 Don DeLillo, *Falling Man* (New York: Picador, 2007).
25 As Nancy may put it. For Nancy, the "inoperative community" is marked by the "wasting away of liberty, of speech, or of simple happiness." See Jean-Luc Nancy, *The Inoperative Community* (Minneapolis: University of Minnesota Press, 1991), p. 1. Might we read DeLillo's *Falling Man* as a Nancyan fable about the rendering impossible or unworkable of the late-modern community?
26 DeLillo, *Falling Man*, pp. 159–68.
27 *Washington Post*, "Battling back: Stories of the victims," Boston Marathon-bombings blog, available at www.washingtonpost.com/wp-srv/special/national/boston-marathon-bombing-victims/.
28 See, for example, *CBS Boston online*, "Doctors: Most victims of bombing have injuries to lower extremities," April 16, 2013, available at http://boston.cbslocal.com/2013/04/16/mgh-doctors-most-victims-of-bombing-have-injuries-to-lower-extremities/.
29 Talal Asad, *On Suicide Bombing* (New York: Columbia University Press, 2007), p. 68.
30 Stanley Cavell, *The Claim of Reason* (Oxford: Oxford University Press, 1999), p. 419.
31 Asad, *On Suicide Bombing*, p. 68.
32 Debrix and Barder, *Beyond Biopolitics*, pp. 22.
33 See Rey Chow, *The Age of the World Target: Self-Referentiality in War, Theory, and Comparative Work* (Durham: Duke University Press, 2006), p. 31.
34 Asad, *On Suicide Bombing*, pp. 68–69.
35 Ibid., p. 68.
36 Cavarero, *Horrorism*, p. 9.
37 Ibid., p. 9.
38 Asad, *On Suicide Bombing*, p. 69.
39 Cavarero, *Horrorism*, p. 9.
40 Asad, *On Suicide Bombing*, p. 70.
41 Cavarero, *Horrorism*, p. 54.
42 Asad, *On Suicide Bombing*, p. 70.
43 Rosi Braidotti, *The Posthuman* (Cambridge: Polity, 2013), p. 91.
44 Esposito had already anticipated this indistinguishable determination between life and death. Roberto Esposito, *Immunitas: The Protection and Negation of Life* (Cambridge: Polity, 2011).
45 On the vitality/vibrancy of things, see Jane Bennett, *Vibrant Matter: A Political Ecology of Things* (Durham: Duke University Press, 2010).
46 Asad, *On Suicide Bombing*, p. 76.
47 Rancière, *The Future of the Image*, pp. 123–30.
48 Jean-François Lyotard, *Lessons on the Analytic of the Sublime* (Stanford: Stanford University Press, 1994).
49 Rancière, *The Future of the Image*, p. 123.
50 Ibid., p. 123.
51 Ibid., p. 123.
52 Ibid., p. 127.
53 Ibid., p. 127.
54 Ibid., p. 128.
55 Ibid., p. 128.
56 Ibid., p. 128.
57 See, in particular, Jean Baudrillard, "The Violence of the Global," *CTheory.Net*, article a129, published May 20, 2003, available at www.ctheory.net/articles.aspx?id=385.
58 Rancière, *The Future of the Image*, p. 128.
59 Rancière, *The Future of the Image*, p. 129.
60 Brett Kashmere, *Valery's Ankle*, digital video, 2006, available at http://vimeo.com/63041317.
61 Brett Kashmere's own description of *Valery's Ankle* on his website: www.brettkashmere.com.

62 As critic Thomas Waugh puts it about Valery's Ankle. See www.brettkashmere.com.

63 Quote from Brett Kashmere, taken from www.brettkashmere.com.

64 Quote from Brett Kashmere, taken from www.brettkashmere.com.

65 Quote from Brett Kashmere, taken from www.brettkashmere.com.

66 As May Joseph puts it about Rancière's theory of the "unrepresentable." May Joseph, "Fascia and the Grimace of Catastrophe," in Patricia Ticineto Clough and Craig Willse (eds), *Beyond Biopolitics: Essays on the Governance of Life and Death* (Durham: Duke University Press, 2011), p. 333.

67 Jean Baudrillard, *Simulations* (New York: Semiotext(e), 1983), pp. 9–10.

4

SEVERING HEADS

Deconstruction *hors texte,* or what remains of the human

We are as attached to our heads as if our lives depended on it.[1]

Gentlemen, with my machine, I can make your head roll in the wink of an eye . . . The mechanism drops like lightning, the head flies, the blood spurts, the man is no more.[2]

This image, perhaps even an iconic photograph . . . [is] really one of the most disturbing, stomach-turning, grotesque photographs ever displayed. [It is the image] of a 7 year-old child holding a severed head up with pride and with the support and encouragement of a parent, with brothers there . . . That child should be in school, that child should be out learning about a future, that child should be playing with other kids, not holding a severed head . . .[3]

People take human heads; people donate their own heads; people display heads and come to see them: when you start to look, severed heads are everywhere, here and now.[4]

The return of beheadings

The recent rise of the Islamic State (IS, also known as ISIS or ISIL) in Syria and Iraq has placed severed heads at the center of contemporary international relations, foreign policy, and security discourses about the ever present danger of "radical Islam" or "jihadism" in the long post-9/11 era. One of the telltale signs of IS, if we are to believe Western politicians, pundits, and security experts, is the "horror" of beheadings.[5] In its ever expanding campaign of terror, IS and its sympathizers capture many of their enemies (Westerners, Middle Easterners from nations allied with the United States, Israel, or Europe, other Muslims, etc.) for ransom or to terrorize them. IS also takes over lands and cities in Syria and Iraq (primarily) and, in its path of conquest, exterminates many who stand in its way or whose deaths are believed to send a political message of fear and submission to the populations of the region and, by extension, to the Western world.[6] Whether its actions are geared towards the West or they are aimed at imposing terror on local populations, the outcome is often seen to be the same: more and more bodies decapitated in front of cameras; more and more severed heads displayed throughout territories conquered by IS.

This association of IS's rule of terror with severed heads is not inaccurate. IS's sustained campaigns of gruesome killing and dismantling of what it perceives as enemy, profane, or unworthy bodies in the course of establishing what it believes to be the rule of the Caliphate in the Middle East are undeniable and, often, horrifying. While images or videos of IS's public decapitations and dismemberments are commonplace and seem to define for the West what IS is and does, what is equally dominant among Western publics today—and often takes over discussions in foreign-policy circles—is a fascination with the beheadings on the part of counter-terrorism, security, and anti-fundamentalism scholars. Undoubtedly, photos and videos of beheadings evoke disgust and what many simply call horror. They are meant to shock and, judging by reactions from Western audiences, they often succeed. But while it may be claimed that beheadings are far more common today since IS has launched its reign of terror, beheadings are not a novel phenomenon in the war on terror. A decade or so ago, lynchings, decapitations, and dismemberments of Western journalists and private contractors in Iraq, in the months that followed the US invasion, were not unusual occurrences.[7] At the time, it was not uncommon for Western media to depict these seemingly inhuman acts as evidence that terrorism and Islamic fundamentalism were daunting threats to Western values, thus justifying sustained US military actions in Iraq.

Since 2003–4, and until today with IS, it has been fairly typical for Western experts, observers, and politicians to see the beheadings as the mark of "radical" or "jihadist" Islam, or perhaps of "Islamic extremism."[8] While "radicalized Islamists" are those who bring terror to and commit terrorist acts in the West (the attacks against the satirical newspaper *Charlie Hebdo* and a kosher grocery store in Paris in January 2015 are some of the latest illustrations of this phenomenon, we are told[9]), when these terrorists and extremists operate in the Middle East—Syria and Iraq, above all—they reveal themselves to be not just terrorists, but also agents of "horror."[10] Thus, in many contemporary Western discourses on the threat of "radical Islam," beheadings are not just the mark of jihadi or Islamic terrorists' proven mastery of horror. They further demarcate the West (or Western civilization) from the non-West, which, in this case, is represented by "radical Islamists" attempting to establish a foothold of terror/horror in the Middle East. Images and videos of beheadings, in other words, help Western publics to understand that the version of Islam that has embraced terror and horror has no respect for the value or dignity of the individual or human person, or for humanity in general. What "we" are meant to see, then, is that IS and other "Islamic fundamentalist" groups are fighting a war not just against the West but against humanity as a whole.[11] And what better way to show this than with images and stories of brutal dismemberments of human bodies, or of severed body parts—often heads—through the streets of the villages and cities IS fighters have taken over. By contrast, typically shown as the victims of these gruesome acts, Westerners (even though many more non-Westerners have been decapitated by IS) and the West in general are left to stand as the last defenders of humanity, as the champions of the respect, dignity, and integrity of the individual and human person and of the human body. Beheadings, then, are depicted as an attack on the human, an attack that can only emanate from those who, mastering terror and horror, presumably can never be reconciled with the West and its ideals or values.

In this general discourse about the West re-securing its identity or image as the last bastion of humanity's protection,[12] as the ultimate champion of humankind, as a result of its victimization at the hands of IS and other "jihadists" and of its geo-political stand-off against the horror of decapitations, Western pundits, scholars, and politicians show obvious signs of historical amnesia. After all, there is a long, and, at times, revered tradition of beheadings and decapitations in the West.[13] This tradition is rarely recalled in the West today. Still, what may be taken to be Western civilization has had a long-standing affection for and fascination with severed heads, particularly when Westerners were the head-cutters or the head-hunters. Haphazard, accidental, customary, symbolic, ritualized, fictionalized, institutionalized, or, indeed, legalized decapitations have often been central to Western pre-modern, modern, and even late-modern social, political, and cultural practices. Institutions in Western societies such as the military, the state, and the law have at times relied on recognized and respected modalities and techniques of beheading.[14] Decapitations, historically, have been used by Western populations to achieve different social, political, economic, and cultural outcomes, too. At key junctures in the West's history, beheadings have been crucial to the development or refinement of democratic, liberal, and allegedly pluralistic political institutions.

However, it is not my purpose in this chapter to trace a history of the West's long-standing attachment to beheadings and severed heads. I am not trying to argue that practices and techniques of decapitation emerged out of so-called Western civilization, even if there are good reasons to suggest that Western societies, at key moments in their histories, played a determinant part in structuring, instituting, and imposing cultural as well as political meanings to some forms of decapitation. Rather, my point here—one of several arguments in this chapter—is to point out an obvious irony in contemporary Western discourses, particularly in narratives by so-called security or anti-terrorism specialists, who insist on linking the value of defending humanity to the West and the West's contemporary challenge to "radical Islam" and to this Islam's recent instances of beheading of Westerners. Part of the fascination of Western scholars, pundits, and politicians with IS's and other groups' apparent insistence on cutting heads off and on making them available for public display may be explained not just by an interest in a certain version of Islam's inhumanity or monstrosity but also by Western culture's long history of attraction to severing and severed heads and, in some cases, by an obsession with deciding which heads may be cut and, by contrast, which heads need to remain attached to human bodies. While contemporary Western foreign-policy makers like US Secretary of State John Kerry may try to tell us that images of beheadings are "the most disturbing, stomach-turning, grotesque photos ever displayed,"[15] the fascination of Western social, cultural, and political elites with decapitations is nothing new.

Victor Hugo once described the spectacle of the guillotine as possessing "something about it which produces hallucination . . . [It is] a vision . . ."[16]

This chapter seeks to provide a beginning to understanding contemporary "hallucinated" narratives among Western foreign-policy, security, and anti-terrorism elites, experts, and intellectuals about beheadings and about the role these narratives play in today's geopolitical context, particularly with regard to Western concerns with security and terror. The chapter does not wish, exactly, to investigate why so much emphasis is being placed on the sight of beheadings and severed heads (there are likely to be many possible answers, none of them definitive): it is driven by a slightly different concern. If, as I argued in the previous chapter, the fallen body or victim of terrorism—"Fallen man"—has become "our" (Western) icon of terror, has the head detached from bodies captured by "Islamic radical" groups in the Middle East not become "our" (again, Western) icon of horror? This question calls for a supplementary one: if the severed head has become "our" icon of horror, why is it important for Western discourses of terror and security to evoke horror in this manner? Might this insistence on the severed head be about making horror—what some may think of as the "unrepresentable" (as discussed in Chapter 3)—into something that can or should be represented, at least at times, depending on who is doing the cutting or on what the cutting of heads may enable or justify? Could beheadings and severed heads, despite the claim among Western elites and experts that these acts and their representations are "grotesque" or "stomach-turning," function productively as a system of signification or meaning-making? Are "we," Western subjects and bodies, not also seeking to reconstruct or solidify "our" version of humanity, "our" vision of the human person, individual, and body, away from the disseminated bits and pieces of fallen and, in some cases, pulverized bodies and body parts, starting with the severed head? Are "we" not perversely interested in collecting images and stories of cut-off heads (if not the heads themselves) in order to tell "ourselves" and others (non-Westerners, often) that "our" stories and visions about the human and humanity still have value, still matter, and can still define human life the world over in the twenty-first century?

I suggest in this chapter that there may be a way to think about the West's recent (re)turn to an interest in beheadings (the act of cutting heads off) and in severed heads (the outcome, after the heads have been forcefully removed from the rest of the body) as an act of discursive and representational reconstruction, as an attempt to fend off and rebuild the seemingly fateful horror of the sight of the dismantled and disseminated human body that, as I argued in previous chapters, takes hold as a result of terrorist attacks (in the West, in particular) or of suicide bombings (often, outside the West), among other horrifying scenes. In a certain fashion, a discursive and representational insistence on the horror of the severed head and of severing heads is about admitting, as I have suggested in previous chapters, that terror is never really antithetical to contemporary Western security policies and politics. For discourses and representations of security, the primary target, the main objective, but also the most insurmountable opponent, is horror. I have argued that security policies and politics and their discourses can accommodate terror. Terror, in the end, can and does justify or boost security politics. But what security politics cannot deal with, because it is already beyond the threshold of human substance, of representation, and of politics, is horror. As I intimate in this chapter, however, if there were to be a way to tame or capture horror, if the horror of the dismantling of the human could ever be made representable, visible, and intelligible, there could possibly be some rekindled hope for the fate of the human, for humanity, for human survivability or over-living (*survivance*).[17] There possibly could be some new hope for the durability of the West's values, ideals, and overall metaphysical project, perhaps beyond the West, too (including in those territories where Westerners are beheaded). Perhaps just as importantly, there could still be some political as well as ideological purpose for security politics and policies and for the maintenance of the political and ideological linkage between security (securing humanity/the West, above all) and terror/terrorism.

As this chapter also details, there may be some ways of reading contemporary displays of horror, such as the showcasing of severed heads in some parts of the Middle East, to suggest that the apparent attempt to undo the human by removing the head from the rest of the body may not need to be seen as a total, absolute, or uncompromising challenge against the idea of humanity. In this manner, unlike instances of suicide bombing, for example, severing heads and severed heads may never completely amount to a rejection, deconstruction, or even destruction of the metaphysics of substance,[18] to a wholesale negation of the Western metaphysical assumption and belief that there must always be a human body in order for social life and political being to make sense, to exist. Severing and severed heads may be a version of horror that, in a perverse way, "we" Westerners may be able to accept, perhaps because, as indicated above, "we" have a long tradition of cutting heads off. With this mode of horror, with severed heads and severing heads, "we" Westerners may still find, or hope to find, some vitality, some over-living, or, perhaps, some signs of vibrancy in the remains of the human/humanity.

And yet, while there may be some strange accommodation of beheadings in the West that may help "us, Westerners," to think that "we" can recuperate this modality of terror and horror, this chapter also maintains that there are risks involved in wanting to see some beheadings and some severed heads as ultimately compatible with remnants of humanity, including remnants of humanity and humanism that can be found in certain modern and late-modern traditions of Western thought and critique.[19] One of the risks is to not take horror for itself but to want to colonize it as yet another part of the Western humanistic tradition about man or the subject. The risk would be to assume that the horror of beheadings always signifies something from the perspective of "our" Western humanity. But what if horror signifies for itself, or for nothing, irrespective of whether there are human bodies to be seen or saved? What if the severed head is no longer reattachable to the metaphysics of human substance and can no longer produce meaning in the context of an ontological primacy allegedly to be given to the human/humanity? The next section of this chapter starts to examine these questions by exposing some of the connections between cut-off heads and the idea of humanity.

Fascinating severed heads

In a recent overview of IS, its ideology, and its operations, US foreign-policy experts Jessica Stern and J. M. Berger write in details about beheadings. Here is an excerpt from their text:

> The scene cut to an image of James Foley, an American reporter who had been kidnapped in Syria in 2012 ... Foley was kneeling in the desert sun, arms bound behind him, dressed in an orange jumpsuit meant to invoke the garb worn by jihadist prisoners of the United States in Guantanamo Bay and in Iraq during the American occupation ... A small, black microphone, of the sort used in Western news broadcasts, was clipped to the collar of his shirt ... Foley painfully reproached his family, including his brother, a member of the US military, referencing US strikes against ISIS ... Foley said he wished he had more time ... The ISIS fighter then took over. He spoke in a British accent, accusing the United States of aggression against ISIS ... The fighter bent to Foley and put a knife to his throat and began to saw. The video cut away before blood began to flow. When the picture resumed, the camera panned over Foley's dead body, his head severed and placed on the small of his back. In the final scene, the fighter reappeared, gripping another hostage, an American journalist named Steven Sotloff, by the collar of his orange jumpsuit. "The life of this American citizen, Obama, depends on your next decision," the fighter said as the video concluded, an excruciating cliffhanger that promised more agony to come ... In the weeks that followed, the short script would repeat itself over and over again, one hostage after another executed as the world watched in horror ... By October, ISIS had beheaded three more Westerners, each installment concluding with a new hostage whose life was placed on the line ... If these victims shared any common quality other than the English language and their white faces, it was their uncommon goodness. Each victim had been carrying out work that ultimately helped Syrians suffering in the civil war ... The American journalists ... were among the few who braved the terrible risks of reporting on the ground during the conflict. David Haines and Alan Henning were [British] aid workers selflessly helping Syrians in dire need ... It seems no one was safe against the knives of ISIS, no matter how kind or how much they had done for Muslims ...[20]

Beheadings, or better yet, the elaborate video recordings of beheadings, are made by Stern and Berger into the defining characteristic of IS. Beheadings are both the technique by which IS, or "Islamic radicals," or "jihadists" (terms used interchangeably in many of these narratives), antagonize the West ("English-speaking white faces," as Stern and Berger put it) and the phenomenon/event that, in its very graphic and non-human nature, opposes what the West is supposed to stand for. These beheadings define IS as much as they define the West/Westerners. Stern and Berger open their study with the following statement:

> In the Western world, in the twenty-first century, the idea of a beheading was something unreal, archaic, a vaguely understood and little contemplated relic of a distant past . . . We [Westerners] have grown used to a less barbaric world so that when the media bring pictures of terrorists' deliberate savagery to our attention, we recoil.[21]

If beheadings of Western citizens define IS "jihadists" as barbaric, archaic, savage, or, indeed, primitive ("medieval-minded killers" is another term used by Stern and Berger to describe IS fighters[22]), those same gruesome acts inscribe the West/Westerners as modern, developed, enlightened, and morally advanced. Orientalist themes are in abundance throughout this and other Western narratives about IS and its reign of terror/horror in Syria and Iraq. Orientalist descriptions and assumptions, as Edward Said famously detailed, are laden with ideological depictions about the way a Western identity/imagery wants or needs to represent and position so-called backward, barbarian, or savage non-Western oriental cultures, habits, and practices.[23] The West orients and establishes itself geopolitically, culturally, and morally by deploying imaginative geographies about what the orient and oriental people allegedly are and do.[24] Narratives about IS beheadings are a contemporary reprise of this old but persistent ideological scheme. Not only are these narratives meant to remind us of the violently primitive "nature" and moral depravity of the oriental, but they also reaffirm the geopolitical superiority of the West at a time when Western publics are faced with gruesome images of "white-faced" and "English-speaking" individuals with their heads cut off.

Another well worn orientalist theme is the attachment of humanity, or the idea of the human, to Western values and traditions and the parallel inability of non-Western cultures to be able to accept or adapt to Western ideas and ideals about humanity and humanism.[25] As Stern and Berger reveal, Western humanity is what is at stake in IS's beheadings. Humanity and humanism are callings that compel "uncommonly good" Westerners—journalists, aid workers—to go to Syria and help their fellow beings in need of assistance. Summary decapitations of Western journalists and aid workers are thus not just a message sent to the United States about its politics and presence in the Middle East. They are not just about making geopolitical statements. They are also, and, perhaps, primarily, immoral and inhumane messages about the wholesale rejection of Western values and ideals, starting with the value/ideal of the respect for and recognition of the integrity and unity of the human person/individual/body. Thus, implicitly, metaphysical statements about humanity (and about the West as humanity's champion) are conveyed each time IS cuts off a Westerner's head.

This orientalist theme about the West's attachment to humanity/humanism versus the non-West/Middle East's detachment (quite literally) from what Western narratives perceive to be universal values by way of beheadings is much more interesting than the insistence in contemporary Western (orientalist) foreign policy/security experts' texts on depicting "jihadist" or "Muslim radical" head-cutters as savage, archaic, barbarian, or uncivilized (since, unfortunately, that form of orientalist discourse is not new). After all, the backwardness or "medievalism" of IS fighters is never guaranteed, not even by Western pundits, since, in those same expert narratives about IS beheadings, the executioners are also depicted as media-savvy, having access to and knowledge of all sorts of social media for propaganda purposes, and well versed in public-perception strategies in order to ensure the greatest possible impact of their cleverly choreographed actions.[26] How can those savages from a "distant past," according to Western anti-terrorism specialists, also be astute "marketers," "manipulators," and "recruiters" of a politics of terror and horror?[27] How can IS head-hunters be at once uncivilized non-Westerners and skillful in their deployment of allegedly Western technologies against the West itself? Orientalist assumptions and beliefs about the backwardness and unenlightened nature of the oriental—here, the oriental terrorist—fall by the wayside in the face of beheadings staged/made possible through the machinery of Western-made or Western-initiated media technology. Thus, orientalist beliefs about IS are quickly revealed to be nothing more than invectives and insults (I'll leave it to the reader to decide if they are justified or not), proffered by Western experts in anti-terrorism or foreign policy who are fascinated by but cannot quite make sense of those beheadings and what they may be about. Or, to put it differently, what the orientalist insistence on savagery and backwardness betrays is an unwillingness to confront a double fact: first, that beheadings, by "Islamic radicals," but possibly by others, too, are always intended to be an attack on humanity, human integrity, and, indeed, human bodily integrality (an idea that, once again, is at the heart of Western metaphysical as well as ideological projects); and, second, in what it means and does to the human, beheadings are not just about non-Western others, or even about the West's very distant past, but rather are very much part of "our" contemporary imaginative geographies about the West and non-West that "we, Westerners" ceaselessly seek to produce.

In a recent historical study of the fascination (mostly in the West) with severed heads and their collection, anthropologist Frances Larson offers two important observations. First, she writes that "severed heads have long had a value, or place, in our society; even if that value is contested or troubling."[28] Second, she asserts that "severed heads demand our attention" because they "remind us of our own fragility [as] . . . they draw us in to peer inside ourselves and invite us to survey the limits of our humanity."[29] Similar to Berger and Stern on IS, the "our" or "us" mobilized by Larson here is decidedly Western and late-modern. The society in question is "ours" today, and the "humanity" supposedly interrogated by the presence of the severed head is no doubt taken to be a highly prized Western value. Part of the reason why the head is seen as so crucial to our humanity, to our society and culture, and more so than any other body part, it seems, is that, as Larson suggests, ancestral cultural beliefs have been keen to associate the head with the center of human life, the core of the person or individual.[30] Not only is the head the "command center" of the human body and, indeed, of the thinking self (the ego as *cogito*, as in Descartes' famous formula[31]), but it is also taken to be the vital center, the place in the human body from which an individual life force emanates. As Larson puts it, "a person's life force seems to reside in their head more than in other parts of their body."[32] Moreover, it is thanks to the head that this vital life force of and about the human has any meaning. The head makes the vital life force meaningful and purposeful and the body whole (and meaningful only as whole, as human integrality). From past rituals of feasting on the brains of the dead or defeated enemies among some tribes of Papua New Guinea, for example,[33] to the distinction in modern medicine and, often, in modern law too between "brain" or "cerebral" death (the brain has shut down and the voluntary as well as involuntary functions needed to "sustain life" are no longer available) and what is sometimes referred as "circulatory" or "respiratory" death (the heart can no longer pump blood to the rest of the body's organs),[34] an anthropologically humanist view of life insists on seeing human existence as residing primarily in the head, or in what the head enables or cradles. Thus, when the head is no more, neither is human life/being, even if the rest of the organs can still be sound and in good health (and, in some cases, can be harvested for future uses in other humans—for other human lives, for example).

Larson further sentimentalizes this story about the assumed anthropological primacy of the human head by bringing up another key feature of the head: its face. The face, a crucial attribute of the head, is also what makes a body human. The face betrays the humanity of the head and of humans in general. Put differently, the face is what all humans share (sometimes, some animals do too, as some human beings want to believe when they choose to anthropomorphize animals, pets above all). Larson writes: "we cannot confront another person's head without sharing an understanding: face to face, we are peering into ourselves."[35] The face/head allows us to see ourselves in other human faces and heads and vice versa. The commonality, the common bond that is our shared humanity, is apparently realized because of the face.[36] Face, brain, *cogito* are all about the head, humanistically inspired anthropologists wish to tell us. Becoming headless implies becoming faceless, brainless, and without a rational capacity to think. But becoming headless also implies an incapacity to be human and, moreover, to share one's humanity with others, to recognize oneself in others and others in oneself, and to empathize with other human bodies, all qualities that, thanks to the head, are taken to be "naturally" human.

To sever another human body's head, then, is to deprive that body of its humanity. It is a matter of interrupting that body's life, but, more crucially, it is seen by humans (who recognize and empathize with each other's faces, we are told) as depriving it of a vital life force that is uniquely human, that makes it human. To lose one's head—literally, as in the case of decapitations, or figuratively, as in the metaphor commonly used to describe someone who has gone insane or become irrational— is often represented as a loss of one's humanity (or, in some cases—for example, with some criminals or madmen—as evidence that the person was never fully human to start with). A body without a head, as we saw above, is no longer human or, at least, it has lost its humanity. Its vital life force has been taken away. It is no longer an individual human body since, as Laure Murat reminds us, "an individual, literally, is one who cannot be divided."[37] A head without a body is no longer human and no longer amounts to a person or an individual since, more than likely, the brain has ceased to function (or, at least, its function has been dissociated from the rest of the body), the skull might have been bashed in, or the face may have been disfigured. Yet, more than the body left without its head, the head left without a body seems to retain human features that, in some situations, can continue to fascinate living or surviving human bodies/individuals.

Larson offers an interesting explanation for why a human head detached from a body can still be compelling to human beings—to a sense of humanity, even— and why, in fact, many living human beings insist on retrieving, collecting, holding, or, indeed, staring at a dead head or human skull. She intimates that a severed human head, by depriving the rest of the human body of its life force, makes the body, body parts, and organs into things.[38] For Larson, anthropocentrically speaking, a human's "lost body" (her term) no longer remains a person. It also no longer remains one single, unique, integral, individual, recognizable, identifiable body. Quickly after the head has been removed, it becomes a thing. And things, for Larson, as for many Western anthropologists, biologists, and philosophers, cannot have or be human bodies. Of course, the severed head, left by itself, detached from an integral human body, can become a thing as well. And yet Larson believes that the severed head's status as a thing or collection of things is far more ambiguous and, in her view, far more disturbing than the leftover or "lost" human body. As she puts it, the head or skull, by itself, "is simultaneously a person and a thing. It is always both and neither."[39] Herein lies a possible source of disturbance supposedly caused by the detached (and possibly gathered, collected, and displayed) head. What troubles and, possibly, horrifies living human beings about the severed head is that, beyond any sign of extant life force/vitality, it retains fundamentally visible human traits (the face, the cavity where a human brain used to be, the recollection that this once was where the *cogito* resided, etc.), remnants or traces of a human individuality perhaps. Simultaneously, the detached head or skull negates the presence or maintenance of the human person/humanity. It is a thing too; it can become an object. You can turn a skull into a drinking cup (there is a long historical tradition of drinking out of the skull of one's former enemies). You can use a severed head or skull as an educational tool, an instrument of learning, or a toy. Of course, you can turn a cut-off head into a trophy, a totem, or a mascot (the practice among American GIs during World War II to collect and showcase the severed heads or skulls of killed Japanese soldiers as mementos has been well documented[40]). You can give the detached head different shapes and forms (you can shrink it, for example). You can even use the decapitated head as a soccer ball (as apparently was done on a few occasions by some drug cartels' members in Mexico[41]). As Larson indicates, "the severed head is compelling—and horrific—because it denies one of the most basic dichotomies we use to understand our world: that people and objects are defined in opposition to each other."[42]

The analysis offered by Larson has historical precedents. For example, the disturbing part about the vision/presence of a severed head and its transformation into something else—no longer quite human yet not completely foreign to humanity, either—after it has been separated from the rest of the body, gave rise to a series of debates during and after the French Revolution, at a time when public executions by way of the guillotine (starting with the execution of the King, the head of the state) became commonplace. Literary theorist and French historian Murat recounts that a pressing argument among politicians, doctors, philosophers, and even members of the public at the time had to do with the status of the severed head right after it had been detached from a condemned individual's body.[43] Both executioners and onlookers told tales of how they clearly saw continued movements in the face of the executed person or changes in the complexion of the severed head (a blushing of the cheeks, for example, was famously reported in the case of Charlotte Corday's execution[44]). Could it be that the severed head retained some sort of life force, some sort of liminal humanity, after the death of the condemned body by way of the guillotine? Could it be that, to use Larson's dichotomy between the head as person and the head as thing, the severed head was neither? Defenders of the guillotine tried to fend off the debate and the troubling questions it raised by providing an analogy with animal bodies. Yet this analogy further blurred the question regarding the status of the humanity of the (formerly alive) person. To explain that the human life force of the condemned body was indeed no more, even if movements of the head or face could still be perceived at times, supporters of the guillotine argued that the recently cut-off head was more like the chopped head of an animal. In a way, it was "animal-like" (if not exactly "thing-like," as Larson might suggest). It was stated that, like chickens that sometimes go on running after their necks have been chopped, guillotined heads could contain an animal-like vitality located in "muscles and nerves."[45] This animal vitality of the severed head, however, was not to be confused with the human vitality or life force present in an integral, individual living person. But this explanation did not manage to close fully the debate about the status of the severed head. In fact, the introduction of another vitality (animal-like, this time) was an additional source of confusion, concern, and possibly horror.[46] How long did the vitality of muscles, nerves, and tissues remain? Was it not part of the human life force of a full human body? Could it be the key to human life in general? Is there an animality about life, including human life, that can persist beyond the fact of death, and, in particular, beyond the separation of the head from the rest of the body? And who might possess this other vitality? Severed heads, like decapitated animals, seem to have it. Could things and objects have it too? If so, might it not reveal a "consciousness that [could] outlive the flesh,"[47] or the *cogito*, or even humanity? These kinds of question, initiated in France during and after the Revolutionary era, have continued until today and are at the heart of debates regarding human torture or the death penalty, for example.[48]

If we follow Larson's analysis and recall debates such as those surrounding the status of the guillotined head, the reason why our humanity may be at stake or threatened with every visible instance of beheading and, further, with the displayed detached head is that instances of severing of heads and images of severed heads appear to introduce doubts about the anthropologically and metaphysically affirmed primacy of the head and, by extension, about the ontological priority of the human body as an integral, unitary, and individual body capable of sharing a humanity in common with other like bodies with heads, brains, and faces. "Our" so-called humanity is challenged by the act of beheading. What was meant to be the mark of "our" humanity, of life as human life (integral, unique, yet commonly shared), is now, potentially, given another "life" or another meaning, one that may no longer be attached to the fact of being human once the head, cut off from the rest of the body, is turned into something else: a thing, an object, an animal-like movement/reflex, or, perhaps, mere organic matter whose extant condition may no longer have anything special or, at least, uniquely human about it. Thus, what I think Larson is suggesting when she posits the dichotomy between the head as person (while the human body is alive *and* integral) and the head as thing (once it has been severed and is available for display by itself and, perhaps, for itself) is that we are in the presence of something horrifying—of horror itself, perhaps. We are faced with horror in the presence of the severed head and the act/image of beheading not simply because the sight or story displays the termination of a life force or the forceful removal of a human face from a commonly shared humanity. Rather, the matter of horror in this performance or display is that our humanity—the humanity attached to the image and idea of the integral/complete human body with a head/face/brain/*cogito* on top and in charge—has now become useful, interesting, meaningful as something else, as something that is as much if not more about the world of things and objects (or about the world of animals and beasts, with a vitality found in muscles, nerves, and tendons, but not in the head) as it is about the anthropocentric realm of persons, beings, and individuals—about humanity. Going back to a theme encountered with suicide bombings in the previous chapter, the horror of severing heads and of severed heads is not just about introducing a blatant visual negation of the idea of humanity, of the belief in the primacy and superiority of the human (and his/her head). It is also, and, perhaps, more crucially, about the revelation that the human, no longer as a unitary whole but now as a series of parts and bits that are at once things and traces of former human persons/lives, can produce meaning and give rise to affects, even though or, better yet, because it has lost or been deprived of its center, of its vital force, of its head. Severed heads and skulls may no longer be human; they may have become things or thing-like (or, perhaps, animal-like). But they are still vibrant, energetic, and potentially active.[49] Thus, if we push Larson's and others' anthropologically centered analyses a bit further (as I have sought to do here), we may understand that beheadings can horrify "us," humans, because they can give us a glimpse into other kinds of force that may not need to be about the human person, about human life, in order to make things happen or, for better or worse, in order to have an impact in the world, even if they make use of "our" heads to do so.

Signifying horror

It is tempting to conclude from the above analysis that severed heads/beheadings signify horror: the horror of the dismantling of the human, the horror of the loss of the primacy of the head, and, perhaps, the horror of the confusion between heads as persons and heads as things. There is a theoretical tradition that supports this line of thinking. Of late, it has been advanced by authors like Julia Kristeva, Giorgio Agamben, and Adriana Cavarero (more on them later). But a possibly lesser-known thinker, literary theorist Regina Janes, deserves as much credit for trying to make sense of decapitation as a matter of signification or as a sign system.

In a compelling study on the role/place of beheadings in Western culture and literature, Janes adopts a semiotic approach to the topic of cutting and cut-off human heads. Janes states that "[b]eheading always signifies," and she adds that "the head is a sign."[50] Her work dissects several cultural instances of signification achieved by way of severed heads, actual or fictional. While Janes is intent on showing that there is a wide range of cultural significations that may be realized by cutting heads off or by narrating the presence/irruption of severed heads (she writes that beheading "always signifies differently within specific codes supplied by culture"[51]), thus suggesting that the meaning of beheadings is always subject to an understanding of cultural context and to dominant social and discursive codes, she nonetheless leaves us with one key argument. Beheadings and severed heads are signs that, when mobilized, "abuse" a dominant "order of meaning."[52] Moreover, the horror of beheadings is precisely to be found in this abuse of meaning. Thus, there is never really such a thing as a "natural social horror" about the severed head. Rather, what is horrifying about beheadings is the result of a cultural, literary, linguistic, and representational intervention at the level of signification.

Janes' argument is not incompatible with Larson's conclusions about the horror of beheadings. Ultimately, what horrifies is the absolute confusion, disturbance, or dismantling of allegedly metaphysically secured categories of meaning and being. But Janes, unlike Larson, does not need to have recourse to an anthropologically naturalized belief in a so-called ontological priority of the integral human body, or of humanity in general, in order to make her point about the horror of beheadings. For Janes, horror is in the modality of signification (the sign itself), not in the referent (the natural human body, a humanity capped by a head/face/*cogito*) that is supposedly on display in the act of beheading or in the sight of or narrative about the detached head. One might ask in passing if, in their terribly skillful staging of Westerners' beheadings, IS fighters have not managed to capture, and thus have understood, too (perhaps better than some Western analysts and experts), the principle according to which the power of horror present in beheadings resides in its sign-function rather than in its supposedly anthropological nature.

Beheading, or the severed head, for Janes, is a semiotic figure. Still, it is a semiotic figure that involves processes of signification at two complementary levels: at the level of the body and at the level of the visual. Put differently, beheading is signification by and for human bodies. But for this signification to be captured, it must be visually perceived, too (although linguistic and narrative forms of beheading—written or spoken accounts of and about severed heads—can have a similar semiotic function, often because the language of beheadings evokes visual "hallucinations" or "visions," as Hugo once again thought). The name Janes gives to beheading as a semiotic figure is "catachresis." Catachresis, as a grammatical intervention and literary operation, Janes explains, is what goes "against common use" or normal "grammar," and thus what destabilizes or "shocks."[53] Catachresis is a modality of signification and representation that "wrenches words from their proper contexts and puts them where they do not belong."[54] At the level of the body, the severed head is a catachresis because it "violates the rules of the body's grammar."[55] It takes the head as that body part that unites and identifies a human body, that gives us an individual or a person, or that guarantees the presence of a human life force, and places it somewhere else, somewhere unexpected, where it does not belong, and against conventional uses of the body, of the head, and of the human. The severed head as catachresis undoes the confidence in the presence of an integral human form by putting the head, detached from the body, side by side with the leftover or "lost" body, or on a decapitated body's back, torso, or legs, or simply on display by itself (for example, on a tray, as in Andrea Solario's famous paintings of Saint John the Baptist[56]), or perhaps cast aside as some sort of excess stuff or waste (human or not). Where the head does not belong but is nonetheless taken after it has been severed is beyond the human body, beyond human vitality, and beyond the community of humans. This is more or less what Janes argues when she writes that "catachreses undo the claims of community founded on sympathetic identification with others who define us."[57] The severed head as catachresis is an "aborted communication" (Janes' turn of phrase) and the mark of a no-longer-operational human community, because heads, faces, and *cogitos* are not available anymore to ensure the kind of "sympathetic identification" that, in Janes' view (but also in Larson's opinion, as we saw above), is key to any form of "social identity."[58]

Perhaps there is no more reviled catachretic figure than the Greek mythological Gorgon, "a trophy head rising on its own."[59] The Gorgon comes back from the beheading—and continues to signify beyond the beheading or precisely because it has been beheaded—to unleash horror and fury. While some insist on seeing the Gorgon as "the guardian of the underworld,"[60] the Gorgon is not just the haunting or vengeful face of violently killed humans. The Gorgon is not the return of the dead (as in a ghost, a spectrally reappearing form, hauntingly coming back in whole or in parts). Rather, beyond death and beyond any hope for resurrected life (since only a furious head remains visible), the Gorgon is a hallucinated aberration, a horrific disturbance and interruption, a nothing that nonetheless insists on signifying, even if what it signifies is not only "against common uses" but also seems to make no sense at all. Thus, the Gorgon "cannot be viewed."[61] It is said that the Gorgon's look petrifies. Medusa, possibly the most infamous of all Gorgons, is a "slimy, swollen" head, a "black hole," says Kristeva.[62] But Medusa is also another kind of presence, perhaps another kind of body or vitality. Cavarero states that Medusa does not "generate horror" but "directly . . . incarnates it."[63] The wounded, gaping hole that is the Gorgon's face/head is horror in the flesh.[64] Indeed, Cavarero notes that

> it alludes to a violence that, tearing furiously at the body, works not simply to take away its life but to undo its figural unity, to wound and dismember, to detach its head. On the other hand, as a head, it emphasizes that the uniqueness of the person, which the Greeks located in that part of the body, is being attacked.[65]

Cavarero's reading of Medusa is compelling. But we can go further. With the figure of the Gorgon, and with Medusa, in particular, the severed head as the body's catachresis reaches an additional layer, a surplus of signification or, rather, of nonsignification. Here, it is perhaps no longer a confrontation with the horror of a deconstructed humanity, of a detached/dismantled body (with the head and the rest of the body no longer forming a unitary whole) that we are dealing with. It is perhaps now about a peering into horror itself, with or without humans being present or at stake, with or without humanity being called in to witness it.

Horror, like Medusa, may be "what lets [itself] be seen once [the human] is decapitated."[66] When any attachment (metaphysical or otherwise) to human integrity has been removed, horror reigns. Kristeva provocatively suggests that, with Gorgons, it is no longer the gaze of living/surviving humans (with their full and individual bodies) that is cast onto the severed head. Rather, a reversal of signification, representation, and violence onto the human is starting to take shape.[67] Indeed, it is the severed head, Medusa itself, that is now looking at us, living/surviving humans. And when Medusa places her gaze onto us, there is nothing for us to see in Medusa's gaze. But, critically, Medusa sees nothing in us as well: no humanity, no community, no social identity. There is nothing in Medusa's gaze that we can sympathize with or recognize. What we may see instead is the abyss of "our" human condition, of "our" identity, of "our" human ontological priority. And this is precisely what her gaze reflects—that is to say, what Medusa seems to see in us, humans.

Medusa's horrifying reversed gaze, the one that looks at us as much as we look at it but no longer reflects anything (including anything in and about us, living/surviving human bodies and persons), is the kind of gaze that Agamben attributes to the *Muselmann*, the name that he and a few others have given to the Auschwitz concentration-camp dweller that has reached a point in "camp-life" that positions it in a zone of total undecidability with regard to "man and non-man," humanity and inhumanity, and death and non-death.[68] Similar to a Gorgon-like figure, Agamben characterizes the *Muselmann* as an "indefinite being."[69] Like Medusa, this indefinite figure/form is mostly defined by its gaze and its face, a gaze and face that reveal an open chasm, an arresting nothingness, but never just death or the end of life (a "corpse without death," says Agamben poignantly[70]). But it is also defined by its gaze and face because "no one wants to see the *Muselmann*."[71] There is an "impossibility of gazing upon" this figure, of facing it and comprehending it.[72] And yet the "impossible vision" of the *Muselmann* in the camp is "at the same time absolutely inevitable" since it is insistent and terrifyingly all too common.[73] This "inevitable impossibility" of the *Muselmann*'s gaze is that of horror, I believe, a horror that gazes upon us when we inevitably see it, that looks at us, and that reflects upon us (and upon what it appears to see in us), but without any depth or distance, not even the distance that may be afforded by death. The horror of the Gorgon-like *Muselmann*'s gaze is not just about seeing the horror of the camp, incarnating it, and, in this fashion, being the main figure that "brings horror to the camp," as Agamben puts it.[74] It is also about a horrifying gaze beyond the camp,[75] a gaze that, by staring at us and not finding anything more, anything different, or anything other (starting with reasons why human bodies, persons, and individuals created the inhuman condition/experiment of the camp), "brings the horror of the camp to the world."[76] The gaze of the *Muselmann* is thus a gaze of and about horror, a horror about the world that "we, humans" inhabit and fill with our claims to community, communication, and social identity and that, from the perspective of the Gorgon-like *Muselmann*'s face, is not clearly distinguishable from the domain of the camp.

Similar to what Agamben seems to suggest, Kristeva wonders whether Medusa's gaze, whether the severed head that looks at us when we think we are the ones looking at it, in all its non-human monstrosity, is not just a destructive gaze (since it decomposes everything that claims some sort of human ontological privilege) but also a leveling or equalizing gaze. Might not Medusa staring at us "invert the human gaze," Kristeva asks,[77] and in so doing seek to own all that the human gaze and the human head claimed they were masters at capturing, possessing, and dominating, including a monopoly on violence, on destruction, on terror? "Who is looking at whom? Who is killing whom?" Kristeva inquisitively incants.[78] One may not want to go so far as to claim that Medusa's gaze, the *Muselmann*'s face, and the severed heads of other figures of bodily catachresis have a salvific function with regard to violence, destruction, or terror. But they are perhaps signifying a leveling or evening out of the plane of horror by gazing back from nothingness, from the wounded hole, from a non-human flesh, onto us, humans, onto our human bodies (our own flesh and bones), and onto our humanity. They are perhaps asking who is causing horror, who has a monopoly on the horrific, and by what stratagem do we, humans, not see that horror's violence is always potentially on the side of humanity, too. The horror of the Gorgon's head and face is that they "capture" but also "freeze" and seek to "eliminate" horror as something that must be fundamentally beyond the human condition.[79] Instead, by gazing onto "humans" from a seemingly no-longer-human place (or with a no-longer-human mode of signification/representation), the Gorgon evens the scores, and it positions horror on all sides. Horror is no longer beyond the human pale; it never was. Horror is no longer the privilege of typically orientalized non-human, monstrous, barbarian half-beasts who decapitate, terrorize, commit suicide attacks, torture, or decompose Western human beings' bodies; it never was, either. Horror, then, becomes a sign system or language that enables us to think and talk about what happens, malevolently as well as benevolently (to the extent that such a distinction still makes any sense), in the world when categories of signification beholden to a metaphysics of human substance are done away with. This is why, I think, for Agamben, it is imperative that "we learn to gaze … upon the Gorgon" and not avoid its stare.[80] Failing to confront the *Muselmann*, failing to look at the Gorgon's severed head, will prevent us from "understanding what Auschwitz is" and from facing the horrifyingly intimate connections between Auschwitz and our human world (as if, somehow, Auschwitz were not of this world).[81]

From such a "horrorist" perspective on the severed head and beheadings, when Medusa's head or the *Muselmann's* gaze distributes horror across all fields of signification (even those beholden to the primacy of human meaning and being), are we not, living/surviving humans who are fascinated or captivated by images or tales of cut-off heads, compelled to ask, and to ask ourselves first, why "our" contemporary narratives about beheadings in Syria, Iraq, or elsewhere by "jidahists" or "radical Islamists," starting with IS fighters, insist on mobilizing a language of horror (coupled with orientalist sentiments about these decapitators' archaic culture and anti-human nature, as we saw above) when, in parts of the world not far removed from where those non-human monsters operate, "we, Westerners," in the name of "our" humanist and human values, are launching dehumanizing "unmanned" aerial drone attacks, seemingly out of nowhere, dropped from the sky, on populations— terrorists, "jihadi" fighters, Taliban sympathizers, but also, and far too often, civilians— often with the objective of destroying their bodies and lives in an instant and typically with the consequence of pulverizing their heads and faces?[82] Who, indeed, has a monopoly on horror and non-humanity, one may ask, when one reads stories (stories because here, unlike with IS beheadings, images often fail or are missing) like the one about the disappeared head of 68-year-old Pakistani grandmother Mamana Bibi, whose face was blown to pieces by a US attack drone in front of her grandchildren while working in the fields of North Waziristan in October 2012?[83] There were no images for us to see, as is often the case with drone attacks. Incidentally, some US attack drones with a capacity to launch "hellfire" missiles onto targets, often human targets, can capture and record images (images that supposedly remain under the tight control of the US military and government). Some of those drones have been aptly and horrifyingly named "Gorgon Stare" drones by the US military since they can take a snapshot of the "kill" as it hits its target[84] but also because to stare in the face of this drone implies immediate annihilation. In North Waziristan, in October 2012, another Gorgonian gaze made it certain that no human image/ representation would remain of the faceless/headless body of the targeted Pakistani grandmother. Mamana Bibi, one can assume, suddenly, out of nowhere, faced the Gorgon/horror, but so did her surviving grandchildren, for whom horror in the faceless form of an attack drone entered the world, their world.[85]

As Cavarero and Agamben have noted (drawing their insights from, among other sources, Primo Levi's accounts of "life" in the concentration camps[86]), those who see the Gorgon or, perhaps, confront the *Muselmann* and are caught by its gaze, rarely come back to tell about it. Colonel Kurtz-like (in the famous cinemato- graphic and literary rendition of the Gorgon's tale[87]), or like Mamana Bibi in a field in Pakistan, they "have gone to the heart of the horror,"[88] for which there is almost always no return. Yet, while it is believed that one's humanity may be preserved by not looking into the face of the Gorgon, by not succumbing to horror's petrification of one's body, life, and humanity, might we not, perversely perhaps, and provocatively as well, ask what may be lost by not seeing the Gorgon, by not looking at its face? Again, this is what I think was Agamben's key concern about the vision of the *Muselmann*. Put differently, what might speaking the language of horror, and thus recognizing horror's distribution on the side of the non-human *and* the human, enable us to understand about the contemporary geopolitics of beheading and defacement? What might horror—the Gorgon, Medusa, the *Muselmann*—tell us about the destruction and fury that is unleashed not only by those who apparently reject humanity and human life (by cutting human heads, particularly "white-faced" and "English-speaking" heads[89]), but also by those— Westerners, defenders of humanity, and protectors of the rights of the human person—who are in the business, less commonly visible, to be sure, but just as choreographed, of dismantling other humans' bodies and making their heads and faces unrecognizable and unidentifiable as well?

As we saw in previous sections of this chapter, what Kristeva elegantly but also dreadfully calls "the perpetual progress of Medusan horror" is not and has never been the privileged realm of non-Western, oriental barbarian others.[90] More generally, it is not the privilege of a non-humanity or anti-humanity, either. Horror, then, is not just an assault on the human and human heads. It can be and, in fact, often is an assault *by* the human, *by* human bodies (Western as well as non-Western), and *by* human heads on others' lives, bodies, heads, and faces. What the severed head—the incarnation of horror, perhaps—can do, then, is not just provide a memento or memorial for the loss and mourning of the human body, a grieving ritual for a disappearing metaphysics of human substance, but also initiate a redistribution of the modes of signification, representation, and cultural/political thinking about horror and about who or what gets to speak it, find it, and name it.[91] The semiotic work of catachresis, the work of the severed head, is an opening onto but also *of* horror. It opens up what horror is, does, and means. Methodologically speaking, it may also appear to be a work of deconstruction, starting with the deconstruction of the human and its head. But here it is a work of deconstruction that goes beyond just thinking about the integral human body that, in some unfortunate and sometimes appalling circumstances, is being dismantled when a human head is violently and forcefully separated from the rest of a human body. As catachresis, it may be as a matter of deconstruction, both in the text (linguistically, semiotically, representationally) and *hors texte* (as a violent abuse of a "body's grammar," form, and image), that the severed head can be of critical importance. Janes may thus be right when she writes that "beheadings used to provide dramatic endings," but "[t]hey are now where we [need to] begin."[92]

Yet it is also not clear whether modalities of deconstruction and catachretic figures are capable of offering us a perspective on the severed head that can effect a radical redistribution of the modes and systems of signification and representation about horror. Put differently, I wonder whether deconstruction is up to the task of enabling us, living/surviving humans, to stare at the Gorgon. The next section addresses some of the ambiguities and ambivalences of the work of deconstruction with regard to human beheadings and severed heads. It questions whether deconstruction, beyond its generally critical or, better yet, anti-foundational impulses, is not in fact a remnant of humanism, or at least a somewhat hidden refuge for the human and human heads (even if/when human heads are seemingly deconstructed or disseminated).

Free heads on deconstructed bodies

Janes writes that, nowadays, the severed head "has become an obsessive, almost comic trope for the vulnerability of the modern self."[93] The contemporary fascination with beheadings evidenced in many Western discourses on security, foreign policy, and terror, and, particularly, the fascination with the beheadings performed by so-called barbaric and oriental others, may well be a way of signifying an obsession with or an angst about the vulnerability of "our" integral self, "our" person, "our" individuality, and, indeed, "our" humanity. Larson had already intimated as much. Stories about and images of severed heads may be the mark of a deep discomfort in the West, among experts, pundits, politicians, and scholars, but perhaps in the general public as well, about the status of "our" humanity in the face of something "we" like to call horror, both a horror that "others" can and do unleash onto Westerners but also a horror possibly stemming from the sentiment that security and anti-terror strategies and technologies used by the West and Westerners can be very skilled at obliterating heads or faces too.[94] But might there be something else about this resurgence of a Western obsession with severed heads and beheadings, something more perverse, perhaps, or at least something that often dare not be said or seen? Might the return of an old Western curiosity about cutting heads off be related to a secret desire on the part of the human person, perhaps a visceral impulse, even, to unburden oneself or one's body of the metaphysical weight of the human, at least of the human as defined and led by the head? Might there not be in Gorgonian confrontations with detached heads an unreasonable or unthinkable (unreasonable and unthinkable because to really think or reason about it would paradoxically require that one has "lost" one's head) wish to relieve bodies of all the hierarchical impositions that come with the idea of the human/humanity?[95]

Janes tries to connect the semiotic dimensions of decapitation in Western culture and literature to a desire on the part of the modern Western subject for some sort of ecstatic or, perhaps, excessive form of liberation, for an opening onto total freedom. She suggests that, for many modern and late-modern Western thinkers, "losing one's head has a pleasant aura of liberation."[96] Recalling some of Georges Bataille's writings and Bataille's notion of the *Acéphale* in particular (*Acéphale*, acephalic man, is a brainless/headless man),[97] Janes tracks within Western thought and literature a reactionary current that appears as a revolt against the belief in the ontological priority given to human integrity and integrality, with a human body necessarily steered by a head/brain/*cogito*. The theme of headlessness as a radically liberating motif is not foreign to Western culture and social/political critique. In fact, the thought about headlessness, she suggests, enables in the modern and late-modern era the affirmation of a different kind of vitality. For Janes, based on her reading of Bataille and other twentieth-century critical and/or deconstructive thinkers (Roland Barthes, Jacques Derrida), there is a body vitality that can be expressed only when the body is no longer made to depend upon the head.[98] While Janes identifies the presence of this critical and radically liberating motif of headlessness in twentieth-century continental thought, starting with Bataille, it may already have been at work in the eighteenth century. After all, did the French *Tiers-État* not understand the decapitations of Louis XVI and Marie Antoinette as the necessary removal of the head of the state without which the liberation of the social body would not be possible?[99]

Acéphale, Janes tells us, "freed from his head ... plunges into a world without foundation and without head."[100] It seems that what Janes and perhaps Bataille find in the removal of the head and the deconstruction of the whole body commanded by a head is the possibility of an ideological opening or challenge (I would suggest, once again, that such a challenge made possible by the removal of the head was already at stake at the time of the French Revolution, even if that challenge quickly descended into its own terror/*terreur*). What the removal of the head challenges is the idea that the ultimate referent to a signifying system that seeks to establish any sort of social, cultural, political, and ethical meaning must be a head (or must have a top, a cap, a heading, a captain, a leader, a center of command, a brain, a *cogito*, etc.) and, in particular, a human head. As Janes states, "dominance of the head, the *cephalos* ... transmute[s] man as a physical object into a symbolic object of value."[101] In other words, according to Janes, it is modern man himself that gets to be valued in modern processes of signification and representation, thanks to the omnipresence of the head. Deconstructing the relationship between the body and the head, mobilizing the severed head as catachresis, is a way, ideologically and semiotically, to undermine the belief according to which modern man—the modern male human body with a rational capacity to think and lead—must be at the center of all things that matter and must remain present and unchallenged in order to provide meaning and direction to human life.

Janes' account of the deconstructive take on the liberated and headless body seems compelling. The radically critical (even if often only metaphorical and textual) possibility of removing heads may offer a plausible, even if somewhat perverse, explanation for the unrelenting fascination in the West, historically and today, with headlessness/beheadings. It may also cast beheadings not as acts that must be abject but, rather, as signs and sights that may have emancipatory potentials, particularly for the sake of the rest of the body, and away from the domination of human heads.[102] In a way, Janes' account of the deconstruction/displacement of the head for the sake of a radically liberated body takes us back to modern and late-modern Western thought, culture, and literature to try to find there an alternate story about severed heads, one that may be more life-affirming and body-affirming than the Gorgonian perspective on the horror of severed heads.

Yet, unlike Kristeva, Cavarero, and Agamben on the severed head and beheading, the deconstructive perspective on head removal discussed by Janes never really comes close to thinking head-cutting in relation to horror. In fact, in Janes' reading, the deconstructive perspective on headlessness for radically liberating purposes may become a way of seeking to fend off the possibility of horror. Here, the deconstructive work of catachresis seems to reveal its limits. Put differently, when Janes introduces acephalic bodies, heads have been let loose, and the semiotic as well as ideological primacy given to the male human subject/self governed by a head has been challenged. But the threshold of the human/humanity has never completely been crossed. This inability to cross the human body's threshold is affirmed when, for example, Janes notes that there is a vitality to the body that can finally be released (but also preserved) once the "colonial" mastery of the head/brain/*cogito* is finally done with. Thus, the vital life force, unshackled from the domination of the head, can now be shown to reside in and across the human body, in and through multiple body parts, whose energy and creativity are finally set free. As Janes puts it: "[h]eadlessness affirms the vitality moving the hierarchical structures of institutions and endorses the indefinite potential of the body, its power, energy, life, longing for release, demanding release, breaking through, breaking away."[103]

Janes' insistence on this deconstructive yet decidedly vitalist scenario requires an ideological struggle against the head as a command center. It champions a catachretic approach to removing heads from bodies (which, at this point, she prefers to call headlessness rather than beheading) on behalf of the body and its potentialities or in the name of pluralized and disseminated life forces. Still, in a vitalist spirit, this deconstruction/dissemination of human heads also imposes some limitations on the severing or removal of heads, since human bodies must still be present, visible, often alive, energetic, and at stake for this version of the vital life force to be expressed, to be experienced, and, indeed, to exist. Liberation from the head may not be in the name of man or the human subject/self. But it is still—it must still be—on behalf of bodies and body energies, forces, and potentialities. And those liberated bodies may still be allowed to define themselves as human and, in fact, may be rediscovered and re-emphasized as human now that the head is no longer in charge.[104] In Janes' account, the critical move towards a deconstruction of the head may be precisely to preserve and reaffirm humanity, but this time from the standpoint of the leftover body (or the "lost" body, in Larson's parlance), a body that can now celebrate the loss of its former head.

This critical modality of deconstruction of heads, perhaps deconstruction *tout court*, does not have much to do with horror, nor even with the possibility that horror may bring with it some leveling or evening out sort of gaze. The deconstructive yet vitalist perspective on headlessness/beheading cannot accommodate horror, and, in fact, it may seek to buffer the vitality of the leftover body from horror's gaze. Here, deconstruction marks its difference from what one may call (following Cavarero's lead) a "horrorist" perspective. Deconstruction's objective seems to be to replace the head with a disseminated body, or with finally unbridled bodily vitalities and energies. Yet, as we saw in the previous section, horror is not just about displacing centers or heads in order to, perhaps, down the line, discover other centers or vitalities, other multiple ways of identifying or recognizing the human/humanity. To wish to displace the head and to try to replace it with several other but still human forms or energies is to remain within human-centered modalities of signification and representation. To celebrate the removal or loss of heads may offer critical potentials for rethinking humanity and human presence in a plural way, as a matter of dissemination. But it cannot undo the metaphysics of human substance (again, it mainly pluralizes it). In so doing, it does not prepare us to confront horror, to stare at the Gorgon, and to capture the distributed powers of the horrific that, as we saw above, are equally to be found on the side of the non-human and the human.

Derrida, perhaps the most inspiring thinker on matters of deconstruction, has offered a reading of beheading/headlessness that seems to confirm the limitations found in Janes' account. Famously (and as Janes recalls), Derrida wrote that "to lose one's head, no longer to know where one's head is, such is perhaps the effect of dissemination."[105] While dissemination may initiate a pluralization of the body and of the body's grammar, it cannot offer any guarantee that the pluralized body, left without a head, will not seek once again to rediscover head-like attributes somewhere else, maybe in other "vital" organs, or maybe in other bits and pieces suddenly taken to be the source of a new vitality or life force. Derrida's take on the notion of "heading" (*cap*) in his essay on the future of Europe and the European continent is indicative of the presence of the specter of reconstruction—perhaps the reconstruction of the human or of some values attached to the human—that appears to haunt the work of deconstruction, particularly when deconstruction strays *hors texte* or is catachretically applied to human bodies and heads.[106]

Reflecting on his purposeful selection of the phrase "the other heading" to call for a new, more plural and pluralistic way of thinking about the meaning of Europe, in its culture and, perhaps above all, in its geopolitical dimensions and contours, Derrida launches into a deconstruction of the term "heading," or *cap* in French. Heading, or *cap*, is an insistent term and a pressing concern in questions that European politicians asked, and asked themselves, in the 1990s, at the time of Derrida's intervention, and are still asking today. The question posed then and still today is: where is Europe headed?[107] Back in the 1990s, this was a question prompted by, among other geopolitical and geocultural concerns, the collapse of the Soviet Union and communist Eastern Europe, demands by Eastern and Southern European nations to join the soon-to-become European Union, the growing diversification and multi-culturalism of Western European populations, and the increasing flows of migrants from Africa and Asia landing on Europe's shores. As Derrida notes,

> the word *cap* [heading] . . . refers, as you well know, to the head, or the extremity of the extreme, the aim and the end, the ultimate, the last . . . It here assigns to navigation the pole, the end, the *telos* of an oriented, calculated, deliberate, voluntary, ordered movement: ordered most often by the *man* in charge . . . [I]t is a *man* who decides on the heading.[108]

What Derrida indicates here is reminiscent of what Janes described. A heading, or *cap*, a steering in a certain, determined, and indeed deliberate direction, towards a reflected or "calculated" objective or finality, is the work of a head, a man's head (a "headman," adds Derrida[109]). Europe's finality, its *telos*, is the work of men and their heads. It is these men (European politicians and bureaucrats, for example) and their heads that set Europe's trajectory, decide what Europe is and means, where it resides and where it ends, and who or what belongs to it and who or what does not.

To step out of this way of configuring Europe, a different set of heads is required, Derrida intimates. Another heading, but a heading still, must be advanced. Another *cap*/head must be offered. Some men must lose their heads. Or, at least, those men's heads, those headmen, must be pushed aside so that other heads can take charge, lead Europe, and think its future. Derrida writes: "The expression 'The Other Heading' can ... suggest that another direction is in the offing ... To change direction can mean to change goals, to decide on another heading, or else to change captains."[110] He adds that another heading/*cap* can

> mean to recall that there is another heading, the heading being not only ours (*le nôtre*) but the other (*l'autre*), not only that which we identify, calculate, and decide upon, but the heading of the other [*le cap de l'autre*] ... the heading of the other being perhaps the first condition of an identity or identification that is not an egocentrism destructive of oneself and the other.[111]

Derrida's sentiment is laudable. It calls for a change to Europe's heading, for an opening of Europe onto the other, away from Europe itself, or at least away from Europe's former and current identities as determined and directed by Europe's former and current leaders ("captains" and "headmen") and their heads. Derrida invites Europe and Europeans to think about "other" headings, headings/*caps* decided and plotted by other men and other heads, perhaps. This implies a geo-political turn or redirection for Europe that would still be headed somewhere, but, perhaps, without the necessary presence of men leading the way. It seems clear here that Derrida's othering of Europe's heading/*cap* is intended to open Europe to or for the other but also to disseminate the meaning/identity of Europe by no longer having "an aim and an end" to the heading. Once again, with this instance of deconstruction (a deconstruction of Europe's direction, future, and *telos*), there is a pluralization and dissemination of political, cultural, and ethical possibilities. But headings/*caps*, it appears, remain. Thus, this "other heading" may not be about removing heads altogether. It may be about othering the head and the heading, displacing heads, men, leaders, and captains so that others (and possibly other men and other heads too) may chart the paths ahead, may decide on multiple new directions for Europe.

Derrida's other heading may be a matter of taking us "beyond *our heading*,"[112] but it remains ambiguous about the possibility of giving up on headings and *caps*. Even with others and other headings at play, is it ever about losing or removing headings and heads? Is there not a tethering by heads/headings and to heads/headings that remains crucial here, one that perhaps prevents Derrida from calling for the total obliteration of headings and *caps*, if only so that the other may be given a chance to steer as well? If some heads are no longer there for Europe and for what is to come for a European identity, others may be able to step in. Or does Derrida leave open the possibility, perhaps to the detriment of the other ever to become a headman, that the call to move "beyond our heading" will become a call to move beyond *any* heading? When Derrida writes that what is at stake is the need "to recall ourselves not only to the *other heading*, and especially to the *heading of the other*, but also perhaps to the *other of the heading*,"[113] he appears to be tempted to push the work of deconstruction beyond heads and headings or beyond steering and directing altogether. Indeed, the "other of the heading" suggests that what is at stake here is perhaps not the displacement of headmanship and its replacement with another, with the other, and possibly for the other. In a way that recalls some of Janes' discussions, Derrida adds that it is about making way for what is always other to heads, to headings, and to *caps* or, as he puts it, for a "relation of identity with the other that no longer obeys the form, the sign, or the logic of the heading, nor even of the *anti-heading*— of beheading, of decapitation."[114] Thus, in Derrida's logic of deconstruction of heads and headings, other heads will remain. Or, if they are not to remain (at least not to remain as headings/*caps*), something about or for the other—what he calls a "relation of identity with the other"—will still be aimed at. The deconstruction of heads and headings for Derrida, similar to some of the sentiments expressed by Janes, cannot just amount to "anti-headings," even those that may take the horrific form of beheadings.[115] There must be more to the deconstruction of heads/headings, remnants to the dissemination of heads.

Deconstruction at the level of the body, when targeting heads or headings, seems to have limits or, at least, to take place within limits (even if these limits are not openly stated). A threshold, once again—perhaps, a human or humanist threshold—may not be crossed, even by deconstructive thinking or disseminated language. For Derrida, in *The Other Heading*, what deconstruction may not be allowed to touch and possibly may never be able to undo is the other, the other as the guarantee that there will be more or other headings, or as the condition of possibility for future relations, identities, and, perhaps, for a humanity to-come (here, a humanity to and for Europe, achieved thanks to the other to-come). In a way, the deconstruction of heads and headings needs to preserve the potential for reconstruction, at least as long as heads and headings are at stake or, in their temporary absence or displacement, as long as the other remains in sight. Deconstruction may liberate (the body, vital forces/energies, the other, heads and headings) by way of dissemination. But, as Derrida intimates, it may not be able to think the "anti-heading," an "anti-heading" that for him is beheading or decapitation. Thus, deconstruction does not allow itself to think about the horror of the severed head. In this way, the deconstruction/dissemination of heads, I would suggest, remains wedded to a Western humanistic tradition.

By contrast, as I indicated above, what horror may invoke is a mode of writing and thinking that is neither about deconstruction nor about reconstruction, and possibly a mode of writing and thinking that takes the deconstruction/reconstruction distinction (or, perhaps, continuum) as pointless. Once again, one can call this modality of writing and thinking "horrorist." The next section pushes these non-deconstructive as well as non-reconstructive horrorist possibilities further. It considers whether these different possibilities for writing and thinking can assist us in facing horror and, in the process, give us a bit more insight into "our" ongoing fascination with severed heads.

A thought that gazes upon the Gorgon

American novelist Robert Olen Butler does not hide his fascination with severed heads. His 2006 collection of short stories *Severance* is a series of 240-word-long "last thoughts" by famous as well as lesser known, primarily human, severed heads.[116] Starting from the double premise that a cut-off head allegedly remains conscious for about 90 seconds (a debatable claim) and that, in an extreme emotional state, humans supposedly can speak at a rate of 160 words per minute, Butler offers the thoughts/expressions right after their beheadings of "individuals" as varied as Medusa, Cicero, St John the Baptist, Anne Boleyn, Sir Walter Raleigh, Marie Antoinette, Maximilien Robespierre, Jayne Mansfield, a chicken, Yukio Mishima, a woman beheaded during the collapse of the World Trade Center on September 11, a female suicide bomber who exploded her body in 2003, an American civilian contractor killed in Iraq in 2004, and the author, Robert Olen Butler himself, announcing his own imagined beheading. The thoughts are errant, rapid, and somewhat disjointed (as disjointed perhaps as the protagonists' heads). They are flashes that rush back to the suddenly separated head in a flow of images, memories, feelings, regrets, longings, hopes, desires, and so on. They are also intersected and at times influenced by strange feelings. Butler's stories mix brief recollections of past events in the life of the beheaded bodies (some very recent events, like the metallic sensation of the cutting blade on the neck, others more distant) with inner secrets, unfulfilled desires, or ultimate remembrances of pains as well as pleasures (including sometimes the pain or pleasure of the severing). The beheaded protagonists' "last" thoughts, in Butler's writing, are never really confessions. Rather, they appear as traces or, again, as flashes of a life that once lived, of a body that once was. They are thoughts, memories, fragments, traces, and trances all at once.

Central to Butler's quick succession of vignettes about cut-off heads are the human sentiments and human sensations that flood back in an instant, even if technically post-mortem. Remnants of a human consciousness (even in the case of non-human severed heads) that ecstatically insists on living or, at least, on talking, thinking, expressing feelings or regrets, and sensing take center stage. Love and life, in particular, expressed from a human-centric perspective, sometimes a lost love or a past life, sometimes a love and a life vividly recalled and embraced, are insistent themes. For example, Lois Kennerly, the woman beheaded on 9/11, thinks:

> and I've just married him but this is the moment I know I love him for sure,
> us smoking outside alone, and the snow is falling beyond my window I have

awakened and I know it's time for my baby she's ready though my water hasn't broken yet and I'm not in any pain I know this is the day and it's still snowing beyond the hospital window the flakes look big as her hands and she's taking my milk and Sam is singing *you're having my baby* and I think him a damn fool, she's mine, and I can hardly see, the lights are so bright, and an arm slips around my waist *put your head on my shoulder*"[117]

(Butler's stories have almost no punctuation, an effort to reflect the speed of thought in moments of extreme emotion). The female Middle Eastern law student who initiates the suicide bombing and loses her head in the process makes several references to her pregnancy, to mothers, to other pregnant women whose lives and babies she is taking away.[118] Criminal François-Pierre Lacenaire, executed in 1836, confuses the touch of the guillotine with that of his past lovers and experiences his beheading as an ultimate climactic moment of love-making.[119] And even Medusa's petrification of those (mostly men) who dare to look at her turns into a desire for love, for loving others, and for loving children above all (perhaps her own):

I love my living hair these serpents whisper when men come close each strand with a split tongue hissing my desire for them I shake my dear children my tresses down and they curl back up their black eyes flashing and the man cries out at my beauty . . . but my children are my true loves rooted in my brain and gathered sleeping against my face muttering sibilant dreams of love.[120]

Reading Butler's stories of severance, one might come to understand that having one's head cut off is part of the human condition. Perhaps it is, it can be, the pinnacle of being human. In the moment of head severance, an exalted human consciousness reveals itself. At that moment, or shortly thereafter, a humanity is lost (when the head rolls), but it also flashes brilliantly. Butler's delicate and precise writing seeks to leave us with traces and trances of the human, of and perhaps for a humanity to-come, traces and trances that celebrate human life and human love. One critic claims that, in *Severance*, Butler brings "the dead back to life through the will of his imagination."[121] But death is never really part of the stories (or, when it is, is merely anecdotal). Rather, human consciousness, once again, never fades away, despite the loss of the head. And the perpetuation of human consciousness guarantees the stubborn presence of human life, of a vital force and energy that can only be human or be about humanity. Interviewed about his intention when writing *Severance*, Butler confesses: "I caught a dramatic moment in which a human soul reevaluates its life. In this extraordinary, dynamic, and dramatic moment, a person is compelled to do something which is essential to his life, to review his life."[122] As Butler further explains, the act of severance is, for him, irrelevant. At best, it is a moment that guarantees a heightening of life. The human "person" (his term) and his/her life continues or lives on—changed, to be sure (it must now continue without a head), but intensified and celebratory of a life and love, of a human body, that will always be (note in passing Butler's transmutation of the human head into a human "soul," as he puts it).

Butler's take on severed heads and beheadings is interesting because it seems to express the view that severed heads/beheadings do not have to destabilize the metaphysics of human substance. Here, a will to believe in the endless existence and persistence of humanity and human life is crucial. It is a will to believe in a human consciousness that, even without a physical head attached to a human body, can continue to fulfill the functions and attributes of the head in its absence. In a way, for the human, in life and in death, with or without a head, humanity's life force is universal and eternal. The severed head as catachresis is conjured away by Butler, even if, along the way, the physically decapitated human head has to be transfigured into a human soul. Put differently, the physicality of human heads, attached to bodies or detached from them, does not matter as long as the functions and attributes of the human head (consciousness, life-affirming force, humanity) are somehow perpetuated.

Likewise, a deconstructive perspective on headlessness/beheading, as described by Janes or championed by Derrida, is accepted and, in fact, embraced by Butler. Heads, headings, *caps* may be removed or may fall. But no beheading or decapitation will ever prevent human persons, human bodies, human lives, and human souls from remaining vibrant and shining through. As for Derrida, head severance for Butler cannot be, will never be, an anti-heading. Disseminated (as with Janes or Derrida) or transfigured (as with Butler), the metaphysics of (human) substance must be preserved. To mobilize another concept borrowed from Derrida's arsenal of deconstructive thinking, in order to maintain humanity's capacity to remain open to other heads and to others' heads, Butler's severed heads and the stories they tell must be placed in a state of *survivance*, or over-living. For Derrida, as Bonnie Honig explains, *survivance*, or over-living, is beyond survival (thus, in a way, beyond life and death). It is "a dividend—that surprise extra, the gift that exceeds rightful expectations, the surplus that exceeds causality."[123] It is also both "more life and more than [mere] life" since "it seeks to orient us . . . toward the gifts of life . . . the unearned . . . toward that which cannot be earned."[124]

Even the Gorgon, Medusa, is placed by Butler into a state of over-living, of "more life" as well as "more than life." Medusa, in Butler's reading, cries for life and love, for children—her children, perhaps. Butler's Medusa shuns horror. She kills and petrifies those who stare at her. But she craves human life, to be human, to be reattached to a body and to humanity. As Butler insists, the Gorgon "was human at one point. She started off as a human being."[125] If there can be hope for Medusa to retrieve her humanity, if not her body, might this not cancel out her horrifying gaze? Might the *survivance* of Butler's human severed heads not provide a guarantee against horror? Might the transmutation or transfiguration of the (human) head into a (human) soul not mark the ultimate victory of humanity, of the metaphysics of substance, over horror? Is that perhaps what, with Robert Olen Butler, we humans are supposed to or want to believe? Is that why we remain fascinated by sights of beheadings and severed heads, because, instead of pointing to an ultimate violation of the ontological dignity of the human person, they reveal something more, a more to life and a more than life? Is our fascination with severed heads and beheadings, then, a will to believe in over-living, or *survivance*?

What Butler's take on severed heads seems to reveal is the presence of some sort of strange kinship, if not some outright complicity, between the idea of the onto-logical primacy or superiority of the human and his/her head (the metaphysics of substance), catachretic or deconstructive perspectives on headlessness, and quasi-theological attempts at transmuting or transfiguring cut-off human heads into eter-nal human souls (with, at times, a desperate insistence on over-living). One may think of this odd kinship or complicity as a rallying cry against horror and its powers. Perhaps it is a sacred union against the apparent non-sense or loss of meaning that comes with horror or that emerges with the sight of the Gorgon (although clearly not Robert Olen Butler's version of the Gorgon/Medusa). But perhaps, as we saw above, and as "horroristic" readings of beheadings can help us figure out, this sacred union between a metaphysics of human heads, disseminated/deconstructive headlessness, and transfiguration as *survivance* seeks to fend off horror's leveling effects, too—that is to say, its equalizing distribution of seemingly senseless violence across the realms of the non-human and the human. In the name of the human/humanity, the new holy trinity that forms itself against the horror of severed heads and beheadings cannot allow perspectives traditionally placed (by humans and their heads) on the side of the inhuman or the non-human or anti-human to become part and parcel of humanity, to be confused with humanity, or, worse yet, to be revealed as what humanity was always already about. Once again, unlike decon-struction or catachresis, what "horroristic" readings enable is a recognition that the Gorgon must be faced if one is to comprehend that the human/humanity is also about horror and is often about removing/destroying heads and bodies. This is what really unsettles about horror and "horroristic" thinking. And this is a form of unsettling or radical disturbance that proponents and defenders of the metaphysics of human substance—even the most deconstructive thinkers among them—cannot accept or face.

Some of Eugene Thacker's recent writings may help us to understand this com-plicity or holy alliance against horror and "horroristic" thought. Affirming that "horror is about the paradoxical thought of the unthinkable,"[126] Thacker connects horror to a seemingly incomprehensible and unacceptable rejection of humanity. Understood to be "about the limits of the human," horror is a Gorgonian confrontation with a world that can be seen or witnessed and yet is not for humans or, as Thacker claims, is not made for us.[127] Horror's "negative philosophy" (Thacker's turn of phrase[128]) is an insistent attempt at placing us, humans, face to face with a world that is not just or is no longer for us, a "world-without-us."[129] The main aim of this "world-without-us" revealed by horror is to unsettle the belief that the world must exist for us, for humans and their bodies (with heads attached), and can only be with us and perhaps because of us (our physical as well as metaphysical presence, even if post-mortem). Put differently, the "world-with-us" outlook is that the world cannot be, or cannot make sense, if we cannot think it, if it is not a measure of our human thought and human heads, or, at least, if thought is not to be here for us, reserved for us humans. Although he does not quite put it this way, Thacker's "world-with-us" or "world-for-us" is akin to what in this study I have called the metaphysics of substance, a concept that, as Judith Butler reminded us, captures the way "a number of philosophical ontologies [are]... trapped within certain illusions of 'Being' and 'Substance'."[130] Philosophy is indeed guilty of or, at the very least, complicit in this imposition of ontology (the ontology of human substance) onto thought and prior to thought. This is also why, for Thacker, the task of horror is philosophical, albeit a negative one. Or, as Thacker insists, horror is "*a non-philosophical attempt to think about the world-without-us philosophically.*"[131]

Thacker's "world-without-us" is, like horror itself, a great equalizer or leveler. In this negatively thought world, things may look "bad" for humans or, at least, from a human perspective. Things in this "world-without-us" may well be horrific or horrifying, as we humans like to put it. After all, as novelist and literary theorist David Peak puts it, both culturally and philosophically, horror is "concerned with the cosmic paralysis of humanity."[132] But just as horror is indifferent with regard to the human and the non-human (it does not recognize this dualism), so is the "world-without-us." To that world and that thought, the presence or absence of the human is, at best, an afterthought. To the "world-without-us," human substance or presence is an afterthought because, as Thacker puts it, the "world-without-us"/ horror has already subtracted the human from it.[133] Or, as I preferred to put it above, horror has affirmed its presence, its sight, equally on the side of the human and the non-human (thus often rendering the human, including so-called humanity's own version of head severance and bodily pulverization—for example, by way of "Gorgon Stare" drone attacks—indistinguishable from the non-human or from the alleged anti-humanity of others who are not like us). But, as Thacker clarifies, this subtraction of the human from the world and from thought is not just "antagonistic to the human," since to antagonize the human would be merely "to put things in human terms."[134] Thus, the distinction between human and non-human can no longer hold. And yet the human/humanity still plays a crucial part in horror. Here again, we can turn to Thacker, who adds that the "world-without-us" is not just neutral towards the human, because to invoke a neutrality of the world with regard to humanity would presume that one is able to think for or as the world-itself.[135] Moreover, claiming a neutrality about the "world-without-us" vis-à-vis humanity would fail to recognize that horror actively targets the human (and the human head, as we saw above), even if it does not oppose or antagonize it. Thus, the possibility of the "world-without-us" is horrifying, or is about horror, because it hangs (by itself, like a floating detached head, perhaps) "somewhere in between" the human and the world, "in a nebulous zone that is impersonal and horrific,"[136] possibly because it prevents any reattachment of the human body to a world it could claim for itself. More than neutral or even indifferent, then, the "world-without-us," its thought, and its horror are undecidable. Indeed, the "world-without-us" actively un-decides what is human and what is not, what is horrific and what is not, where horror is to reside and where it is not to be found (for example, "horrific" beheadings can take place "over there," in the non-West, but also "in-here," in the West, and by the West, as we saw above), and what has or does not have ontological priority (and, one might add, the "world-without-us" renders undecidable the question of whether the world can exist or be meaningful if humans and their heads are subtracted from it).

If horror allows us a glimpse into the "world-without-us," if that world that does not need us, humans, is a horrifying vision that nonetheless we may not escape (as Agamben claimed about the sight of the *Muselmann*), what is made undecidable is precisely what needs to be captured and faced if one is to step away from the metaphysics of substance (its ideology, its hegemony, and its violence) but also if one is to make sure that substance can remain in this "nebulous zone" (as Thacker puts it), where attempts at reclaiming an ontological priority for humanity will be undermined. Thus, horror's "philosophical negativity," its proliferation of undecidability (not to be confused with a deconstructive dissemination of headlessness, as we saw above), is a critical guarantee. It is the guarantee that humanity's ontological priority and superiority will no longer be claimed with metaphysical and political certainty when it comes to selecting which human heads may be cut and which severed heads represent a violation of human dignity or of the human person/body, or whose tradition of beheading is to be accepted, understood, and perhaps revered, and whose modality of head removal is to be seen as barbaric, savage, oriental, unacceptable, and inhuman. Put somewhat differently, horror's undecidability must be confronted because it can help us and the world to question how much of an ontological difference there actually is between preserving heads or mourning for some lost heads, on the one hand, and cutting heads off, on the other. From a "world-with-us" or a "world-for-us" perspective, the distinction matters a lot and helps to determine where the ontological stakes are (allegedly, on the side of the human and of the preservation of some human heads). But from a "world-without-us" perspective, where the thought of horror is introduced, the insistence on the preservation of heads attached to integral human bodies and the forceful severing of heads are both driven by the metaphysics of substance. Both are about preserving the human and its priority (even through its beheading, as we saw in Robert Olen Butler's stories). Or, at least, both are about making claims about humanity and about using human heads in order to establish political and ideological preferences, often political and ideological preferences with regard to what humanity should be like. Thus, the opposition between executioners, or head-cutters, on one side, and head preservers, on the other (an opposition that only matters from the perspective of the "world-with-us," of a human versus non-human duality, once again) is perhaps nothing more than an opposition between two seemingly different views about the "world-with-us" and two apparently divergent strategies about how to go about imposing those views, with humanity always at stake. Thought this way, with horror in sight, the difference between those who mourn the savage loss of human (allegedly, mostly Western) heads and those who supposedly champion cutting human heads off is not really a metaphysical difference. It may be an ideological difference (what is the preferred way, politically, strategically, culturally, of advancing humanity). But it is mostly a difference of method with regard to how to preserve or establish the metaphysics of substance. And this is perhaps also why, fundamentally, the severing of heads, in contemporary as well as past beheadings, fascinates us, humans. Head severances fascinate because they are part of a play of political and ideological choices and strategies. They are about differential methods chosen to try to achieve political and ideological (but still human) objectives. Put differently, that beheadings remain fascinating for us, and must remain so, is the guarantee that we are still operating—or at least, we want to believe that we are—within a world made for us and by us, with our heads and others' still in charge but also, at times, in danger. As long as beheadings continue to fascinate us this way, we may be able to manage not to think of horror, not to confront or face it.

Thus, what horror is not allowed to reveal, what we do not want to see in the Gorgon's gaze, is the rupture of this fascination with severed heads and beheadings, of this fascination with disseminated headlessness, in a way. What we, humans, cannot afford to face is the non-differentiation or undecidability between two allegedly different (but, in a way, complicit, since one always needs the other—the human needs the so-called non-human or anti-human) regimes of preservation/ destruction of human heads. What cannot be faced, what horror brings with it, in its glimpse of a "world-without-us," is the unthinkable, as Thacker puts it, a thought not thought from the perspective of the human. Thus, in common discourses as well as expert ones about beheadings and fallen heads, what is unthinkable is precisely a thought that would force us to think the non-differentiation between us and them, between what we, today, in the West, take humans and their heads to be and mean and what we claim they, so-called orientals who sever heads, believe or think about human bodies, human persons, and human heads. Yet, I would suggest, the unthinkable is exactly what needs to be thought, with or without us. To force through the thought of the unthinkable, or horror's negative philosophy, Thacker advances the challenge of what he calls "demontology." "Demontology," as some sort of demonic ontology, would replace human ontology, the priority given to the "world-with-us" and the "world-for-us," and the metaphysics of substance. Where "ontology deals with the minimal relation being/non-being, ... demontology would undertake the thought of nothingness (a negative definition), but a nothing- ness that is also not simply non-being (a privative definition)," writes Thacker.[137] Demontology's task, Thacker intimates, would be to "rethink the world as unthinkable," and thus to enable the conditions of possibility for a thought that would think "in the absence of a human-centric point of view,"[138] although perhaps not without humans altogether (perhaps with humans still, but humans no longer tethered— often by their heads—to a metaphysics of substance).

As suggested above, beheadings and severed heads, despite our commonly human and humanistic claims (particularly in the West), are often not about horror. Or, if and when they are, they are about a horror that fascinates, and consequently that can be contained and deflected towards those so-called inhuman practices carried out by barbaric and savage others. As we saw, contemporary discourses by Western security, foreign-policy, and anti-terror experts about beheadings (by IS or other "radical Islamist" groups) in the Middle East are replete with this weak version of horror, this weak sense of what horror is and does. Very often, these typically orientalist discourses, posing as rallying calls on behalf of humanity, are content with creating or reinforcing false oppositions between humanity (in the West) and horror (in the non-West).[139] Thus, most narratives or depictions of beheadings and severed heads do not radically unsettle the ontological view about the priority of the human and human substance. In fact, perversely perhaps, they maintain it or affirm it all over again. But there is a glimpse of horror that still comes with the severed head, with the Gorgonian gaze, and with a leveling of possibilities (often, violent possibilities) shown to be indifferently about the human and the non-human, if one is ready to face it, see it, and think it "horroristically" or, better yet, "demontologically." Thinking "demontologically," thinking the unthinkable, about us, about humans, about human heads, about the world ("our" world), is horror's demand, not because the unthinkable is impossible or out of reach, but rather because it is often present, though not always visible or willingly represented, in the midst of "our" world, a world supposedly made with and for humans. A world, with or without us, in which neither "they" (whoever "they," barbaric head-cutters, may be) nor "we" (whoever "we," so-called defenders of a certain vision of humanity, the human body, and human life, may wish to be) have a prerogative over brutal and gruesome ways of doing away with human heads.

Notes

1 Regina Janes, *Losing Our Heads: Beheadings in Literature and Culture* (New York: NYU Press, 2005), p. 195.
2 Doctor Louis Guillotin, quoted in Julia Kristeva, *The Severed Head: Capital Visions* (New York: Columbia University Press, 2012), p. 92.
3 US Secretary of State John Kerry talking about a seven-year-old Australian child, whose father, Khaled Sharrouf, of Sydney, Australia, had joined ISIS and moved his family to Syria. Quoted in *USA Today*, "Kerry Condemns Image of Boy with Severed Head," August 12, 2014.
4 Frances Larson, *Severed: A History of Heads Lost and Heads Found* (New York: Liveright Publishing, 2014), p. 3.
5 See, for example, Associated Press, "Kerry Condemns Image of Boy with Severed Head," August 12. See also Erick Stakelbeck, *ISIS Exposed: Beheadings, Slavery, and the Hellish Reality of Radical Islam* (Washington, DC: Regnery Publishing, 2015); and Rukmini Kallimachi, "The Horror before the Beheadings: ISIS Hostages Endured Torture and Dashed Hopes, Freed Cellmates Say," *New York Times*, October 26, 2014, p. A1.
6 The last few years have witnessed an explosion of popular and tabloid publications on IS and its reign of terror. See, for example, Jay Sekulow, *Rise of ISIS: A Threat We Can't Ignore* (New York: Simon and Schuster, 2014); Michael Weiss and Hassan Hassan, *ISIS: Inside the Army of Terror* (New York: Regan Arts, 2015); William McCants, *The ISIS Apocalypse: The History, Strategy, and Doomsday Vision of the Islamic State* (New York: St Martin's Press, 2015); and Joseph Micallef, *Islamic State: Its History, Ideology, and Challenge* (Vancouver: Antioch Downs, 2015).
7 See, for example, *Washington Times*, "Beheading Videos Fascinate Public," October 18, 2004, available at www.washingtontimes.com/news/2004/oct/18/20041018-103745-2585r/?page=all. See also Evan Osnos, "American Contractor Beheaded in Iraq," *Chicago Tribune*, September 21, 2004, available at http://articles.chicagotribune.com/2004-09-21/news/0409210334_1_beheading-american-contractor-masked.

8 See, for example, Daniel Benjamin and Steven Simon, *The Age of Scared Terror: Radical Islam's War against America* (New York: Random House, 2004); Shmuel Bar, *Warrant for Terror: The Fatwas of Radical Islam and the Duty to Jihad* (Lanham, MD: Rowman and Littlefield, 2008); or Stakelbeck, *ISIS Exposed: Beheadings, Slavery, and the Hellish Reality of Radical Islam.*

9 See, for example, Tammy Bruce, "Four Lessons from Paris Attacks: What Must Happen Now to Stop Radical Islam," *Fox News online*, opinion section, January 12, 2015, available at www.foxnews.com/opinion/2015/01/12/four-lessons-from-paris-attacks-what-must-happen-now-to-stop-radical-islam.html. See also Dan Bilefsky and Maia de la Baume, "French Premier Declares 'War' on Radical Islam as Paris Girds for Rally," *New York Times*, January 10, 2015, available online at www.nytimes.com/2015/01/11/world/europe/paris-terrorist-attacks.html?_r=0.

10 See David French, "How Should Christians Expect Our Nation to Respond to ISIS? With Wrath and Vengeance," *National Review*, online edition, September 3, 2014, available at www.nationalreview.com/corner/386960/how-should-christians-expect-our-nation-respond-isis-wrath-and-vengeance-david-french. See also Adam Chandler, "Mosul under ISIS: Clean Streets and Horror," *The Atlantic*, online edition, June 10, 2015, available at www.theatlantic.com/international/archive/2015/06/isis-mosul-iraq/395531/.

11 As, for example, US Senator and presidential candidate Lindsey Graham recently put it about IS and its acts of terror/horror. See Pam Key, "Graham: ISIS War against Humanity same as Nazis," *Breitbar News*, March 2, 2015; available at www.breitbart.com/video/2015/03/02/graham-isis-war-against-humanity-same-as-nazis/. Lindsey merely reprised a slogan that had been popular a decade earlier when used by then US President George W. Bush describing Iraqi insurgents. George W. Bush, "President Discusses War on Terror at National Endowment for Democracy," October 6, 2005, available at www.whitehouse.gov/news/releases/2005/10/20051006-3.html.

12 For more on the West's quest to re-secure or re-center its identity in the early twenty-first century, see François Debrix, "The Centrality of Tabloid Geopolitics: Western Discourses of Terror and the Defacing of the Other," in Scott Nelson and Nevzat Soguk (eds), *The Ashgate Research Companion to Modern Theory, Modern Power, and World Politics* (Farnham, UK: Ashgate Publishing, 2015), pp. 129–48.

13 On beheadings and Western civilization and culture, see Larson, *Severed: A History of Heads Lost and Found*. See also Larissa Tracy and Jeff Massey (eds), *Heads Will Roll: Decapitation in the Medieval and Early Modern Imagination* (Boston: Brill, 2012).

14 And none more so than the guillotine. On the social, political, and legal uses and misuses of the guillotine, see Allister Kershaw, *A History of the Guillotine* (New York: Barnes and Noble, 1993); see also Paul Friedland, *Seeing Justice Done: The Age of Spectacular Capital Punishment in France* (Oxford: Oxford University Press, 2012).

15 See once again Associated Press, "Kerry Condemns Image of Boy with Severed Head," August 12, 2014.

16 Victor Hugo, *Les Misérables* (New York: Thomas Crowell, 1887), p. 15; also quoted in Laure Murat, *The Man Who Thought He Was Napoleon: Toward a Political History of Madness* (Chicago: University of Chicago Press, 2014), p. 57.

17 On "over-living" or *survivance*, see Bonnie Honig, *Emergency Politics: Paradox, Law, Democracy* (Princeton: Princeton University Press, 2009), pp. 7–10. See also Jacques Derrida, "Living On. Borderlines," in Harold Bloom *et al.*, *Deconstruction and Criticism* (London: Routledge & Kegan Paul), pp. 75–176; and Judith Butler, *Frames of War: When Is Life Grievable?* (London: Verso, 2009), pp. 59–62.

18 The concept of the metaphysics of substance in the context of this study was introduced and explained in the previous chapters. On the metaphysics of substance, see also Judith Butler, *Gender Trouble: Feminism and the Subversion of Identity* (London: Routledge, 1990), p. 10; and Elizabeth Povinelli, *Economies of Abandonment: Social Belonging and Endurance in Late Liberalism* (Durham, NC: Duke University Press, 2011), pp. 106–7.

19 Here, I have in mind not only post-Marxism or variants of Frankfurt School Critical Theory (whose critical brands of humanism have been detailed and debated by many studies before) but also some forms of post-structural thinking, including deconstruction. More will be said about the "remnants of humanity/humanism" in deconstruction later in this chapter.

20 Jessica Stern and J.M. Berger, *ISIS: The State of Terror* (New York: Harper Collins, 2015), pp. 120–3.

21 Ibid., p. 2.

22 Ibid., p. 5.

23 See Edward Said, *Orientalism* (New York: Vintage Books, 1979).

24 Ibid., pp. 54–5.

25 For Said, this disconnection or severance of the oriental subject from Western humanity/ humanism does not just betray the hegemony of the West over the non-West but also explains why and how, in many Western (orientalist) discourses about the non-West and non-Western subjects, orientals are "rarely seen or looked at . . . as citizens, or even people, but [rather] as problems to be solved or confined or—as the colonial powers openly coveted their territory—taken over." See Said, *Orientalism*, p. 207. Of course, the belief that non-Western cultures and people are "lagging behind," if not downright inferior when it comes to their access to (or capacity to access) values and ideals about humanity/ humanism, was and continues to be a key ideological and racial theme in Western colonialist/imperialist projects. On this point, see, for example, Walter Mignolo, *The Darker Side of Western Modernity: Global Futures, Decolonial Options* (Durham, NC: Duke University Press, 2011), pp. 81–6.

26 On the technological and media expertise of IS and its members, see Abdel Bari Atwan, *Islamic State: The Digital Caliphate* (Berkeley, CA: University of California Press, 2015).

27 These are comments about IS deployed by Stern and Berger to describe IS. See Stern and Berger, *ISIS: The State of Terror*, p. 3.

28 Larson, *Severed*, p. 2.

29 Ibid., p. 275.

30 Ibid., pp. 10-11.

31 René Descartes, *Discourse on Method*, third edition (Indianapolis, IN: Hackett Publishing, 1998).

32 Larson, *Severed*, p. 11.

33 See, for example, Robert Glasse, "Cannibalism in the Kuru Region of New Guinea," *Transactions of the New York Academy of Sciences*, Vol. 29, No. 6 (1967), pp. 748–54.

34 See, for example, Xavier Ducrocq *et al.*, "Consensus Opinion on Diagnosis of Cerebral Circulatory Arrest Using Doppler-Sonography," *Journal of Neurological Sciences*, Vol. 159, No. 2 (1998), pp. 145–50.

35 Larson, *Severed*, p. 9.

36 For more on the politics and imagery of the face, see Jenny Edkins, *Face Politics* (London: Routledge, 2015).

37 Murat, *The Man Who Thought He Was Napoleon*, p. 31.

38 Larson, *Severed*, p. 9.

39 Ibid., p. 9.

40 As reported by Larson. See Larson, *Severed*, pp. 50-52. See also Simon Harrison, *Dark Trophies: Hunting and the Enemy Body in Modern War* (Oxford: Berghahn Books, 2012).

41 On this topic, see Ed Vulliamy, *Amexica: War along the Borderline* (New York: Picador, 2011).

42 Larson, *Severed*, p. 9.

43 Murat, *The Man Who Thought He Was Napoleon*, pp. 30–1.

44 Female French revolutionary Charlotte Corday famously assassinated Jacobin ideologue and political leader Jean-Paul Marat on July 13, 1793. Corday was guillotined four days later.

45 Pierre Jean Georges Cabanis, *Notes sur le supplice de la guillotine* [Notes on the supplice of the guillotine] (Orleans: Orient, 2007), p. 60, quoted in Murat, *The Man Who Thought He Was Napoleon*, p. 31.

46 Murat, *The Man Who Thought He Was Napoleon*, p. 31.

47 Ibid., p. 31.

48 Some of these debates are covered by Austin Sarat in his volume *Gruesome Spectacles: Botched Executions and America's Death Penalty* (Stanford: Stanford University Press, 2014).

49 I understand the "vibrancy" of severed heads and skulls here along the lines of what Bennett has referred to as "vibrant matter." The "vibrant matter" of things for Bennett suggests that there is "an energetic vitality inside each of these things" and that, as a consequence, things that are vibrant are "vivid entities not entirely reducible to the contexts in which (human) subjects set them, never entirely exhausted by their semiotics." Jane Bennett, *Vibrant Matter: A Political Ecology of Things* (Durham, NC: Duke University Press, 2010), p. 5.

50 Janes, *Losing Our Heads*, p. 12.

51 Ibid., p. 12.

52 Ibid., p. 12.

53 Ibid., p. 12.

54 Ibid., p. 12.

55 Ibid., p. 12.

56 One of Solario's most famous paintings is titled "Head of Saint John the Baptist, 1507." It depicts the peaceful severed head of John the Baptist resting on a serving tray. No sign of violent death or forceful dismemberment (not even a drop of blood) is visible. Solario composed other such paintings displaying the same severed head held or brandished by Salome or displayed on a platter. Herod, Roman ruler over Galilee from 6 to 39 AD, ordered the execution of John the Baptist by decollation. Textual accounts suggest that the request for Saint John the Baptist's execution came to Herod from his stepdaughter Salome. See Barbara Baert, "The Head of Saint John the Baptist on a Platter: The Gaze of Death," *IKON: Journal of Iconographic Studies*, Vol. 4 (2011), pp. 163–74.

57 Janes, *Losing Our Heads*, p. 12.

58 Ibid., pp. 12-13.

59 Ibid., p. 27.

60 Jean-Pierre Vernant, *Mortals and Immortals: Collected Essays* (Princeton: Princeton University Press, 1991), p. 121.

61 Kristeva, *The Severed Head*, p. 29.

62 Ibid., p. 29.

63 Adriana Cavarero, *Horrorism: Naming Contemporary Violence* (New York: Columbia University Press, 2009), p. 15.

64 Lacan also saw the Gorgon/Medusa as an absolute threat to the Symbolic Order and to meaning in general. Associating Medusa's head/face/gaze with the sight of the female sexual organs, Lacan referred to Medusa as "unnameable," an "unlocatable form," or an "abyss" or "gulf ... in which everything is swallowed up." Jacques Lacan, *The Second Seminar: The Ego in Freud's Theory and in the Technique of Psychoanalysis, 1954–1955* (New York: Norton, 1991), p. 164.

65 Ibid., p. 15.

66 Kristeva, *The Severed Head*, p. 30.

67 Ibid., p. 30.

68 Giorgio Agamben, *Remnants of Auschwitz: The Witness and the Archive* (New York: Zone Books, 2002), p. 47. On the figure of the *Muselmann*, see also Wolfgang Sofsky, *The Order of Terror: The Concentration Camp* (Princeton: Princeton University Press, 1997); Bruno Bettelheim, *The Informed Heart* (New York: Free Press, 1960); and Primo Levi, *Survival in Auschwitz* (New York: Touchstone Books, 1996).

69 Agamben, *Remnants of Auschwitz*, p. 48.

70 Ibid., p. 72.

71 Ibid., p. 40. Agamben here directly quotes Aldo Carpi, *Diario di Gusen* (Turin: Einaudi, 1993), p. 33.
72 Agamben, *Remnants of Auschwitz*, p. 50.
73 Ibid., p. 53.
74 Ibid., p. 70.
75 Perhaps, by being in excess of the camp's spatiality, the power of this horrifying gaze is topological, too (as we saw in Chapter 1).
76 Ibid., p. 70.
77 Kristeva, *The Severed Head*, p. 30.
78 Ibid., p. 30.
79 Ibid., p. 30.
80 Agamben, *Remnants of Auschwitz*, p. 52.
81 Ibid., p. 52.
82 On military drones and drone attacks, see Grégoire Chamayou, *A Theory of the Drone* (New York: The New Press, 2015); Adam Rothstein, *Drone* (London: Bloomsbury, 2015), pp. 19–34; and Medea Benjamin, *Drone Warfare: Killing by Remote Control* (London: Verso, 2013). Tellingly, some of the more "targeted" drone attacks are sometimes referred to by the military and security/defense experts as "decapitation strikes," a phrase reserved not just for aerial drone assaults (other weapons have been and can be used to "remove the head" of an enemy group or nation) but recently revived in the context of the long global war on terror as a result, in particular, of the attack "flexibility" provided by drones.
83 See *Time online*, "Amnesty International and Human Rights Watch Blast US Drone Strikes," October 22, 2013, available at http://world.time.com/2013/10/22/amnesty-international-and-human-rights-watch-blast-u-s-drone-strikes/.
84 On the "Gorgon Stare" drone, see, for example, Chamayou, *A Theory of the Drone*, p. 43 and p. 236.
85 One can also see that populations that are constantly subjected to the gaze of the attack drone experience a condition of "inevitable impossibility" with regard to this gaze, one that is not unlike the confrontation with the *Muselmann* in the concentration camp. Recently, Pakistani populations in areas commonly targeted by US drones were quoted as saying that, "when you can hear the drone circling in the sky, you think it might strike you . . . We always have this fear in our head." The presence of drones (visual and auditory), like the presence of the *Muselmann* in the camp, forces one to lose one's sense of reality, one's humanity, and, perhaps, one's head. As another civilian puts it in reference to his neighbors, who constantly sense that they are under the threat of drones: they "have lost their mental balance." In a way, they have lost their head and their mind already, whether they are still alive or already dead. See Stanford International Human Rights and Conflict Resolution Clinic, *Living under Drones: Death, Injury, and Trauma in Civilians from US Drone Practices in Pakistan*, September 2012, cited and quoted by Chamayou, *A Theory of the Drone*, pp. 44–5.
86 Levi, *Survival in Auschwitz*. See also Primo Levi, *The Drowned and the Saved* (New York: Vintage, 1989).
87 There seems to be a way of reading Joseph Conrad's *Heart of Darkness,* but perhaps even more so Francis Ford Coppola's cinematographic revisiting of Conrad's novel (the movie *Apocalypse Now*), as a tale of gradual and, for most humans involved, eventually fateful and fatal confrontation with the horror of the Gorgon's head, face, and stare. Janes offers a reading of Conrad's novel in relation to her description of Western representations of severed African heads, but she never allows herself to bring the figure of the Gorgon into her account of *Heart of Darkness.* She makes no mention of *Apocalypse Now*, either. Janes, *Losing Our Heads*, pp. 139–42. A closer connection between the Gorgon's horror and Colonel Kurtz (at least the Kurtz of *Heart of Darkness*) is suggested by Cavarero in an appendix to her book *Horrorism* (but still without a mention of *Apocalypse Now*). Cavarero, *Horrorism*, pp. 116–24.
88 Cavarero, *Horrorism*, p. 34.
89 Stern and Berger's terms, once again.

90 Kristeva, *The Severed Head*, p. 116.
91 I sought to make a similar point about horror in Chapter 2 by evoking Walter Benjamin's notion of the return of the history of the repressed as a violent moment, as a flash or glimpse into another reality or modality of representation of human life.
92 Janes, *Losing Our Heads*, p. 40.
93 Ibid., p. 194.
94 Edkins remarks on this kind of discomfort by stating that "dismantling the face" is often seen to "open up a world of unreason … It is a world, potentially, of horror." Jenny Edkins, *Face Politics* (London: Routledge, 2015), p. 6.
95 This questioning is reminiscent of some of Georges Bataille's challenges to the human/humanity, or what Thacker has called Bataille's "darkening of the human," an imaginative and textual operation that, for Bataille, consists of "undoing the human by paradoxically revealing the shadows and nothingness at its core." Eugene Thacker, *Starry Speculative Corpse: Horror of Philosophy, Vol. 2* (Washington, DC: Zero Books, 2015), p. 38. See also Georges Bataille, *The Accursed Share* (New York: Zone Books, 1991).
96 Janes, *Losing Our Heads*, p. 186.
97 See, in particular, Georges Bataille, *Visions of Excess* (Minneapolis: University of Minnesota Press, 1985).
98 Janes, *Losing Our Heads*, pp. 186–97.
99 On the French Revolution and the sense of freedom achieved by the populace with the removal of aristocrats' and royals' heads, see Murat, *The Man Who Thought He Was Napoleon*, pp. 23–6.
100 Janes, *Losing Our Heads*, p. 178.
101 Ibid., p. 181.
102 As Hillman and Mazzio also note, "the rejection of all forms of totality, including the corporeal, is one of the defining characteristics of postmodernism." David Hillman and Carla Mazzio, "Introduction: Individual Parts," in David Hillman and Carla Mazzio (eds), *The Body in Parts: Fantasies of Corporeality in Early Modern Europe* (New York: Routledge, 1997), p. xii.
103 Ibid., p. 187.
104 These bodies may even be re-experienced as "all too human," as the vitalist Nietzsche may have wanted to put it. Friedrich Nietzsche, *Human, All Too Human: A Book for Free Spirits* (Lincoln, NE: University of Nebraska Press, 1984).
105 Jacques Derrida, *Dissemination* (Chicago: University of Chicago Press, 1981), p. 20.
106 Jacques Derrida, *The Other Heading: Reflections on Today's Europe* (Bloomington, IN: Indiana University Press, 1992).
107 Ibid., pp. 5-10.
108 Ibid., p. 14.
109 Ibid., p. 14.
110 Ibid., pp. 14-15.
111 Ibid., p. 15.
112 Ibid., p. 15.
113 Ibid., p. 15.
114 Ibid., p. 15.
115 This is why, once again, similar to Janes who gestured towards a distinction between headlessness and beheading, Derrida's "other heading" cannot be a decapitation.
116 Robert Olen Butler, *Severance* (San Francisco: Chronicle Books, 2006).
117 Ibid., p. 225.
118 Ibid., p. 233.
119 Ibid., p. 125.
120 Ibid., p. 17.
121 Tom Barbash, "Dead Heads," *The New York Times, Sunday Book Review*, September 3, 2006, available at www.nytimes.com/2006/09/03/books/review/Barbash.t.html?_r=0.
122 Mark Budman, "From Where You Dream: A Conversation with Robert Olen Butler," *Del Sol Literary Dialogues*, available at www.webdelsol.com/Literary_Dialogues/interview-wds-butler.htm.

123 Bonnie Honig, *Emergency Politics: Paradox, Law, Democracy*, p. 10.

124 Ibid., p. 10.

125 Butler in Budman, "From Where You Dream," no page given.

126 Eugene Thacker, *In the Dust of this Planet: Horror of Philosophy, Vol. 1* (Winchester: Zero Books, 2011), p. 9.

127 Ibid., p. 8.

128 Ibid., p. 9.

129 Ibid., p. 5.

130 Judith Butler, *Gender Trouble: Feminism and the Subversion of Identity*, p. 20.

131 Thacker, *In the Dust of this Planet*, p. 9; author's own emphasis.

132 David Peak, *The Spectacle of the Void* (San Bernardino, CA: Schism Press, 2014), p. 15.

133 Thacker, *In the Dust of this Planet*, p. 5.

134 Ibid., p. 5.

135 Ibid., p. 6.

136 Ibid., p. 6. This nebulous "in-betweenness" of the "world-without-us" would also be, as David Peak suggests, a "post-communicative plane of thought" where human language substituting itself for thought and serving as the condition of possibility for thought would be pushed aside. This would be "thinking without language," as Peak further puts it, and the "contradictory filters of inarticulate lucidity and articulate confusion" would become conditions of communication in this "world-without-us." See Peak, *The Spectacle of the Void*, p. 15.

137 Thacker, *In the Dust of this Planet*, p. 46.

138 Ibid., p. 48. In a sequel to his *In the Dust of this Planet*, Thacker connects the task of demontology, or the rethinking of the world as unthinkable and away from human-centric thought and language, to a series of historical figures, philosophers, and contemporary thinkers. One key demontological line of thought is provided by Georges Bataille's writings, here not so much his writings on acephalous man (Acéphale, as we saw above), but rather his thoughts on mysticism, or what Thacker labels Bataille's "darkening of the human." Thacker writes:

> Bataille's texts opt to darken the human, to undo the human by paradoxically revealing the shadows and nothingness at its core, to move not towards a renewed knowledge of the human, but towards something we can only call an unknowing of the human, or really, the *unhuman*.

I suggest that demontology's calling is indeed this "unknowing of the human," which, admittedly, Bataille's thinking had already announced. Eugene Thacker, *Starry Speculative Corpse: Horror of Philosophy*, Vol. 2 (Winchester, UK: Zero Books, 2015), p. 38. Note also in passing here the mobilization of Bataille's writings for horroristic rather than deconstructive purposes.

139 Another recent instance of this constructed opposition between humanity and the so-called horror of orientalist beheadings was seen in Western media's reactions to the reported torture and beheading by ISIS of a Syrian archeologist who had attempted to hide and protect antiquities (including "Roman treasures," as many news outlets would put it) in the city of Palmyra from ISIS fighters' assault on these traces of ancient civilization, or humanity's heritage. See, for example, Ben Hubbard, "Syrian Expert Who Shielded Palmyra Antiquities Meets a Grisly Death at ISIS' Hands," *The New York Times*, August 20, 2015, p. A1.

EPILOGUE

Fusing remnants at the 9/11 Memorial Museum

In his essay "In the Face of Disappearance," Jacques Rancière warns against the danger of *Vernichtung*, the German term for "the extreme form of [the] will" to deny that human tragedy ever happened.[1] *Vernichtung*, for Rancière, is not just negation but the negation of the negation, or "the annihilation of that annihilation, the disappearance of its traces, the disappearance of its very name."[2] Rancière's call to avoid *Vernichtung* may remind us of Agamben's challenge to not look away in the presence of the *Muselmann*,[3] to learn to accept that we need to face horror, to recognize that horror is also of this world, or to come face to face with the realization that humanity and horror may not be so distinguishable after all (as I suggested in Chapter 4). Avoiding *Vernichtung* is a necessary reminder that horror is both about a world without us, as Thacker might suggest,[4] and about a world with and for us.

And yet, when Rancière evokes *Vernichtung*, or at least its avoidance, is he not also calling for an ultimate form of resistance against the horrifying possibility of the disappearance of the human/humanity? Is the annihilation of the annihilation not, for Rancière, a recognition of the powers of horror and, simultaneously, an opportunity to give humanity a final chance, even if the world is no longer and perhaps never was for, with, or about us? To avoid *Vernichtung* is to avoid rendering horror invisible. But it is also a not so secret wish to avoid invisibility *tout court*, to leave something visible about the world, or at least to claim that even invisibility can be made visible (even if, as Rancière goes on to affirm, "only art can reveal something that is invisible"[5]). If horror, the non-human, the not-to-be seen (like the Gorgon's stare, for example) can be made visible, through art, in particular, might there not be, deep in the abyss of horror, a hope for a trace of the human/humanity, a trace of the human/humanity that may no longer be able to claim any sort of ontological privilege or superiority (and may no longer reign triumphant behind a metaphysics of substance) but that, within horror, may get one last chance to exist or, at least, to avoid total negation? This could be what Rancière, in this same essay concerned with the danger of *Vernichtung*, has in mind when he invokes Walter Benjamin's messianic power so that, through art, through the image, something may still be given a faint chance to "shine in the present instant in order to ignite a spark of hope."[6] Here, not unlike what we saw towards the end of Chapter 2 with Benjamin's eschatological time/history of the oppressed,[7] horror, invisibility (the not-to-be-seen), or, indeed, the "world-without-us" is reconfigured by Rancière in such a way that it is only horror itself, only invisibility, and only the "world-without-us" that can now redeem humanity or, better yet, that can rediscover remnants of the human (even if, or precisely because, these human remnants are deprived of a humanity or, at least, are no longer visible in their expected and ontologically assumed human totality, integrity, or uniformity). Could it be, Rancière appears to suggest, that horror, the invisible/not-to-be-seen, or the "world-without-us" is now the only possibility for the human? Could it be that making horror visible, the invisible visible, and the "world-without-us" visible will reveal them to us (horrifying as they may be) but will also offer a few fleeting chances (or flashes, as Judith Butler had said about Benjamin[8]) to resist the annihilation of the annihilation and, in the process, to give some sort of decomposed humanity a "spark of hope"?

I recently visited the National September 11 Memorial Museum at the World Trade Center in New York City's Lower Manhattan. Pondering what I saw there, I was left to wonder if there was not a way of making sense of the 9/11 Memorial Museum, its structure, its exhibits, its displays, and its artifacts precisely as attempts to harness the powers of horror in a way that could resist *Vernichtung* and, in the process, give traces of a decomposed or undone humanity a "spark of hope." Or, I wondered, could it be instead that, despite an attempt to avoid the disappearance of the disappearance at the 9/11 Memorial Museum, the work of negation, the crushing "demontological" (to use Thacker's term[9]) work of horror, was irremediable, without recourse, even for fragments of the human? Opened on September 11, 2011 on the exact site where the twin towers of the World Trade Center stood prior to September 11, 2001, the 9/11 Memorial Museum seeks to "attest to the triumph of human dignity over human depravity and [to affirm] an unwavering commitment to the fundamental value of human life."[10] Overtly visual (text and narrative are minimal throughout the museum; captions next to objects or photos are clear but concise), the 9/11 Memorial Museum is spectacular, graphic, and at times vivid. Audio recordings are often used as supports for or enhancements of the images, and they tend to intensify the primarily visual experience of the museum. Five main visual media are mobilized throughout the museum: displays of large, severely damaged structures (remnants of steel columns or concrete staircases; burnt and distorted metal beams that used to anchor the buildings' façades); object exhibits, some large (rescue vehicles), others small (wallets, pens, keys, subway cards, personal mementos that belonged to the victims and first responders), some largely destroyed, others oddly intact; photos (portraits of victims, rescuers, and survivors; photojournalistic stills of various scenes of chaos and disaster from that day and afterwards); video recordings (often taken from news media and their live reports from 9/11/2001 and subsequent days and weeks); and paintings and other artworks by local as well as international artists. The visitor meanders through the museum's large halls, ambling through objects, structures, mementos, and images, going into areas that are visually and acoustically saturated (a lot to see, a lot to hear) and through other sections that are quieter, darker, and with softer colors, tones, and lighting, thus inviting reflection, remembrance, or respite. Almost at the very center of the museum's lower level, between the main halls where the two towers once stood, is a large wall made of blue tiles (the piece is by New York artist Spencer Finch and is titled "Trying to Remember the Color of the Sky on that September Day"), with a large quote by Roman poet Virgil inscribed across it that reads: "No Day Shall Erase You from the Memory of Time." Inaccessible to visitors, behind this blue tiled wall is a repository for the remains of many of the 9/11 victims (many of whom are still unidentified to this day).

The 9/11 Memorial Museum is a work of fusion and confusion. Humans and objects, human matter and thing matter come together, have been merged into one another, and often serve as substitutes for one another. This is a poignant rendition of what took place on 9/11 on this very site, at Ground Zero—a visual testimony of the disappearance on "that September Day." It is also, through art, through the image, through the visible, a rendition/representation of the invisible, of what cannot be seen or looked at, even if what cannot be seen—human pulverization on 9/11— is still largely out of sight behind the big blue wall. Thus, the 9/11 Memorial Museum's main message to its visitors seems to be that there is a way to capture horror, perhaps to be one with it for the human/humanity, and yet also to resist *Vernichtung*. Put somewhat differently, the vibrancy of objects and structures, the "actancy of thing-power" (as Jane Bennett might say),[11] takes center stage at the museum and, enhanced by human-made visual displays and boosted by human-driven strategies about the most effective way to make powerful use of images, it is granted the task of speaking for and representing human matter and humanity (both for the survivors and for all the human victims who perished on 9/11 and whose bodies and body parts may have been dismantled somewhere around Ground Zero). In *Vibrant Matter*, Bennett writes that "each human is a heterogeneous compound of wonderfully vibrant, dangerously vibrant, matter."[12] She adds that, "[i]f matter itself is lively, then not only is the difference between subjects and objects minimized, but the status of the shared materiality of all things is elevated."[13] The 9/11 Memorial Museum seems to have chosen to "bear solemn witness" (as its visitors' brochure claims) to the annihilation that took place that day by championing the liveliness of all matter, irrespective of its origin and, perhaps, irrespective of whether its vibrancy is human or not. Indeed, what Bennett calls a "shared materiality" of subjects and objects takes pride of place there, as objects often tell stories, show trauma, reveal loss, and speak of a horror that, on that fateful day, befell human and non-human matter alike. And while one might cynically (but probably correctly) suggest that objects are rendered visibly vibrant at the museum so they could speak of and for humans (particularly, for those human remains that are hidden behind the big blue wall), or so they could give us a glimpse of a horror that affected "our" world, one might wonder whether the "shared materiality," or what I called, above, the fusion and confusion, does not also undermine any belief that humans and humanity are being restored to their ontological priority by way of a clever (human-made) visual/artistic manipulation of objects. In other words, what sort of humanity, what remnants of human matter re-emerge alongside horror, alongside the fusion and confusion of destroyed and recombined objects and subjects, at the 9/11 Memorial Museum?

I think that it is possible to argue that what is celebrated by the 9/11 Memorial Museum displays is not a redeemed or rediscovered (or excavated, as it were) human matter. It is also not the resilient thing-power of objects or inorganic matter. Rather, what is celebrated at this museum is fusion/confusion itself, or the inability to tell if what is left, if what remains visible despite the negation, is a human subject or an object/thing. Interestingly, the undecidability of lively matter, what the fusion/confusion of the human and non-human as a result of the 9/11 disaster represents, is no longer something to be dreaded here, something to be horrified by (as it might have been with the outcome of suicide-bombing attacks, as we saw in Chapter 3). Rather, such an undecidability of matter, such a sharing or putting in common of bodies and parts (whether human or not), horrifying as it may be from a human-centric perspective, now seems to be a somewhat hopeful embrace of horror itself. In a way, Bennett is correct when she writes that "[a]ll bodies [human and non-human alike] are more than mere objects."[14] But all the matter and its remnants on display at the 9/11 Memorial Museum are more than mere (human) subjects. In their irresistible confusion, fusion, and immanent substitution, the various bodies or parts of bodies throughout the museum (whether they are visible or removed from the visitor's sight) are horrifying *and* hopeful. They offer us a look into a horror that decomposes, fuses, and recombines matter and, in so doing, rediscovers or reshapes objects and subjects, humans and non-humans, away from any sense of ontological priority or privilege that would have to be granted to humanity or the human body, away from any metaphysics of (human) substance. Might this be the "spark of hope" for a no longer only human humanity that Rancière was looking for? Or, as we saw with the horror of pulverized and recomposed bodies and body parts of suicide bombing attacks (in Chapter 3), might this no longer have anything to do with humanity at all, even with a decomposed but seemingly still hopeful humanity? Unlike Rancière, perhaps, I would be more tempted to leave this question open, unresolved, and undecidable.

Two instances of the fusion and confusion of the human and the non-human jumped out at me when I visited the 9/11 Memorial Museum. The first was on display in the museum but also in a ceremonial that took place months after 9/11 and was replayed on several of the video screens in one of the museum's exhibits. The display in question, the "Last Column," was about the last of the large collapsed steel structures of the former World Trade Center towers to be removed by the recovery workers in charge of clearing the massive field of debris at Ground Zero. The Last Column was removed from the rubble of the World Trade Center in May 2002, and, like all matter that was piled on and around the site after the 9/11 disaster, it was taken to the infamously named Fresh Kills landfill on Staten Island, where the

FBI, the New York Police Department, and other forensic experts sorted through all the agglomerated materials (organic and inorganic) for years after 9/11. In 2009, the column returned to Ground Zero, in the space under construction that would become the Foundation Hall of the 9/11 Memorial Museum. Right in the middle of the Foundation Hall, it now stands as a "proud symbol of resilience" in the face of terror/terrorism.[15] More interesting than the column itself, which is nothing exceptional and whose symbolism is far from novel (the erection of phallic structures and monuments to commemorate or celebrate national resilience, prowess, and vigor is a very common motif) is the museum's exhibit, around the corner from the Foundation Hall, that showcases via video montage the ceremonial cutting down, removal, and departure of the Last Column on May 28 and 29, 2002. In a graphic fashion that eerily anticipates images following the US invasion of Iraq (although the Iraq images were not as visible), when the first dead American soldiers' bodies would be repatriated back home, one can see the meticulous lowering down at dawn of the column on a truck, draped neatly in a giant American flag, with rescuers, Ground Zero workers, and onlookers silently and pensively watching the scene while paying homage to this last remnant of the World Trade Center to be hauled away. The brief video montage also shows overhead footage from a helicopter of the truck with the flag-draped column slowly escorted away from Lower Manhattan all the way to the Staten Island landfill. It is hard to watch this footage without thinking that what is on the truck (this column that, in the museum, now stands erect only a few feet away), is a giant coffin of sorts, and what we are meant to see here is a ritualized remake of other US national mourning ceremonials—the JFK funeral and the procession of his American-flag-draped coffin through the District of Columbia to Arlington Cemetery, caskets of fallen US soldiers shipped back from Vietnam, Afghanistan, or Iraq and landing at Dover Air Force Base—that, usually, have (dead) human bodies as their main subjects. The last remaining large structure from the Word Trade Center is taken by those who witness the ritual (on site or via the video) to stand for everything and everyone that perished on 9/11, everything and everyone that has been destroyed, cut off from life, and abruptly taken away. And so, the museum's video intimates, as we watch the Last Column go from the place where it used to stand, we can no longer tell if we are dealing with a human or a non-human form. It no longer matters what or who is under this giant flag and what or who will find its way to the Fresh Kills landfill. To use Bennett's turns of phrase again, it is a shared materiality, a vibrant matter, that we are meant to celebrate and mourn. What we are looking at and paying tribute to is an undecidable fusion/confusion of remains and remnants in which what is left of the human is expressed by way of a chopped-down steel column.

The place to where the column was sent (before it was brought back in 2009 to stand erect as one of the 9/11 Memorial Museum's centerpieces) is worth considering too. In September 2001, the Fresh Kills landfill on Staten Island became another Ground Zero, the location to where all that was pulverized on 9/11 was taken in order to be sorted out and, perhaps, reconstituted. But it soon became clear that Fresh Kills would not be a location where life or lives would be reconstructed, where organic unities would be rediscovered and reassembled, away from the indiscriminate mass of things. While Ground Zero in Lower Manhattan would gradually be cleared and cleaned up and made into a gaping hole (where the 9/11 Memorial—itself a hole of a monument—and the 9/11 Memorial Museum would eventually be built), Fresh Kills, as a landfill (and, now, as *the* 9/11 landfill), would be the place where all sorts of matter and materials would proliferate, often in complete disregard for what would remain as human and what would not. For those who worked at Fresh Kills, even though identification was supposed to be the guiding forensic principle, un-identification, confusion, combination, juxtaposition, and proliferation would become the dominant experiences and conditions of life and work there. Mark Schaming, the Director of the New York State Museum in Albany, NY, was asked to participate in the recovery/identification work at Fresh Kills. Schaming also took several photos of artifacts/materials in the landfill (similar photos by other Fresh Kills forensic specialists are on display at the 9/11 Memorial Museum). One of Schaming's main observations about Fresh Kills was that everything was mixed up with everything else: "[o]bjects were found in the sorting sheds, on the field and in vehicles, alongside human remains."[16] At Fresh Kills, as at Ground Zero (and, as we saw above, at the 9/11 Memorial Museum too), human remains did not hold any special status. They were like any matter, all part of the rubble. Human and non-human matter, indistinguishable from one another, combined together, "was buried at the landfill."[17] In fact, Schaming admits that, for the forensic expert, "the artifact became a surrogate remain,"[18] particularly as it was obvious that "human remains were part of the dust and [were] embedded debris attached to most objects."[19] In a manner that invokes a mode of thinking about thing-power that post-human theorists may champion, Schaming has no choice but to conclude that "objects have a life much greater than us."[20]

In a way, the horrific (dis)organization principle encountered at the Fresh Kills landfill, in all its confusion of matter, its mixing of life and destruction, and its recognition that what may remain of humanity may be inseparable from things and objects, has become precisely the model of organization, presentation, and visual display that has been privileged by the designers and curators of the 9/11 Memorial Museum. At the museum, just like at Fresh Kills, the artifact is primarily seen as a "surrogate remain," and human remains and remnants of things are indistinguishable from one another. In fact, they are not meant to be distinguished. In opposition to any form of metaphysical certainty (about the status of the one and the other; indeed, who is one and who or what is other at Ground Zero, at Fresh Kills, and at the museum?), and away from any credible ontological reconstruction or restructuring (of the human and his/her body, in particular),[21] a horrifying liveliness of undifferentiated matter is oddly proclaimed. And, alongside such undifferentiated matter, a sense of hopefulness through recombined things and objects is perhaps introduced too, despite horror or, rather, because of horror (might the horror of Ground Zero and Fresh Kills not also give rise to what may be seen as hopeful at the 9/11 Memorial Museum?).

This possible combination of horror and a "spark of hope" (as Rancière, via Benjamin, once again, puts it) leads me to the second instance of fusion/confusion of the human and non-human that I found arresting at the 9/11 Memorial Museum. In a rather dark corner of the "Historical Exhibition" section of the museum, not far from the Last Column video montage, stands a large grey object (at first glance, it looks like a big boulder) called a "composite." This 9/11 composite, like others found at Ground Zero and Fresh Kills, is an amalgamation of about five collapsed floors from one of the towers that have been melted and molded together as a result of the force of the explosion, the extreme heat of the fire, and the pressure of the destruction from the crushed buildings.[22] Schaming, who came across several of the composites in his forensic and documentary work at Fresh Kills, notes that they are made up of "a variety of building material, office furnishings, paper, rings, cards and, among it all, human remains."[23] A caption next to the large composite in the museum mentions that, while forensic testing has not been able to find the presence of human remains in it, it is actually not possible to determine whether human matter is present in this object/thing or not. Crucially, composites are objects that do not exist anywhere else (composites are "unique to this event and site," says a 9/11 Museum Planning Report[24]). They are a combination of matter and materials that the 9/11 disaster created. Composites are new matter that has resulted from the explosion, the combustion, and the collapse. This is raw matter emanating or birthed from horror, with humans and non-humans alike used as the foundation for something new, something that has imploded any "ontological divide between persons and things."[25]

It may be tempting to claim that the composite is the closest the 9/11 Memorial Museum comes to displaying human remains (since, once again, we are meant to assume that most 9/11 human remains have been returned to families and loved ones, are behind the big blue wall, or still lie somewhere in the Fresh Kills landfill). Might we not think of the 9/11 composite as some sort of sarcophagus, reminiscent, perhaps, of those sepultures that have been collected and put on display in natural-history or science museums worldwide? Might they be seen as the last repository of some mummified human body or human parts? This is precisely what Schaming wants (us) to believe when he declares that the "value" of these composites resides in the fact that they are "containers of the remains of people killed."[26] Nevertheless, the 9/11 Memorial Museum's own study refutes the belief that the composite is to be taken as a container for human life (or death).[27] While it may have traces of human matter in its making, what the human matter that has been combusted, crushed, melted, and molded with many other things has given rise to is something that has never been experienced before: a new form, a new matter, a new life, perhaps. Here, with the composite, we encounter something new and different in the fusion and confusion between human and non-human matter. Unlike the Last Column, it is not a question of seeing remnants of human life or traces of humanity "shining through" in combination with things or objects. It may also not be about hopefulness with or in horror anymore. Rather, the fusion/confusion of the composite is about horror creating a new matter, a new vibrant thing-power, with effects on and affects about everything and everyone around it. With this new, unique composite matter birthed out of horror (the horror of the human and the non-human alike), it may become more difficult to find the "spark of hope" in some recomposed humanity that Rancière was looking for. Indeed, with the composite—and differently from objects and things given (human) life—neither objects nor subjects are recomposed. Neither humans nor non-humans are recombined. Rather, some other, new, as of yet unseen material emerges and comes to life (or, perhaps, to liveliness).

I wonder if the composite does not open yet another possibility within the horror of the visual, within the field of vision and artistic representation that, as Rancière suggested, enables the invisible to be made visible. The possibility here would be not only to see the fusion/confusion of the human and the non-human as undecidable but also to see the undecidable as that which precisely can give rise to a new materiality, a new vibrancy, or a new liveliness in which neither the human subject (and its remains) nor the non-human object (and its remnants) are to be found. I wonder, too, if this composite form or matter is not an approximation of the "nothingness that is not simply non-being" that Thacker was invoking when he introduced the possibility of thinking and seeing things (and the world) "demonto-logically."[28] Finally, I wonder if this new, composite "demontological" matter or "aliveness", in its incommensurability with regard to both human and non-human remains/remnants, is not the reason why it is relegated to a small dark corner of the 9/11 Memorial Museum, whereas other fused/confused artifacts and displays—starting with the Last Column—take center stage.[29]

Upon leaving the 9/11 Memorial Museum and stepping outside the building, one comes across the 9/11 Memorial itself. The 9/11 Memorial, conceived and designed by architect Michael Arad, is titled "Reflecting Absence." It is a two-part structure, at the exact location of the Twin Towers (the bulk of the 9/11 Memorial Museum actually lies in between and underneath the Memorial). Arad's "Reflecting Absence" is made up of two very large square holes with water streaming down from the four sides and dropping into the recesses of the memorial. As art historian and critic Thomas Stubblefield explains, Arad's 9/11 Memorial "not only establishes absence as its central design feature, but [it also] presents this idiom in terms of an undetermined and neutral space whose lack of material presence eschews symbolic coding."[30] For Arad, the counter-monumentality of these open, swallowing holes, through their alleged absence of signs, symbols, images, texts, forms, and, perhaps, meanings, are meant to enable "therapy, transparency, and participation."[31] And, perhaps, in opposition to official discourses, they are supposed to encourage "individual processes of healing and reflection."[32] My point here is not to decide if Arad's memorial actually manages to be therapeutic or participatory. Rather, I wish to suggest that the 9/11 Memorial Museum can be seen as a contrast to the 9/11 Memorial.

As I suggested above, the 9/11 Memorial Museum is not interested in "reflecting absence." Instead, its efforts are geared towards celebrating the remaining presence of matter and materials, even if only by means of traces, images, objects, pieces of structures, and, perhaps, composites. Through its celebration of the proliferation, fusion/confusion, and, indeed, undecidability of matter, the 9/11 Memorial Museum is perhaps not supposed to be therapeutic, at least not primarily so. Rather than therapeutic or healing, I would argue that the museum at Ground Zero is revelatory and possibly messianic. It reveals, announces, and perhaps invokes a horror (that it does make visible) that is not without flashes of hopefulness and, as such, is also not without traces of a recombined humanity (even if such humanity has been deprived of any sense of ontological certainty or superiority). Yet the horror tinged with some "spark of hope" for a new modality of and perhaps for the human at the museum is never assured. As we saw, newly composed or composite matter is also revealed as a new sort of no longer just human creation, as some kind of "demon-tological" aliveness or vibrancy. Thus, any hope for a recombined humanity/human matter at the heart of horror must contend with this radical negative possibility, too, with the possibility not so much that *Vernichtung* will not be overcome but that overcoming *Vernichtung* may well be revelatory of some new materiality for which the human is but a distant memory.

This is why the presence of hope, of traces of humanity, and, indeed, of horror through all sorts of materialities and material combinations and fusions at Ground Zero, at Fresh Kills, and at the 9/11 Memorial Museum can only be messianic. Reading Benjamin once again (and as discussed in Chapter 2), Butler explains that messianic power can only emerge "as a sudden and provisional light."[33] She adds that "what we can call the messianic is always on the order of the 'might enter'."[34] That the revelatory power of horror, after it has undone the metaphysics of substance, might bring a new hope for the human is indeed as uncertain as it is destabilizing (it would be "something of a wager," Butler adds[35]). It is a chance that is often not up to us, humans, to take. When confronted with horror, horror befalls us (as some survive with memories and traces of the disappeared while others are reduced to fragments and dust). But if there is to be a hope for a different human/humanity to come, for a different, recombined, or recomposed human matter, we might do well not to look away from horror (as Agamben had already intimated). Rather than trying to reflect on or memorialize the absence or disappearance (as Arad's "Reflecting Absence" Memorial seems to wish to do), perhaps it is more important to stare at the material presence and presentation of horror (as I believe the 9/11 Memorial Museum invites us to do), even if such a glimpse into horror can only provide fleeting or provisional instants of messianic redemption.

Notes

1 Jacques Rancière, *Figures of History* (Cambridge, UK: Polity, 2014), p. 45.
2 Ibid., p. 45.
3 Giorgio Agamben, *Remnants of Auschwitz: The Witness and the Archive* (New York: Zone Books, 2002), p. 52.
4 Eugene Thacker, *In the Dust of this Planet: Horror of Philosophy, Volume I* (Winchester: Zero Books, 2011), p. 5.
5 Rancière, *Figures of History*, p. 50.
6 Ibid., p. 53. The phrase "spark of hope" is taken directly from Benjamin's "Theses on the Philosophy of History."
7 Walter Benjamin, "Theses on the Philosophy of History," in Walter Benjamin, *Illuminations*, ed. Hannah Arendt (New York: Schocken Books, 1968), pp. 253–64.

8 Judith Butler, *Parting Ways: Jewishness and the Critique of Zionism* (New York: Columbia University Press, pp. 102–4).
9 Thacker, *In the Dust of this Planet*, p. 46.
10 As the official 9/11 Memorial Museum map and brochure put it.
11 Jane Bennett, *Vibrant Matter: A Political Ecology of Things* (Durham, NC: Duke University Press, 2010), pp. 8–9.
12 Ibid., pp. 12-13.
13 Ibid., p. 13.
14 Ibid., p. 13.
15 As the 9/11 Memorial Museum website affirms. See 9/11 Memorial Museum, "Last Column: A Symbol of Resilience," available at www.911memorial.org/images-videos/video/last-column-symbol-resilience.
16 Mark Schaming, "From Evidence to Relic to Artefact: Curating in the Aftermath of 11 September 2001," in Brigitte Sion (ed.), *Death Tourism: Disaster Sites as Recreational Landscape* (London: Seagull Books, 2014), pp. 146–7.
17 Ibid., p. 149.
18 Ibid., p. 151.
19 Ibid., p. 152.
20 Ibid., p. 163.
21 The 9/11 Memorial Museum features parts of an Auguste Rodin sculpture recovered from the field of debris at Fresh Kills. The sculpture used to belong to one of the brokerage firms whose offices were located in one of the towers. What is left of Rodin's "The Three Shades" sculpture (on display at the museum) may be taken as symbolic of the undoing of the metaphysics of substance and of the impossibility of rediscovering/reconstructing a human-centered unity or ontological priority. Only a human bust, with one thigh and one arm, remains of the statue. The head has been removed. It was reported that, at Fresh Kills, the remnants of the statue were found near parts of one of the planes that crashed into the World Trade Center (interestingly, Mark Schaming took a picture of this artifact at Fresh Kills, too). The horror for the human on 9/11, displaced to a sculpture representing a human form that has now been mutilated (and, in particular, beheaded), was perhaps perversely foreshadowed by Rodin himself, who had intended for "The Three Shades" to sit atop his "Gates of Hell" project. For more on Rodin's "The Three Shades," see Albert E. Elsen, "The Gates of Hell: What They Are about and Something of Their History," in Albert E. Elsen (ed.), *Rodin Rediscovered* (Washington, DC: National Gallery of Art, 1966), pp. 61–79.
22 See 9/11 Memorial Museum, "2013 Museum Planning Conversation Series Report," p. 4; available at www.911memorial.org/sites/all/files/2013ConversationSeries.pdf.
23 Schaming, "From Evidence to Relic to Artifact," p. 156.
24 "2013 Museum Planning Conversation Series Report," p. 4.
25 Bennett, *Vibrant Matter*, p. 12. Recently, a colleague suggested to me that composites may be akin to what Timothy Morton has called "hyperobjects." Hyperobjects, Morton writes, are creations or phenomena that become "'hyper' in relation to some other [non-human] entity, whether they are directly manufactured by humans or not." Yet, what seems to define hyperobjects for Morton is their capacity to impact the human world and thus to continue to matter in relation to humans/humanity. What hyperobjects are and do in relation to humans is still key to Morton's thinking or, as Morton asserts, hyperobjects are "things that are massively distributed in time and space relative to humans." See Timothy Morton, *Hyperobjects: Philosophy and Ecology after the End of the World* (Minneapolis: University of Minnesota Press, 2013), p. 1.
26 Schaming, "From Evidence to Relic to Artifact," p. 156.
27 "2013 Museum Planning Conversation Series Report," p. 5.
28 Thacker, *In the Dust of this Planet*, p. 46.
29 Horror scholar David Peak evokes a similar suspicion when he mentions that a horror that does not just target and attack the idea of the ontological superiority of the human (the world-with-us) but, further, removes any trace or remnant of humanity is beyond

acceptance or redemptive hope. Peak refers to this horror as a "horror beyond horrors." As we saw above, while Rancière may still find a "spark of hope" in horror, in the unthinkable and the unrepresentable (thanks to art and the visual, primarily), this hopefulness still demands that human traces, beyond ontological certainty, remain. A composite matter in which no longer any shreds of the human can be detected is seemingly unacceptable for Rancière and, in a way, it takes us back to *Vernichtung*, or perhaps to a horror beyond horrors. See David Peak, *The Spectacle of the Void* (New York: Schism Press, 2014), p. 17.
30 Thomas Stubblefield, *9/11 and the Visual Culture of Disaster* (Bloomington, IN: Indiana University Press, 2015), p. 155.
31 Ibid., p. 155.
32 Ibid., p. 163.
33 Butler, *Parting Ways*, p. 102.
34 Ibid., p. 103.
35 Ibid., p. 103.

BIBLIOGRAPHY

9/11 Memorial Museum. "2013 Museum Planning Conversation Series Report," June 18, 2013, available at www.911memorial.org/sites/all/files/2013ConversationSeries.pdf (accessed May 29, 2016).

9/11 Memorial Museum. "Last Column: A Symbol of Resilience," n.d., available at www.911memorial.org/images-videos/video/last-column-symbol-resilience (accessed May 29, 2016).

Agamben, Giorgio. *The Coming Community* (Minneapolis: University of Minnesota Press, 1993).

Agamben, Giorgio. *Homo Sacer: Sovereign Power and Bare Life* (Stanford: Stanford University Press, 1998).

Agamben, Giorgio. *Potentialities: Collected Essays in Philosophy* (Stanford: Stanford University Press, 1999a).

Agamben, Giorgio. *Remnants of Auschwitz: The Witness and the Archive* (New York: Zone Books, 1999b).

Agamben, Giorgio. *Means without End: Notes on Politics* (Minneapolis: University of Minnesota Press, 2000).

Agamben, Giorgio. *The Open: Man and Animal* (Stanford: Stanford University Press, 2004).

Agamben, Giorgio. *The Kingdom and the Glory: For a Theological Genealogy of Economy and Government* (Stanford: Stanford University Press, 2011).

Agier, Michel. *On the Margins of the World: The Refugee Experience Today* (Cambridge: Polity, 2008).

Althusser, Louis. "Ideology and Ideological State Apparatuses," in Louis Althusser (ed.), *Lenin and Philosophy, and Other Essays* (New York: Monthly Review Press, 1971): 127–86.

Amin, Ash. "Spatialities of Globalization," *Environment and Planning A* Vol. 34, No. 3 (2002): 385–99.

Amin, Ash. "Regulating Economic Globalization," *Transactions of the Institute of British Geographers* Vol. 29, No. 2 (2004): 217–33.

Arendt, Hannah. *The Origins of Totalitarianism* (New York: Harcourt, Brace, Jovanovich, 1973).

Arendt, Hannah. *Eichmann in Jerusalem: A Report on the Banality of Evil* (New York: Penguin, 2006).

Asad, Talal. *On Suicide Bombing* (New York: Columbia University Press, 2007).

Atwan, Abdel Bari. *Islamic State: The Digital Caliphate* (Berkeley: University of California Press, 2015).

Baert, Barbara. "The Head of Saint John the Baptist on a Platter: The Gaze of Death," *IKON: Journal of Iconographic Studies* Vol. 4 (2011): 163–74.

Bar, Shmuel. *Warrant for Terror: The Fatwas of Radical Islam and the Duty to Jihad* (Lanham, MD: Rowman and Littlefield, 2008).

Barbash, Tom. "Dead Heads," *New York Times*, Sunday Book Review, September 3, 2006, available at www.nytimes.com/2006/09/03/books/review/Barbash.t.html?_r=0 (accessed May 26, 2016).

Barnett, Thomas. *The Pentagon's New Map: War and Peace in the Twenty-First Century* (New York: Berkley Trade, 2005).

Bataille, Georges. *Visions of Excess* (Minneapolis: University of Minnesota Press, 1985).

Bataille, Georges. *The Accursed Share* (New York: Zone Books, 1991).

Battersby, Matilda. "Image of Terror: 78-year-old Runner Knocked over by Second Boston Marathon Blast," *Independent*, April 16, 2013, available at www.independent.co.uk/news/world/americas/image-of-terror-78yearold-runner-knocked-over-by-second-boston-marathon-blast-8574515.html (accessed October 27, 2013).

Baudrillard, Jean. *Simulations* (New York: Semiotext(e), 1983).

Baudrillard, Jean. *Forget Foucault* (New York: Semiotext(e), 1987).

Baudrillard, Jean. "The Violence of the Global," *CTheory.Net*, article a129, published May 20, 2003, available at www.ctheory.net/articles.aspx?id=385 (accessed May 26, 2016).

Belcher, Oliver, Lisa Martin, Ana Secor, Stephanie Simon, and Tommy Wilson. "Everywhere and Nowhere: The Exception and the Topological Challenge of Geography," *Antipode* Vol. 40, No. 4 (2008): 499–503.

Benjamin, Daniel and Steven Simon. *The Age of Scared Terror: Radical Islam's War against America* (New York: Random House, 2004).

Benjamin, Medea. *Drone Warfare: Killing by Remote Control* (London: Verso, 2013).

Benjamin, Walter. "Theses on the Philosophy of History," in Walter Benjamin (ed.), *Illuminations: Essays and Reflections* (New York: Schocken, 1968): 253–64.

Bennett, Jane. *Vibrant Matter: A Political Ecology of Things* (Durham, NC: Duke University Press, 2010).

Bergson, Henri. *The Two Sources of Morality and Religion* (South Bend: University of Notre Dame Press, 1991).

Berlant, Lauren. *Cruel Optimism* (Durham, NC: Duke University Press, 2011).

Bettelheim, Bruno. *The Informed Heart* (New York: Free Press, 1960).

Bilefsky, Dan and Maia de la Baume. "French Premier Declares 'War' on Radical Islam as Paris Girds for Rally," *New York Times*, January 10, 2015, available at www.nytimes.com/2015/01/11/world/europe/paris-terrorist-attacks.html?_r=0 (accessed May 28, 2016).

Blond, Philip. *Post-Secular Philosophy: Between Philosophy and Theology* (New York: Routledge, 1998).

Blum, Virginia and Ana Secor. "Psychotopologies: Closing the Circuit between Psychic and Material Space," *Environment and Planning D: Society and Space* Vol. 29, No. 6 (2011): 1030–47.

Boston Globe. "102 Hours in Pursuit of Marathon Suspects," April 28, 2013, available at www.bostonglobe.com/metro/2013/04/28/bombreconstruct/VbSZhzHm35yR88EVmVdbDM/story.html (accessed October 27, 2013).

Braidotti, Rosi. *The Posthuman* (Cambridge: Polity, 2013).

Brodzki, Bella. *Can These Bones Live? Translation, Survival, and Cultural Memory* (Stanford: Stanford University Press, 2007).

Brown, Wendy. *Walled States, Waning Sovereignty* (New York: Zone Books, 2010).

Bruce, Tammy. "Four Lessons from Paris Attacks: What Must Happen Now to Stop Radical Islam," *Fox News*, January 12, 2015, available at www.foxnews.com/opinion/2015/01/12/four-lessons-from-paris-attacks-what-must-happen-now-to-stop-radical-islam.html (accessed May 28, 2016).

Budman, Mark. "From Where You Dream: A Conversation with Robert Olen Butler," *Del Sol Literary Dialogues*, n.d., available at www.webdelsol.com/Literary_Dialogues/interview-wds-butler.htm (accessed May 26, 2016).

Bush, George W. "Address to the Nation on the Terrorist Attacks," *The American Presidency Project*, September 11, 2001, available at www.presidency.ucsb.edu/ws/?pid=58057#axzz2iJMceZ4F (accessed October 27, 2013).

Bush, George W. "President Discusses War on Terror at National Endowment for Democracy," October 6, 2005, available at www.whitehouse.gov/news/releases/2005/10/20051006-3.html (accessed April 12, 2015).

Butler, Judith. *Gender Trouble: Feminism and the Subversion of Identity* (London: Routledge, 1990).

Butler, Judith. *Antigone's Claim: Kinship between Life and Death* (New York: Columbia University Press, 2000).

Butler, Judith. *Precarious Life: The Powers of Mourning and Violence* (London: Verso, 2004).

Butler, Judith. *Frames of War: When Is Life Grievable?* (London: Verso, 2009).

Butler, Judith. *Parting Ways: Jewishness and the Critique of Zionism* (New York: Columbia University Press, 2012).

Butler, Robert Olen. *Severance* (San Francisco: Chronicle Books, 2006).

Cabanis, Pierre Jean Georges. *Notes sur le supplice de la guillotine* [Notes on the Supplice of the Guillotine] (Orléans: Orient, 2007).

Campbell, David. *Writing Security: United States Foreign Policy and the Politics of Identity* (Minneapolis: University of Minnesota Press, 1998).

Campbell, David. "The Iconography of Famine," in Geoffrey Batchen, Mick Gidley, Nancy Miller, and Jay Prosser (eds), *Picturing Atrocity: Photography in Crisis* (London: Reaktion Books, 2012): 79–91.

Carpi, Aldo. *Diario di Gusen* (Turin: Einaudi, 1993).

Cavarero, Adriana. *Horrorism: Naming Contemporary Violence* (New York: Columbia University Press, 2009).

Cavell, Stanley. *The Claim of Reason* (Oxford: Oxford University Press, 1999).

CBS Boston. "Doctors: Most Victims of Bombing Have Injuries to Lower Extremities," April 16, 2013, available at http://boston.cbslocal.com/2013/04/16/mgh-doctors-most-victims-of-bombing-have-injuries-to-lower-extremities/ (accessed October 27, 2013).

Chamayou, Grégoire. *A Theory of the Drone* (New York: The New Press, 2015).

Chandler, Adam. "Mosul under ISIS: Clean Streets and Horror," *The Atlantic*, June 10, 2015, available at www.theatlantic.com/international/archive/2015/06/isis-mosul-iraq/395531/ (accessed May 28, 2016).

Chiesa, Lorenzo. "Giorgio Agamben's Franciscan Ontology," *Cosmos and History: The Journal of Natural and Social Philosophy* Vol. 5, No. 1 (2009): 105–16, available at http://cosmosandhistory.org/index.php/journal/article/view/130 (accessed May 27, 2016).

Chow, Rey. *The Age of the World Target: Self-Referentiality in War, Theory, and Comparative Work* (Durham: Duke University Press, 2006).

CNN. "Boston Marathon Terror Attack," April 22, 2013, available at www.cnn.com/interactive/2013/04/us/boston-marathon-terror-attack/ (accessed October 27, 2013).

Coleman, Mathew. "Review: State of Exception," *Environment and Planning D: Society and Space* Vol. 25, No. 1 (2007): 187–90.

Coleman, Mathew and Kevin Grove. "Biopolitics, Biopower, and the Return of Sovereignty," *Environment and Planning D: Society and Space* Vol. 27, No. 3 (2009): 489–507.

Collins, Stephen. *From Divine Cosmos to Sovereign State* (Oxford: Oxford University Press, 1989).

Coole, Diana and Samantha Frost (eds). *New Materialisms: Ontology, Agency, and Politics* (Durham, NC: Duke University Press, 2010).

Danchev, Alex. *On Art and War and Terror* (Edinburgh: Edinburgh University Press, 2011).

Dauphinee, Elizabeth and Cristina Masters (eds). *The Logics of Biopower and the War on Terror: Living, Dying, Surviving* (London: Palgrave, 2006).

Dean, Mitchell. "Demonic Societies: Liberalism, Biopolitics, and Sovereignty," in Thomas Blom Hansen and Finn Stepputat (eds), *States of Imagination: Ethnographic Explorations of the Postcolonial State* (Durham, NC: Duke University Press, 2001): 41–64.

Debrix, François. "Post-Mortem Photography: Gilles Peress and the Taxonomy of Death," *Postmodern Culture* Vol. 9, No. 2 (1999), available at https://muse.jhu.edu/article/27700 (accessed May 26, 2016).

Debrix, François. *Tabloid Terror: War, Culture, and Geopolitics* (New York: Routledge, 2008).

Debrix, François. "Rethinking Democracy's Emergence: Towards New Spaces of Grief and Survivability," *Environment and Planning D: Society and Space* Vol. 29, No. 2 (2009): 369–74.

Debrix, François. "The Virtual Nomos?" in Stephen Legg (ed.), *Spatiality, Sovereignty, and Carl Schmitt* (London: Routledge, 2011): 220–6.

Debrix, François. "The Centrality of Tabloid Geopolitics: Western Discourses of Terror and the Defacing of the Other," in Scott Nelson and Nevzat Soguk (eds), *The Ashgate Research Companion to Modern Theory, Modern Power, and World Politics* (Farnham, UK: Ashgate Publishing, 2016): 129–48.

Debrix, François and Alexander D. Barder. *Beyond Biopolitics: Theory, Violence, and Horror in World Politics* (London: Routledge, 2012).

Debrix, François and Mark J. Lacy (eds), *The Geopolitics of American Insecurity: Terror, Power and Foreign Policy* (London: Routledge, 2009).

De Landa, Miguel. *Intensive Science and Virtual Philosophy* (London: Continuum, 2002).

Deleuze, Gilles. *Difference and Repetition* (New York: Columbia University Press, 1994).

DeLillo, Don. *Falling Man* (New York: Picador, 2007).

Derrida, Jacques. "Living On: Borderlines," in Harold Bloom, Paul de Man, Jacques Derrida, Geoffrey Hartman, and J. Hillis Miller (eds), *Deconstruction and Criticism* (London: Routledge & Kegan Paul, 1979): 75–176.

Derrida, Jacques. *Dissemination* (Chicago: University of Chicago Press, 1981).

Derrida, Jacques. *The Other Heading: Reflections on Today's Europe* (Bloomington, IN: Indiana University Press, 1992).

Derrida, Jacques. *Specters of Marx: The State of the Debt, the Work of Mourning, and the New International* (New York: Routledge, 1994).

Descartes, René. *Discourse on Method* (Indianapolis, IN: Hackett Publishing, 1998).

Diken, Bülent and Carsten Laustsen. *The Culture of Exception: Sociology Facing the Camp* (London: Routledge, 2005).

Dillon, Michael. *Politics of Security: Towards a Political Philosophy of Continental Thought* (New York: Routledge, 1996).

Dillon, Michael. "Governing Terror: The State of Emergency of Biopolitical Emergence," *International Political Sociology* Vol. 1, No. 1 (2007): 7–28.

Dillon, Michael. "Specters of Biopolitics: Finitude, *Eschaton*, and *Katechon*," *The South Atlantic Quarterly* Vol. 110, No. 3 (2011): 780–92.

Dillon, Michael. *Biopolitics of Security: A Political Analysis of Finitude* (London: Routledge, 2015).

Dillon, Michael and Julian Reid. *The Liberal Way of War: Killing to Make Life Live* (London: Routledge, 2009).

Doty, Roxanne. *Imperial Encounters: The Politics of Representation in North-South Relations* (Minneapolis: University of Minnesota Press, 1996).

Ducrocq, Xavier, Werner Hassler, Kouzo Moritake, David W. Newell, Gerhard-Michael von Reutern, Toshiyuki Shiogai, and Robert R. Smith. "Consensus Opinion on Diagnosis of Cerebral Circulatory Arrest Using Doppler-Sonography," *Journal of Neurological Sciences* Vol. 159, No. 2 (1998): 145–50.

Edkins, Jenny. "Sovereign Power, Zones of Indistinction, and the Camp," *Alternatives* Vol. 25, No. 1 (2000): 3–25.

Edkins, Jenny. *Face Politics* (London: Routledge, 2015).

Edkins, Jenny, Veronique Pin-Fat, and Michael Shapiro (eds). *Sovereign Lives: Power in Global Politics* (London: Routledge, 2004).

Elsen, Albert E. "The Gates of Hell: What They Are About and Something of Their History," in Albert E. Elsen (ed.), *Rodin Rediscovered* (Washington, DC: National Gallery of Art, 1966): 61–79.

Esposito, Roberto. *Bios: Biopolitics and Philosophy* (Minneapolis: University of Minnesota Press, 2008).

Esposito, Roberto. *Immunitas: The Protection and Negation of Life* (Cambridge: Polity, 2011).

Evans, Brad. "The Liberal War Thesis: Introducing the Ten Key Principles of Twenty-First Century Biopolitical Warfare," *The South Atlantic Quarterly* Vol. 110, No. 3 (2011): 747–56.

Evans, Brad. *Liberal Terror* (Cambridge: Polity, 2013).

Fassin, Didier. "Ethics of Survival: A Democratic Approach to the Politics of Life," *Humanity* Vol. 1, No. 1 (2010): 81–95.

Foucault, Michel. *Discipline and Punish: The Birth of the Prison* (New York: Vintage Books, 1979).

Foucault, Michel. *"Society Must Be Defended": Lectures at the Collège de France, 1975–1976* (New York: Picador, 2003).

Foucault, Michel. *Security, Territory, Population: Lectures at the Collège de France, 1977–1978* (New York: Picador, 2007).

French, David. "How Should Christians Expect Our Nation to Respond to ISIS? With Wrath and Vengeance," *National Review*, September 3, 2014, available at www.nationalreview.com/corner/386960/how-should-christians-expect-our-nation-respond-isis-wrath-and-vengeance-david-french (accessed May 28, 2016).

Friedland, Paul. *Seeing Justice Done: The Age of Spectacular Capital Punishment in France* (Oxford: Oxford University Press, 2012).

George, Larry N. "American Insecurities and the Ontopolitics of US Pharmacotic Wars," in François Debrix and Mark J. Lacy (eds), *The Geopolitics of American Insecurity: Terror, Power, and Foreign Policy* (New York: Routledge, 2009): 34–53.

Giaccaria, Paolo and Claudio Minca. "Topographies/Topologies of the Camp: Auschwitz as a Spatial Threshold," *Political Geography* Vol. 30, No. 1 (2011): 3–12.

Glasse, Robert. "Cannibalism in the Kuru Region of New Guinea," *Transactions of the New York Academy of Sciences* Vol. 29, No. 6 (1967): 748–54.

Gregory, Derek. *The Colonial Present: Afghanistan, Palestine, Iraq* (London: Blackwell, 2004).

Gregory, Derek. "The Black Flag: Guantanamo Bay and the Space of Exception," *Geografiska Annaler* Vol. 88, No. 4 (2006): 405–27.

Grosz, Elizabeth. *Volatile Bodies: Toward a Corporeal Feminism* (Bloomington: Indiana University Press, 1994).

Grusin, Richard (ed.). *The Nonhuman Turn* (Minneapolis: University of Minnesota Press, 2015).

Haraway, Donna. *When Species Meet* (Minneapolis: University of Minnesota Press, 2007).

Hardt, Michael and Antonio Negri. *Multitude: War and Democracy in the Age of Empire* (New York: Penguin, 2004).

Harrison, Simon. *Dark Trophies: Hunting and the Enemy Body in Modern War* (Oxford: Berghahn Books, 2012).

Hayles, N. Katherine. *How We Became Posthuman: Virtual Bodies in Cybernetics, Literature, and Informatics* (Chicago: University of Chicago Press, 1999).

Hillman, David and Carla Mazzio. "Introduction: Individual Parts," in David Hillman and Carla Mazzio (eds), *The Body in Parts: Fantasies of Corporeality in Early Modern Europe* (New York: Routledge, 1997): xi–xxix.

Hobbes, Thomas. *Leviathan* (New York: Penguin, 1995).

Hollinger, Veronika. "Posthumanism and Cyborg Theory," in Mark Bould, Andrew Butler, Adam Roberts, and Sherryl Vint (eds), *The Routledge Companion to Science Fiction* (London: Routledge, 2009): 267–78.

Honig, Bonnie. *Emergency Politics: Paradox, Law, Democracy* (Princeton: Princeton University Press, 2009).

Hubbard, Ben. "Syrian Expert Who Shielded Palmyra Antiquities Meets a Grisly Death at ISIS' Hands," *New York Times*, August 19, 2015, available at www.nytimes.com/2015/08/20/world/middleeast/isis-palmyra-syria-antiquities-scholar-beheaded.html (accessed May 28, 2016).

Hugo, Victor. *Les Misérables* (New York: Thomas Crowell, 1887).

Hurd, Elizabeth Shakman. "The Political Authority of Secularism in International Relations," *European Journal of International Relations* Vol. 10, No. 2 (2004): 235–62.

Hurd, Elizabeth Shakman. "International Politics after Secularism," *Review of International Studies* Vol. 38, No. 5 (2012): 943–61.

Janes, Regina. *Losing Our Heads: Beheadings in Literature and Culture* (New York: NYU Press, 2005).

Johnson, Scott. "Family, Friends, Dignitaries Pay Tribute to Ambassador Stevens," written for the *Oakland Tribune* and reported in the *San Jose Mercury News*, October 16, 2012, available at www.mercurynews.com/top-stories/ci_21786355/memorial-services-start-ambassador-christopher-stevens (accessed October 27, 2013).

Jones, Martin. "Phase Space: Geography, Relational Thinking, and Beyond," *Progress in Human Geography* Vol. 33, No. 4 (2009): 487–506.

Joseph, May. "Fascia and the Grimace of Catastrophe," in Patricia Ticineto Clough and Craig Willse (eds), *Beyond Biopolitics: Essays on the Governance of Life and Death* (Durham: Duke University Press, 2011): 332–50.

Kallimachi, Rukmini. "The Horror before the Beheadings: ISIS Hostages Endured Torture and Dashed Hopes, Freed Cellmates Say," *New York Times*, October 26, 2014, p. A1.

Kantorowicz, Ernst. *The King's Two Bodies: A Study in Mediaeval Political Theology* (Princeton: Princeton University Press, 1997).

Kaplan, Robert. *Imperial Grunts: On the Ground with the American Military, from Mongolia to the Philippines to Iraq and Beyond* (New York: Vintage, 2006).

Kaplan, Robert. *The Revenge of Geography: What the Map Tells Us About Coming Conflicts and the Battle against Fate* (New York: Random House, 2012).

Kashmere, Brett. *Valery's Ankle*, digital video, 2006, available at http://vimeo.com/63041317 (accessed October 27, 2013).

Kashmere, Brett. www.brettkashmere.com (accessed October 27, 2013).

Kennedy, Liam. *Afterimages: Photography and US Foreign Policy* (Chicago: University of Chicago Press, 2016).

Kershaw, Allister. *A History of the Guillotine* (New York: Barnes and Noble, 1993).

Key, Pam. "Graham: ISIS War against Humanity same as Nazis," *Breitbar News*, March 2, 2015, available at www.breitbart.com/video/2015/03/02/graham-isis-war-against-humanity-same-as-nazis/ (accessed May 28, 2016).

Kohn, Eduardo. *How Forests Think: Toward an Anthropology beyond the Human* (Berkeley: University of California Press, 2013).

Kristeva, Julia. *Powers of Horror: An Essay on Abjection* (New York: Columbia University Press, 1982).

Kristeva, Julia. *The Severed Head: Capital Visions* (New York: Columbia University Press, 2012).

Lacan, Jacques. *The Second Seminar: The Ego in Freud's Theory and in the Technique of Psychoanalysis, 1954–1955* (New York: Norton, 1991).

Larson, Frances. *Severed: A History of Heads Lost and Heads Found* (New York: Liveright Publishing, 2014).

Lefort, Claude. *Democracy and Political Theory* (Cambridge: Polity, 1991).

Levi, Primo. *The Drowned and the Saved* (New York: Vintage, 1989).

Levi, Primo. *Survival in Auschwitz* (New York: Touchstone Books, 1996).

Lobo-Guerrero, Luis. *Insuring Security: Biopolitics, Security and Risk* (London: Routledge, 2012).

Lyotard, Jean-François. *Lessons on the Analytic of the Sublime* (Stanford: Stanford University Press, 1994).

McCants, William. *The ISIS Apocalypse: The History, Strategy, and Doomsday Vision of the Islamic State* (New York: St Martin's Press, 2015).

McKim, Donald. *Westminster Dictionary of Theological Terms* (London: Westminster John Knox Press, 1996).

Malpas, Jeff. "Putting Space in Place: Philosophical Topography and Relational Geography," *Environment and Planning D: Society and Space* Vol. 30, No. 2 (2012): 226–42.

Martel, James. *Divine Violence: Walter Benjamin and the Eschatology of Sovereignty* (London: Routledge, 2012).

Massey, Doreen. *For Space* (Thousand Oaks: Sage, 2005).

Mbembe, Achille. "Necropolitics," *Public Culture* Vol. 15, No. 1 (2003): 11–40.

Meier, Heinrich. *The Lesson of Carl Schmitt: Four Chapters on the Distinction between Political Theology and Political Philosophy* (Chicago: University of Chicago Press, 1998).

Micallef, Joseph. *Islamic State: Its History, Ideology, and Challenge* (Vancouver: Antioch Downs, 2015).

Mignolo, Walter. *The Darker Side of Western Modernity: Global Futures, Decolonial Options* (Durham, NC: Duke University Press, 2011).

Minca, Claudio. "The Return of the Camp," *Progress in Human Geography* Vol. 29, No. 4 (2005): 405–12.

Minca, Claudio. "Giorgio Agamben and the New Biopolitical *Nomos*," *Geografiska Annaler* Vol. 88, No. 4 (2006): 387–403.

Mitchell, Katharyne. "Pre-Black Futures," *Antipode* Vol. 41, No. 1 (2009): 239–61.

Morgenthau, Hans. "Another 'Great Debate': The National Interest of the United States," *American Political Science Review* Vol. 46, No. 4 (1952): 961–88.

Morton, Timothy. *Hyperobjects: Philosophy and Ecology at the End of the World* (Minneapolis: University of Minnesota Press, 2013).

Murat, Laure. *The Man Who Thought He Was Napoleon: Toward a Political History of Madness* (Chicago: University of Chicago Press, 2014).

Murdoch, Jonathan. *Post-Structuralist Geography: A Guide to Relational Space* (Thousand Oaks: Sage, 2005).

Nancy, Jean-Luc. *The Inoperative Community* (Minneapolis: University of Minnesota Press, 1991).

Neocleous, Mark. *Critique of Security* (Montreal: McGill-Queen's University Press, 2008).

Nietzsche, Friedrich. *Human, All too Human: A Book for Free Spirits* (Lincoln, NE: University of Nebraska Press, 1984).

Osnos, Evan. "American Contractor Beheaded in Iraq," *Chicago Tribune*, September 21, 2004, available at http://articles.chicagotribune.com/2004-09-21/news/0409210334_1_beheading-american-contractor-masked (accessed May 28, 2016).

Ó Tuathail, Gearóid. *Critical Geopolitics: The Politics of Writing Global Space* (Minneapolis: University of Minnesota Press, 1996).

Owens, Patricia. "Humanity, Sovereignty, and the Camps," *International Politics* Vol. 45, No. 4 (2008): 522–30.

Peak, David. *The Spectacle of the Void* (San Bernardino, CA: Schism Press, 2014).

Peress, Gilles. *The Silence* (New York: Scalo, 1995).

Peress, Gilles and Eric Stover. *The Graves: Srebrenica and Vukovar* (New York: Scalo, 1998).

Philpott, Daniel. "The Religious Roots of Modern International Relations," *World Politics* Vol. 52, No. 2 (2000): 206–45.

Posen, Barry. *Restraint: A New Foundation for US Grand Strategy* (Ithaca, NY: Cornell University Press, 2015).

Povinelli, Elizabeth. *Economies of Abandonment: Social Belonging and Endurance in Late Liberalism* (Durham, NC: Duke University Press, 2011).

Rancière, Jacques. *The Future of the Image* (London: Verso, 2007).

Rancière, Jacques. *Figures of History* (Cambridge: Polity, 2014).

Redman, Samuel J. *Bone Rooms: From Scientific Racism to Human Prehistory in Museums* (Cambridge, MA: Harvard University Press, 2016).

Reid, Julian. *The Biopolitics of the War on Terror: Life Struggles, Liberal Modernity and the Defence of Logistical Societies* (Manchester: Manchester University Press, 2009).

Reid, Julian. "The Vulnerable Subject of Liberal War," *The South Atlantic Quarterly* Vol. 110, No. 3 (2011): 770–9.

Roden, David. *Posthuman Life: Philosophy at the Edge of the Human* (London: Routledge, 2015).

Rodriguez, Olga. "Mexico Violence: Eight Decomposed Bodies Found Inside Car in North," *Huffington Post*, August 10, 2013, available at: www.thonline.com/news/national_world/article_63c73e1f-94be-5963-96f4-38b217bfff52.html (accessed May 26, 2016).

Rose, Mitch and John Wylie. "Animating Landscape," *Environment and Planning D: Society and Space* Vol. 24, No. 4 (2006): 475–9.

Rose, Nikolas. *The Politics of Life Itself: Biomedicine, Power, and Subjectivity in the Twenty-First Century* (Princeton: Princeton University Press, 2007).

Rosenblatt, Adam. *Digging for the Disappeared: Forensic Science after Atrocity* (Stanford: Stanford University Press, 2015).

Rothstein, Adam. *Drone* (London: Bloomsbury, 2015).

Said, Edward. *Orientalism* (New York: Vintage Books, 1979).

Santner, Eric. *On Creaturely Life: Rilke, Benjamin, Sebald* (Chicago: University of Chicago Press, 2006).

Santner, Eric. *The Royal Remains: The People's Two Bodies and the Endgames of Sovereignty* (Chicago: University of Chicago Press, 2011).

Sarat, Austin. *Gruesome Spectacles: Botched Executions and America's Death Penalty* (Stanford: Stanford University Press, 2014).

Scarry, Elaine. *The Body in Pain: The Making and Unmaking of the World* (Oxford: Oxford University Press, 1985).

Schaming, Mark. "From Evidence to Relic to Artefact: Curating in the Aftermath of 11 September 2001," in Brigitte Sion (ed.), *Death Tourism: Disaster Sites as Recreational Landscape* (London: Seagull Books, 2014): 139–64.

Schmitt, Carl. *The Concept of the Political* (Chicago: University of Chicago Press, 1996).

Schmitt, Carl. *The Nomos of the Earth* (New York: Telos, 2003).

Schmitt, Carl. *Political Theology* (Chicago: University of Chicago Press, 2005).

Sekulow, Jay. *Rise of ISIS: A Threat We Can't Ignore* (New York: Simon and Schuster, 2014).

Sofsky, Wolfgang. *The Order of Terror: The Concentration Camp* (Princeton: Princeton University Press, 1999).

Sontag, Susan. *Regarding the Pain of Others* (New York: Farrar, Straus and Giroux, 2003).

Sparke, Matthew. *In the Space of Theory: Postfoundational Geographies of the Nation-State* (Minneapolis: University of Minnesota Press, 2005).

Stakelbeck, Erick. *ISIS Exposed: Beheadings, Slavery, and the Hellish Reality of Radical Islam* (Washington, DC: Regnery Publishing, 2015).

Stanford International Human Rights and Conflict Resolution Clinic. *Living under Drones: Death, Injury, and Trauma in Civilians from US Drone Practices in Pakistan*, Stanford Law School, September 2012, available at http://chrgj.org/wp-content/uploads/2012/10/Living-Under-Drones.pdf (accessed August 25, 2016).

Steele, Brent. *Ontological Security in International Relations: Self Identity and the IR State* (New York: Routledge, 2008).

Stern, Jessica and J.M. Berger. *ISIS: The State of Terror* (New York: Harper Collins, 2015).

Stubblefield, Thomas. *9/11 and the Visual Culture of Disaster* (Bloomington, IN: Indiana University Press, 2015).

Taubes, Jacob. *Occidental Eschatology* (Stanford: Stanford University Press, 2009).

Telegraph. "Boston Marathon Bombings Victim: It Reminded Me of 9/11," October 21, 2013, available at www.telegraph.co.uk/news/worldnews/northamerica/usa/10020061/Boston-Marathon-bombings-victim-it-reminded-me-of-911.html (accessed October 27, 2013).

Thacker, Eugene. *After Life* (Chicago: University of Chicago Press, 2010).

Thacker, Eugene. *In the Dust of this Planet: Horror of Philosophy, Vol. 1* (Winchester, UK: Zero Books, 2011).

Thacker, Eugene. *Starry Speculative Corpse: Horror of Philosophy, Vol. 2* (Washington, DC: Zero Books, 2015).

Time. "Amnesty International and Human Rights Watch Blast US Drone Strikes," October 22, 2013, available at http://world.time.com/2013/10/22/amnesty-international-and-human-rights-watch-blast-u-s-drone-strikes/ (accessed May 26, 2016).

Tracy, Larissa and Jeff Massey (eds). *Heads Will Roll: Decapitation in the Medieval and Early Modern Imagination* (Boston: Brill, 2012).

Tracy, Marc. "The Fallen Man: Marathons Push Ordinary People To Be Extraordinary. One Photo from Monday's Bombing Made that Clear," *New Republic*, April 15, 2015, available at www.newrepublic.com/article/112927/boston-marathon-bombing-fallen-man-photo (accessed May 28, 2016).

Urry, John. *Global Complexity* (Cambridge: Polity, 2003).

USA Today. "Kerry Condemns Image of Boy with Severed Head," August 12, 2014, available at www.usatoday.com/story/news/world/2014/08/12/kerry-condemns-severed-head-image/13939635/ (accessed May 28, 2016).

Vaughan-Williams, Nick. "The UK Border Security Continuum: Virtual Biopolitics and the Simulation of the Sovereign Ban," *Environment and Planning D: Society and Space* Vol. 28, No. 6 (2010): 1071–83.

Vaughan-Williams, Nick. *Border Politics: The Limits of Sovereign Power* (Edinburgh: Edinburgh University Press, 2012).

Vernant, Jean-Pierre. *Mortals and Immortals: Collected Essays* (Princeton: Princeton University Press, 1991).

Vulliamy, Ed. "The Terror," *Vanity Fair*, October 21, 2010, available at www.vanityfair.com/news/2010/10/drug-wars-in-mexico-201010 (accessed May 26, 2016).

Vulliamy, Ed. *Amexica: War along the Borderline* (New York: Picador, 2011).

Walker, R.B.J. "Security, Sovereignty, and the Challenge of World Politics," *Alternatives* Vol. 15, No. 1 (1990): 3–27.

Walker, R.B.J. *Inside/Outside: International Relations as Political Theory* (Cambridge: Cambridge University Press, 1992).

Walker, R.B.J. "The Subject of Security," in Keith Krause and Michael C. Williams (eds), *Critical Security Studies* (Minneapolis: University of Minnesota Press, 1997): 61–81.

Walker, R.B.J. *After the Globe, before the World* (New York: Routledge, 2010).

Washington Post. "Battling Back: Stories of the Victims," Boston Marathon bombings blog, April 23, 2013, available at www.washingtonpost.com/wp-srv/special/national/boston-marathon-bombing-victims/ (accessed October 27, 2013).

Washington Times. "Beheading Videos Fascinate Public," October 18, 2004, available at www.washingtontimes.com/news/2004/oct/18/20041018-103745-2585r/?page=all (accessed May 28, 2016).

Watson, Janell. "Butler's Biopolitics," *Theory & Event* Vol. 15, No. 2 (2012), available at https://muse.jhu.edu/article/478357 (accessed May 28, 2016).

Weber, Max. "Politics as a Vocation," in Max Weber (ed.), *The Vocation Lectures* (Indianapolis: Hackett Publishing, 2004): 32–94.

Weiss, Michael and Hassan Hassan. *ISIS: Inside the Army of Terror* (New York: Regan Arts, 2015).

Whatmore, Sarah. *Hybrid Geographies: Natures, Cultures, Spaces* (Thousand Oaks: Sage, 2001).

Wolfe, Cary. *What Is Posthumanism?* (Minneapolis: University of Minnesota Press, 2009).

Wool, Zoë. *After War: The Weight of Life at Walter Reed* (Durham, NC: Duke University Press, 2015).

INDEX